The Boost C++ Libraries

Boris Schäling

The Boost C++ Libraries

Disclaimer

The information in this book is provided on an "as is" basis, without warranty. While every effort has been taken by the author and XML Press in the preparation of this book, the author and XML Press shall have neither liability nor responsibility to any person or entity with respect to any loss or damages arising from the information contained in this book.

This book contains links to third-party web sites that are not under the control of the author or XML Press. The author and XML Press are not responsible for the content of any linked site. Inclusion of a link in this book does not imply that the author or XML Press endorses or accepts any responsibility for the content of that third-party site.

Trademarks

XML Press and the XML Press logo are trademarks of XML Press.

All terms mentioned in this book that are known to be trademarks or service marks have been capitalized as appropriate. Use of a term in this book should not be regarded as affecting the validity of any trademark or service mark.

XML Press
24310 Moulton Pkwy, Suite O-175
Laguna Hills, California
http://xmlpress.net

First Edition
ISBN: 978-0-9822191-9-5

Table of Contents

Preface

What you will learn

This book is an introduction to the Boost C++ Libraries. The Boost C++ Libraries complement the C++ standard and add many practical tools that can be of use to any C++ developer and in any C++ project. Because the Boost C++ Libraries are based on the C++ standard, they are implemented using state-of-the-art C++. They are platform independent and are supported on many operating systems, including Windows and Linux, by a large developer community.

The Boost C++ Libraries enable you to boost your productivity as a C++ developer. For example, you can benefit from smart pointers that help you to write more reliable code or use one of the many libraries to develop platform independent network applications. Since many Boost C++ Libraries will be incorporated into the next version of the C++ standard, you can prepare yourself starting today.

What you should know

Since the Boost C++ Libraries are based on, and extend, the C++ standard, you should know the C++ standard well. You should understand and be able to use containers, iterators, and algorithms, and ideally you should have heard of concepts such as RAII, function objects, and predicates. The better you know the C++ standard, the more you will benefit from the Boost C++ Libraries.

Typographical Conventions

The following text styles are used in this book:

`Monospace font`	A Monospace font is used for class names, function names, and keywords — basically for any C++ code. It is also used for code examples, command line options, and program output. For example:

```
int main()
{
}
```

`Monospace bold font`	A Monospace bold font is used for variable names, objects, and user input. For example: A static variable like **done** can be used to do a one-time initialization in a process.

Bold	Commands are marked in bold. For example: To automatically install the Boost C++ Libraries with Boost.Jam, a command line program called **bjam** is used.
Quotes	Quotes are used when a new concept is introduced and mentioned for the first time. For example: After covering the four interfaces of Boost.MultiIndex, the remainder of this section focuses on "key extractors".

Examples

The numbered examples in this book can be downloaded from the book's companion web site: http://xmlpress.net/publications/boost. In most cases, you may copy, change, and use these files in your own programs in any way you want, freely, and without asking permission. The only exceptions would be if you wish to sell or distribute the examples. For more information, send email to mailto:permissions@xmlpress.net.

The examples are provided with NO WARRANTY express or implied.

Acknowledgments

First and foremost, I have to thank the Boost C++ community and all of the developers who make the community so lively and successful. Without the large number of developers from around the world who share and discuss ideas about Boost and spend a lot of time writing code, we wouldn't benefit from so many useful libraries. Not only would this book not exist, but I wouldn't have the many libraries I use in every C++ project I work on. But most importantly – and having met many developers at BoostCon 2011 I can truly say this – we wouldn't have this outstanding community. I especially want to thank Zoltan Juhasz, Beman Dawes, Dave Abrahams, Doug Gregor, Jeff Garland, and John Maddock for their permission to use the Boost C++ logo on the book cover.

Next I have to thank Andreas Masur. When the first version of this book was published online in 2008, it was only available in German. After I announced the publication of this book on the Boost C++ mailing lists, Andreas approached me and offered his help to translate the book from German to English. I wasn't sure if anyone would have the motivation and endurance to translate the entire book. But Andreas did! He spent several months translating and brought the process to a successful conclusion. Without Andreas this book wouldn't have been available in English in 2010 – and maybe not even today. Thank you, Andreas!

Last, but not least, I have to thank Richard Hamilton. Because I use DocBook XML to maintain my book, I was looking for a publishing house that could process DocBook XML files. Fortunately, I found Richard's publishing house, XML Press. Richard not only has extensive experience in DocBook XML and associated technologies like the DocBook XSL stylesheets, he also helped me turn my online book into a professional paper book – improving content, formatting, design, and many other tiny tasks one too easily forgets. Thank you, Dick!

1

Introduction

C++ and Boost

The Boost C++ Libraries[1] are a collection of modern libraries based on the C++ standard. The source code is released under the Boost Software License,[2] which allows anyone to use, modify and distribute the libraries for free. The libraries are platform independent and support most popular compilers, as well as many that are lesser-known.

The Boost community is responsible for developing and publishing the Boost C++ Libraries. It consists of a relatively large group of C++ developers from around the world coordinated through the web site www.boost.org[3] as well as several mailing lists. The mission statement of the community is to develop and collect high-quality libraries that complement the C++ standard. Libraries that prove of value and become important for the development of C++ applications stand a good chance of being included in the C++ standard someday.

The Boost community emerged around 1998 when the first version of the C++ standard was released. It has grown continuously since then and nowadays plays a big role in the standardization of C++. Even though there is no formal relation between the Boost community and the standardization committee, some of the developers are active in both groups. The next version of the C++ standard, which will most likely be approved in 2011, will include a couple of libraries that have their roots in the Boost community.

Boost C++ Libraries are a good choice to increase productivity in C++ projects when your requirements go beyond what is available in the C++ standard. Since the current version of the C++ standard (1998) and Technical Report 1 (2003) were published, Boost C++ Libraries have added many new features. You don't need to wait for the next version of the C++ standard to benefit from progress made in the evolution of C++, thanks to the Boost C++ Libraries.

Due to the excellent reputation of the Boost C++ Libraries, knowing them well can be a valuable skill for engineers. It is not unusual to be asked about the Boost C++ Libraries in an interview,

---

[1] http://www.boost.org/doc/libs/
[2] http://www.boost.org/LICENSE_1_0.txt
[3] http://www.boost.org/

because developers who know these libraries are usually also familiar with the latest innovations in C++ and are able to write and understand modern C++ code.

Development Process

The development of the Boost C++ Libraries is only possible because individual developers and organizations vigorously support them. Because Boost only accepts libraries which solve existing problems, exhibit a convincing design, are developed using modern C++, and are documented in an understandable way, each Boost C++ Library has a lot of work behind it.

C++ developers can participate in the Boost community and propose new libraries. However, in order to convert an idea into a Boost C++ Library, a lot of time and effort needs to be invested. It is of vital importance to discuss the requirements and possible solutions with other developers and potential users on the Boost mailing lists.

Besides new libraries, it is also possible to nominate existing C++ libraries for inclusion into Boost. However, because the requirements for these libraries are the same as for libraries explicitly developed for Boost, changes may be required before new libraries are accepted.

Whether or not a library gets accepted into Boost depends on the outcome of the review process. Developers of libraries can apply for a review, which usually takes place over the course of 10 days. During the review, other developers are asked to rate the library. Based on the number of positive and negative reviews, the review manager decides whether or not to accept the library into Boost. Since some developers are exposed to the library for the first time during their review of the proposal, it is not uncommon for modifications to be required.

If a library is rejected for technical reasons, it is still possible to revise the library and request a new review for an updated version. However, if a library is rejected because it does not solve any practical problem or because it provides an unconvincing solution to an existing problem, there is a good chance that it will be rejected in another review.

Because new libraries can be accepted at any time, a new version of the Boost C++ Libraries is released every three months. This book covers version 1.47.0 of the Boost C++ Libraries, which was released in July, 2011.

Please note that there are additional libraries that have been already accepted but are not yet part of the official release of the Boost C++ Libraries. They must be manually installed until they are included in a release.

Installation

The Boost C++ Libraries come as source code. While most of the libraries consist solely of header files that can be used directly, some of the libraries require compilation. In order to make installation as easy as possible, an automated installation process based on Boost.Jam is available. Instead of validating and compiling individual libraries separately, Boost.Jam installs the complete set automatically. Boost.Jam can be used with many operating systems and compilers and is able to compile each individual library based on appropriate configuration files.

To automatically install the Boost C++ Libraries with Boost.Jam, a command line program called **bjam** is used. The Boost C++ Libraries ship this program as source code and not as an executable.

That's why two steps are required to build and install the Boost C++ Libraries. Change to the Boost directory after you download the Boost C++ Libraries and enter the following commands on the command line:

1. Enter **bootstrap** on Windows and **./bootstrap.sh** on other platforms like Linux to compile **bjam**. The script automatically searches for a C compiler to build **bjam**.

2. Afterwards enter **bjam** on Windows and **./bjam** on other platforms like Linux to start installing the Boost C++ Libraries.

You use **bootstrap** only once to build **bjam**. However, **bjam** might be used more often because **bjam** supports many command line options to build the Boost C++ Libraries differently. If you start **bjam** without any command line options, a default configuration will be used. Because the default configuration is not always appropriate, you should know the most important command line options:

▶ The command line options `stage` and `install` specify whether the Boost C++ Libraries are installed in a subdirectory called `stage` or are made available system-wide. The meaning of system-wide depends on the operating system. On Windows, the target directory is `C:\Boost`; on Linux it is `/usr/local`. The target directory can also be explicitly specified with the `--prefix` option. Starting **bjam** without command line options always means `stage`.

▶ If **bjam** is called without any command line options, it will search for a suitable C++ compiler. A specific compiler can be selected using the `--toolset` option. To select the Microsoft C++ compiler from Visual Studio 2010 on Windows, call **bjam** with `--toolset=msvc-10.0`. To select the GCC compiler on Linux, use `--toolset=gcc`.

▶ The command line option `--build-type` determines which build types of the libraries are created. By default, this option is set to `minimal`, meaning that only release builds are created. This may become an issue for developers who want to create debug builds of their projects with Visual Studio or GCC. Because these compilers automatically try to link against the debug builds of the Boost C++ Libraries, an error message will be displayed. In this case the option `--build-type` should be set to `complete` to generate both debug and release builds of the Boost C++ Libraries. This can take quite some time, which is why `complete` is not used by default.

To create both debug and release builds of the Boost C++ Libraries with the C++ compiler from Visual Studio 2010 and install them in the directory `D:\Boost`, enter the following command:

bjam --toolset=msvc-10.0 --build-type=complete --prefix=D:\Boost install

To build them on Linux and install them in the default directory, the command would be:

bjam --toolset=gcc --build-type=complete install

There are many other command line options that you can use to specify in detail how to compile the Boost C++ Libraries. I typically use the following command on Windows:

bjam --toolset=msvc-10.0 debug release link=static runtime-link=shared install

The `debug` and `release` options cause both debug and release builds to be generated. `link=static` only creates static libraries. `runtime-link=shared` specifies that the C++ runtime library is dynamically linked, which is the default setting for C++ projects in Visual Studio 2010.

Overview

Version 1.47.0 of the Boost C++ Libraries contains more than 100 libraries. This book discusses the following libraries in detail:

Table 1.1 – Covered Libraries

Boost C++ Library	Standard	Short Description
Boost.Any		Boost.Any provides a data type called `boost::any` which stores arbitrary types. For example, a variable of type `boost::any` can first store a value of type `int` before replacing it with a string of type `std::string`.
Boost.Array	TR1	Boost.Array makes it possible to treat C++ arrays just like containers from the C++ standard.
Boost.Asio	TR2	Boost.Asio allows you to develop applications, such as network applications, that process data asynchronously.
Boost.Bimap		Boost.Bimap provides a class called `boost::bimap` which is similar to `std::map`. The crucial difference is that `boost::bimap` allows you to search for both key and value.
Boost.Bind	TR1	Boost.Bind is a kind of adapter to pass functions as template parameters, even if the function signature is incompatible with the template parameter.
Boost.CircularBuffer		Boost.CircularBuffer offers a circular container with a constant memory size.
Boost.Conversion		Boost.Conversion provides three cast operators to perform downcasts and cross casts, and convert between values of different numeric types.
Boost.DateTime		Boost.DateTime can be used to process, read and write date and time values.
Boost.DynamicBitset		Boost.DynamicBitset provides a container similar to `std::bitset`. While the number of bits for `std::bitset` is set at compile time, `boost::dynamic_bitset` allows you to set it at run-time.
Boost.Exception		Boost.Exception allows you to add additional data to thrown exceptions in order to provide more data to `catch` handlers. This makes it easier to debug and respond to exceptions.
Boost.Filesystem	TR2	Boost.Filesystem provides a class to process paths and several functions to access files and directories.

Boost.Foreach		Boost.Foreach provides a macro which is similar to "foreach"-loops in other programming languages. With that macro you can, for example, iterate over a container without using iterators yourself.
Boost.Format		Boost.Format replaces the function `std::printf()` with a type-safe and extendable class, `boost::format`.
Boost.Function	TR1	Boost.Function simplifies the definition of function pointers.
Boost.Interprocess		Boost.Interprocess allows applications to communicate via shared memory in a fast and efficient manner.
Boost.Intrusive		Boost.Intrusive provides "intrusive" containers, which are used like containers from the C++ standard. They provide higher performance, but also have special requirements for the objects they contain.
Boost.Lambda		Boost.Lambda allows the definition of anonymous functions. Code is written down inline where normally a function call would be required to avoid having to define separate functions.
Boost.MinMax		Boost.MinMax provides an algorithm which can find the smallest and greatest value in a container without calling the two functions `std::min()` and `std::max()`.
Boost.MultiArray		Boost.MultiArray simplifies working with multidimensional arrays.
Boost.MultiIndex		Boost.MultiIndex allows you to define new containers that can support multiple interfaces such as the ones from `std::vector` and `std::map`.
Boost.NumericConversion		Boost.NumericConversion provides a cast operator to safely convert between values of different numeric types without generating an overflow or underflow condition.
Boost.Operators		With Boost.Operators many operators can be automatically overloaded with the help of already defined operators.
Boost.PointerContainer		Boost.PointerContainer provides containers which are optimized for managing dynamically allocated objects.
Boost.Ref	TR1	Boost.Ref provides adapters that allow you to pass references to objects that can't be copied to functions that pass parameters by copy.
Boost.Regex	TR1	Boost.Regex provides functions to search strings via regular expressions.
Boost.Serialization		With Boost.Serialization, objects can be serialized and stored in files to be reloaded later.
Boost.Signals2		Boost.Signals2 is a framework for event handling based on the "signal/slot" concept: functions are associated with signals and automatically called when a signal is triggered.

Boost.SmartPoiners	TR1	Boost.SmartPoiners provides a set of smart pointers which simplify managing dynamically allocated objects.
Boost.Spirit		Boost.Spirit allows you to generate parsers using a syntax similar to EBNF (Extended Backus Naur Form).
Boost.StringAlgorithms		Boost.StringAlgorithms provides many stand-alone functions to facilitate string handling.
Boost.System	TR2	Boost.System offers a framework to process system- and application-specific error codes.
Boost.Swap		Boost.Swap defines `boost::swap()` which does the same as `std::swap()` but is optimized for many Boost C++ Libraries.
Boost.Thread	C++0x	Boost.Thread allows you to develop multithreaded applications.
Boost.Tokenizer		Boost.Tokenizer allows you to iterate over tokens in a string.
Boost.Tuple	TR1	Boost.Tuple provides a generalized version of `std::pair` which can not only be used to store two but arbitrary many values.
Boost.Unordered	TR1	Boost.Unordered adds `boost::unordered_set` and `boost::unordered_map` to the containers from the C++ standard.
Boost.Utility		Boost.Utility is a collection of various tools which are too small to be put in their own libraries and don't fit in another library.
Boost.Variant		Boost.Variant permits the definition of data types that, similar to `union`, group multiple data types. The advantage of Boost.Variant over `union` is that you can use classes as well.

Although Technical Report 1 was published in 2003, details about standardization regarding C++0x and Technical Report 2 represent the current status. Because neither the next version of the C++ standard nor the Technical Report 2 have been approved yet, either or both may still change.

2

Smart Pointers

General

The first version of the C++ standard, adopted in 1998, only provides one smart pointer: `std::auto_ptr`. In principle, it behaves like a regular pointer – it provides access to a dynamically allocated object by storing its address. However, `std::auto_ptr` is considered smart as it automatically releases the contained object during destruction by calling the `delete` operator. This requires that you give the pointer the address of the object – returned by the `new` operator – at initialization. Because the `delete` operator is called within the destructor of `std::auto_ptr`, the associated memory for the contained object is guaranteed to be released.

This becomes even more important in conjunction with exceptions. Without smart pointers such as `std::auto_ptr`, every function that allocates dynamic memory would need to catch every possible exception so that it could release memory before passing the exception to its calling function. The library Boost.SmartPointers[1] provides many additional smart pointers that can be used in all kind of situations.

RAII

The principle of smart pointers is based on a common idiom called RAII (Resource Acquisition Is Initialization). Smart pointers are only one example of this idiom, though a very prominent one. Smart pointers are used to ensure that dynamically allocated memory is released properly under all circumstances, freeing the developer from the burden of managing this on her own. This includes scenarios in which the execution of a function is interrupted by an exception, and the instruction to release the memory is skipped. This guarantee is accomplished by initializing a smart pointer with the address of a dynamically allocated object, which in turn is used to release the memory during destruction. Because the destructor is always executed, the contained memory is always released.

---

[1] http://www.boost.org/libs/smart_ptr/

RAII is applied whenever a second instruction is needed to release a resource previously allocated by another instruction. Because many C++ programs require dynamically allocated memory, smart pointers are important RAII classes. RAII itself can be applied in other scenarios, too.

Example 2.1

```cpp
#include <windows.h>

class windows_handle
{
  public:
    windows_handle(HANDLE h) : handle_(h) {}

    ~windows_handle()
    {
      CloseHandle(handle_);
    }

    HANDLE handle() const
    {
      return handle_;
    }

  private:
    HANDLE handle_;
};

int main()
{
  windows_handle h(OpenProcess(PROCESS_SET_INFORMATION, FALSE,
    GetCurrentProcessId()));
  SetPriorityClass(h.handle(), HIGH_PRIORITY_CLASS);
}
```

Example 2.1 defines a class called `windows_handle`, which calls the function `CloseHandle()` in its destructor. Because this is a Windows API function, the program can only be executed on Windows. On Windows, many resources must be opened before being used. This implies that resources should be closed once they are no longer being used. The class `windows_handle` provides a mechanism to ensure just that.

An instance of type `windows_handle` is initialized with a handle. Windows uses handles in order to uniquely identify its resources. For example, the function `OpenProcess()` returns a handle of type `HANDLE` that can be used to access a currently running process. In Example 2.1, the program itself is accessed.

Using the returned handle, the process priority is increased, allowing the application to request more CPU time from the scheduler. This is only for illustration purposes and does not serve any real benefit. The important point here is that the resource opened with `OpenProcess()` does not need to be explicitly closed with `CloseHandle()`. Of course the resource would be closed anyway once the program terminates. However, in more complex programs the class `windows_handle` ensures that a resource is correctly closed when no longer needed. Once a particular resource leaves its visibility scope – in the above example it's **h** at the end of `main()` – the destructor is automatically invoked, which in turn closes the contained resource.

Scoped Pointer

A scoped pointer is a pointer that is the sole owner of a dynamically allocated object. The corresponding class is called `boost::scoped_ptr` and is defined in `boost/scoped_ptr.hpp`. Unlike `std::auto_ptr`, a scoped pointer is not able to transfer ownership of its contained object to another scoped pointer. Once initialized with an address, the dynamically allocated object is released during destruction.

Because a scoped pointer simply stores and solely owns an address, the implementation of `boost::scoped_ptr` is less complex than `std::auto_ptr`. If you don't need to transfer ownership, it is better to use `boost::scoped_ptr` instead of `std::auto_ptr` to avoid inadvertent transfer of ownership.

Example 2.2

```
#include <boost/scoped_ptr.hpp>

int main()
{
  boost::scoped_ptr<int> i(new int);
  *i = 1;
  *i.get() = 2;
  i.reset(new int);
}
```

Once initialized, the contained object of the smart pointer `boost::scoped_ptr` can be accessed through an interface similar to ordinary pointers (see Example 2.2). This is achieved by providing the corresponding operators `operator*`, `operator->`, and `operator bool`. In addition, the member functions `get()` and `reset()` are available. `get()` returns the address of the contained object, and `reset()` reinitializes the smart pointer with a new object. In this case, the contained object is automatically destroyed before the new object is assigned.

The contained object is released with `delete` within the destructor of `boost::scoped_ptr`. This puts an important restriction on the types of objects `boost::scoped_ptr` can use. `boost:scoped_ptr` is not allowed to be initialized with the address of a dynamically allocated array because this would require a call to `delete[]`. In these cases, the class `boost:scoped_array`, which is introduced next, can be used.

Scoped Array

A scoped array is used just like a scoped pointer. The crucial difference is that the destructor of a scoped array uses the operator `delete[]` to release the contained object. Because this operator only applies to arrays, a scoped array must be initialized with the address of a dynamically allocated array.

The corresponding class for scoped arrays is `boost::scoped_array` and is defined in `boost/scoped_array.hpp`.

Example 2.3

```
#include <boost/scoped_array.hpp>

int main()
{
  boost::scoped_array<int> i(new int[2]);
  *i.get() = 1;
  i[1] = 2;
  i.reset(new int[3]);
}
```

The class boost::scoped_array (see Example 2.3) provides overloads for the operators operator[] and operator bool. Using operator[], a specific element of the array can be accessed. Thus, an object of type boost::scoped_array behaves exactly like the array it owns.

Just like boost::scoped_ptr, the member functions get() and reset() are provided to retrieve and reinitialize the address of the contained object.

Shared Pointer

This smart pointer is widely used and was badly missed in the first version of the C++ standard. It has been added in Technical Report 1 (TR1). If a compiler supports TR1, the class std::shared_ptr, which is defined in the header file memory, can be used. In the Boost C++ libraries, the smart pointer is boost::shared_ptr and defined in boost/shared_ptr.hpp.

The smart pointer boost::shared_ptr is similar to boost::scoped_ptr. The key difference is that boost::shared_ptr is not necessarily the exclusive owner of an object. Ownership can be shared with other smart pointers of type boost::shared_ptr. In these cases, the shared object is not released until the last shared pointer referencing the object is destroyed.

Because ownership can be shared with boost::shared_ptr, copies of any shared pointer can be created – unlike boost::scoped_ptr. This lets you store smart pointers in standard containers, something that cannot be done with std::auto_ptr, which transfers ownership when copied.

Example 2.4

```
#include <boost/shared_ptr.hpp>
#include <vector>

int main()
{
  std::vector<boost::shared_ptr<int> > v;
  v.push_back(boost::shared_ptr<int>(new int(1)));
  v.push_back(boost::shared_ptr<int>(new int(2)));
}
```

Thanks to boost::shared_ptr, it is possible to safely use dynamically allocated objects with standard containers as shown in Example 2.4. Because boost::shared_ptr can share ownership of its contained object, copies stored in the container (as well as additional copies in case the container needs to be rearranged) are equal. As outlined before, this is not the case with std::auto_ptr, which should never be stored in a container.

Similar to boost::scoped_ptr, the class boost::shared_ptr provides overloads for the following operators: operator*, operator->, and operator bool. In addition, get() and reset() are available to retrieve and reinitialize the address of the contained object.

Example 2.5

```
#include <boost/shared_ptr.hpp>

int main()
{
  boost::shared_ptr<int> i1(new int(1));
  boost::shared_ptr<int> i2(i1);
  i1.reset(new int(2));
}
```

Example 2.5 defines two shared pointers **i1** and **i2**; both refer to the same object of type int. While **i1** is explicitly initialized with the address returned by new, **i2** is copy-constructed from **i1**. The address of the contained integer of **i1** is then reinitialized by a call to reset(). However, the previously contained object is not released because it is still referenced by **i2**. The smart pointer boost::shared_ptr counts the number of shared pointers currently referencing the same object and releases it only when the last shared pointer loses its scope.

By default, boost::shared_ptr uses the delete operator to destroy the contained object. However, you can specify how to destroy the object as shown in Example 2.6.

Example 2.6

```
#include <boost/shared_ptr.hpp>
#include <windows.h>

int main()
{
  boost::shared_ptr<void> h(OpenProcess(PROCESS_SET_INFORMATION, FALSE,
    GetCurrentProcessId()), CloseHandle);
  SetPriorityClass(h.get(), HIGH_PRIORITY_CLASS);
}
```

The constructor of boost::shared_ptr takes a regular function or a function object as the second parameter, which in turn is used for destruction of the contained object. In Example 2.6, the Windows API function CloseHandle() is passed. Once the variable **h** loses its scope, the passed function is called instead of the delete operator. In order to avoid compiler errors, the function is required to take one parameter of type HANDLE, which is the case with CloseHandle().

Example 2.6 actually behaves the same as Example 2.1, which illustrated the RAII idiom. However, instead of defining a separate class windows_handle, the example takes advantage of the specific characteristics of boost::shared_ptr by passing a function to the constructor which is automatically called once the shared pointer goes out of scope.

Please note that we pass void and not HANDLE as a template parameter to boost::shared_ptr. Because HANDLE is a type definition for void*, it would be wrong to instantiate boost::shared_ptr with HANDLE. After all a smart pointer like boost::shared_ptr expects a complete type like void and not void*.

Example 2.6 only works because HANDLE is defined as void*. You should not expect that you can always use boost::shared_ptr and never need to define utility classes like windows_handle.

As boost::shared_ptr is the most important of all smart pointers provided by the Boost C++ Libraries, the function boost::make_shared() has been defined to create objects of type boost::shared_ptr more efficiently (see Example 2.7).

Example 2.7

```
#include <boost/shared_ptr.hpp>
#include <boost/make_shared.hpp>

int main()
{
  boost::shared_ptr<int> i1 = boost::make_shared<int>(1);
  boost::shared_ptr<int> i2(i1);
  i1.reset(new int(2));
}
```

You should use boost::make_shared() rather than instantiating boost::shared_ptr with a pointer. boost::make_shared() allocates memory for the shared object and the reference counter used internally by the smart pointer in one step. This is more efficient than allocating memory for the shared object with new yourself and letting the smart pointer call new again for the reference counter.

Shared Array

A shared array works essentially the same as a shared pointer. The crucial difference is that the destructor of the shared array uses the delete[] operator to release the contained object. As this operator only applies to arrays, a shared array must be initialized with the address of a dynamically allocated array.

The corresponding class for shared arrays is boost::shared_array and is defined in boost/shared_array.hpp.

Example 2.8

```
#include <boost/shared_array.hpp>
#include <iostream>

int main()
{
  boost::shared_array<int> i1(new int[2]);
  boost::shared_array<int> i2(i1);
  i1[0] = 1;
  std::cout << i2[0] << std::endl;
}
```

Just like with a shared pointer, the ownership of the contained object can be shared with other shared arrays. Example 2.8 defines two variables, **i1** and **i2**, both of which refer to the same dynamically allocated array. The value 1 – stored using operator[] of **i1** – can be referenced and printed to the standard output stream with **i2**.

As with all the smart pointers introduced in this chapter, boost::shared_array also provides the member functions get() and reset(). In addition, operator bool is overloaded.

Weak Pointer

Every smart pointer introduced so far can be used individually in different scenarios. However, weak pointer only makes sense if used in conjunction with a shared pointer. It is defined as boost::weak_ptr in boost/weak_ptr.hpp (see Example 2.9).

Example 2.9

```cpp
#include <windows.h>
#include <boost/shared_ptr.hpp>
#include <boost/weak_ptr.hpp>
#include <iostream>

DWORD WINAPI reset(LPVOID p)
{
  boost::shared_ptr<int> *sh = static_cast<boost::shared_ptr<int>*>(p);
  sh->reset();
  return 0;
}

DWORD WINAPI print(LPVOID p)
{
  boost::weak_ptr<int> *w = static_cast<boost::weak_ptr<int>*>(p);
  boost::shared_ptr<int> sh = w->lock();
  if (sh)
    std::cout << *sh << std::endl;
  return 0;
}

int main()
{
  boost::shared_ptr<int> sh(new int(99));
  boost::weak_ptr<int> w(sh);
  HANDLE threads[2];
  threads[0] = CreateThread(0, 0, reset, &sh, 0, 0);
  threads[1] = CreateThread(0, 0, print, &w, 0, 0);
  WaitForMultipleObjects(2, threads, TRUE, INFINITE);
}
```

boost::weak_ptr must always be initialized with a boost::shared_ptr. Once initialized, it basically provides only one useful member function: lock(). It returns a boost::shared_ptr that shares ownership with the shared pointer used to initialize the weak pointer. In case the shared pointer does not contain any object, the returned one is empty as well.

Weak pointers make sense whenever a function is expected to work with an object managed by a shared pointer, but the lifetime of the object should not depend on the function itself. The function should only use the object as long as it is owned by at least one shared pointer somewhere else in the program. In case the shared pointer is reset, the object should not be kept alive because of an additional shared pointer inside the corresponding function.

Example 2.9 creates two threads in `main()` using functions provided by the Windows API. Thus, the example can only be compiled and run on Windows.

The first thread executes the function `reset()`, which receives the address of a shared pointer. The second thread executes the function `print()`, which receives the address of a weak pointer. This weak pointer has been previously initialized with the shared pointer.

Once the program is launched, both `reset()` and `print()` are executed at the same time. However, the order of execution cannot be predicted. This leads to the potential issue of `reset()` destroying the object while it is being accessed by `print()`.

The weak pointer solves this issue as follows: invoking `lock()` returns a shared pointer which points to a valid object if one exists at the time of the call. If not, the shared pointer is set to 0 and is equivalent to a standard null pointer.

The weak pointer itself does not have any impact on the lifetime of an object. In order to safely access the object within the `print()` function, `lock()` returns a shared pointer. This guarantees that even if a different thread attempts to release the object, it will continue to exist thanks to the returned shared pointer.

Intrusive Pointer

In general, an intrusive pointer works the same as a shared pointer. However, while `boost::shared_ptr` internally keeps track of the number of shared pointers referencing a particular object, the developer has to keep track of this for the intrusive pointer himself. This especially makes sense if classes from frameworks are used that already keep track of the number of times they are referenced.

The intrusive pointer is defined as `boost::intrusive_ptr` in `boost/intrusive_ptr.hpp`.

Example 2.10 uses functions provided by COM (Component Object Model) and thus can only be built and run on Windows. COM objects are a perfect example for `boost::intrusive_ptr` because they keep track of the number of pointers referencing them. The internal reference count can be incremented or decremented by 1 with the member functions `AddRef()` and `Release()`. Once the counter reaches 0, the COM object is automatically destroyed.

The two member functions `AddRef()` and `Release()` are called from within `intrusive_ptr_add_ref()` and `intrusive_ptr_release()`. Boost.Intrusive expects a developer to define these two functions, which are automatically called whenever a reference counter must be incremented or decremented. The parameter passed to these functions is a pointer to the type that was used to instantiate the class template `boost::intrusive_ptr`.

Example 2.10

```cpp
#include <boost/intrusive_ptr.hpp>
#include <atlbase.h>
#include <iostream>

void intrusive_ptr_add_ref(IDispatch *p)
{
  p->AddRef();
}

void intrusive_ptr_release(IDispatch *p)
{
  p->Release();
}

void check_windows_folder()
{
  CLSID clsid;
  CLSIDFromProgID(CComBSTR("Scripting.FileSystemObject"), &clsid);
  void *p;
  CoCreateInstance(clsid, 0, CLSCTX_INPROC_SERVER, __uuidof(IDispatch), &p);
  boost::intrusive_ptr<IDispatch> disp(static_cast<IDispatch*>(p), false);
  CComDispatchDriver dd(disp.get());
  CComVariant arg("C:\\Windows");
  CComVariant ret(false);
  dd.Invoke1(CComBSTR("FolderExists"), &arg, &ret);
  std::cout << (ret.boolVal != 0) << std::endl;
}

void main()
{
  CoInitialize(0);
  check_windows_folder();
  CoUninitialize();
}
```

The COM object used in this example is called FileSystemObject and is available on Windows by default. It provides access to the underlying file system to, for example, check whether a given directory exists. In Example 2.10, the existence of a directory called C:\Windows is checked. How that works internally depends solely on COM and is irrelevant to the functionality of boost::intrusive_ptr. The crucial point is that once the intrusive pointer **disp** goes out of scope at the end of check_windows_folder(), the function intrusive_ptr_release() is called automatically. This in turn will decrement the internal reference counter of the COM object FileSystemObject to 0 and destroy the object.

Pointer Containers

After meeting the different smart pointers of the Boost C++ Libraries, one should be able to write safe code for dynamically allocated objects as well as arrays. Many times, these objects must be stored within a container which, as seen above, is fairly easy to do with boost::shared_ptr and boost::shared_array.

Example 2.11

```
#include <boost/shared_ptr.hpp>
#include <vector>

int main()
{
  std::vector<boost::shared_ptr<int> > v;
  v.push_back(boost::shared_ptr<int>(new int(1)));
  v.push_back(boost::shared_ptr<int>(new int(2)));
}
```

While the code in Example 2.11 is correct, and smart pointers can be used that way, it is impractical for a couple of reasons. For one, the repetitive declaration of boost::shared_ptr requires more typing. In addition, copying the boost::shared_ptr to, from, and within the container requires incrementing and decrementing the internal reference counter continuously and thus is deemed very inefficient. For these reasons, the Boost C++ Libraries provide Boost.PointerContainers[2], which are optimized for managing dynamically allocated objects.

Example 2.12

```
#include <boost/ptr_container/ptr_vector.hpp>

int main()
{
  boost::ptr_vector<int> v;
  v.push_back(new int(1));
  v.push_back(new int(2));
}
```

In Example 2.12, the class boost::ptr_vector is defined in boost/ptr_container/ptr_vector.hpp and works the same way as the container instantiated with boost::shared_ptr in Example 2.11. Because boost::ptr_vector is specialized for dynamically allocated objects, it is easier to use and more efficient. However, because boost::ptr_vector is the sole owner of all contained objects, ownership can't be shared with a shared pointer that isn't stored inside the container, unlike std::vector<boost::shared_ptr<int> >.

Besides boost::ptr_vector, additional containers specialized for managing dynamically allocated objects are available, including: boost::ptr_deque, boost::ptr_list, boost::ptr_set, boost::ptr_map, boost::ptr_unordered_set, and boost::ptr_unordered_map. These containers are equivalent to the ones provided by the C++ standard. The last two containers match the containers std::unordered_set and std::unordered_map in Technical Report 1. They are also implemented as boost::unordered_set and boost::unordered_map and provided by Boost.Unordered.

---

[2] http://www.boost.org/libs/ptr_container/

Exercises

1. Optimize the following program by using an appropriate smart pointer:

   ### Example 2.13

   ```cpp
   #include <iostream>
   #include <cstring>

   char *get(const char *s)
   {
     int size = std::strlen(s);
     char *text = new char[size + 1];
     std::strncpy(text, s, size + 1);
     return text;
   }

   void print(char *text)
   {
     std::cout << text << std::endl;
   }

   int main(int argc, char *argv[])
   {
     if (argc < 2)
     {
       std::cerr << argv[0] << " <data>" << std::endl;
       return 1;
     }

     char *text = get(argv[1]);
     print(text);
     delete[] text;
   }
   ```

2. Optimize the following program:

   ### Example 2.14

   ```cpp
   #include <vector>

   template <typename T>
   T *create()
   {
     return new T;
   }

   int main()
   {
     std::vector<int*> v;
     v.push_back(create<int>());
   }
   ```

3

Function Objects

General

This chapter deals with function objects and could have been called "Functions of higher order" as well. This refers to functions which can be passed to or returned from other functions. Functions of higher order are implemented as function objects in C++, thus the original title still makes sense.

This chapter presents several Boost C++ Libraries that deal with function objects. Boost.Bind[1] replaces the well-known `std::bind1st()` and `std::bind2nd()` functions from the C++ standard, Boost.Function[2] provides a class to encapsulate function pointers, and Boost.Lambda[3] introduces a way to create anonymous functions.

Boost.Bind

Boost.Bind simplifies a feature that is already provided by the C++ standard via the functions `std::bind1st()` and `std::bind2nd()`: It should be possible to pass functions with large numbers of parameters where functions with a specific and different signature are expected. Some of the best examples for such a scenario are the many algorithms defined by the C++ standard.

---

[1] http://www.boost.org/libs/bind/
[2] http://www.boost.org/libs/function/
[3] http://www.boost.org/libs/lambda/

Example 3.1

```
#include <iostream>
#include <vector>
#include <algorithm>

void print(int i)
{
  std::cout << i << std::endl;
}

int main()
{
  std::vector<int> v;
  v.push_back(1);
  v.push_back(3);
  v.push_back(2);

  std::for_each(v.begin(), v.end(), print);
}
```

As its third parameter, the algorithm `std::for_each()` expects a function or function object that accepts exactly one parameter. When `std::for_each()` is called, the values in the container (in Example 3.1, values of type `int`) are passed one-by-one to the `print()` function. However, if a function with a different signature is needed, things get complicated. An example is the function `add()`, shown below, which adds a constant value to each value of the container and displays the result.

```
void add(int i, int j)
{
  std::cout << i + j << std::endl;
}
```

Because `std::for_each()` expects a function that takes only one parameter, the `add()` function cannot be passed directly. Instead, the source code needs to be modified.

Example 3.2

```
#include <iostream>
#include <vector>
#include <algorithm>
#include <functional>

class add
  : public std::binary_function<int, int, void>
{
public:
  void operator()(int i, int j) const
  {
    std::cout << i + j << std::endl;
  }
};

int main()
{
  std::vector<int> v;
```

```
  v.push_back(1);
  v.push_back(3);
  v.push_back(2);

  std::for_each(v.begin(), v.end(), std::bind1st(add(), 10));
}
```

Example 3.2 adds the value 10 to every value of the container **v** and writes the result to the standard output stream. The source code had to be substantially modified to make this possible: The add() function has been converted to a function object derived from std::binary_function.

Boost.Bind simplifies the binding between different functions. It consists of the template function boost::bind(), which is defined in boost/bind.hpp. With this function Example 3.2 can be implemented as shown in Example 3.3.

Example 3.3

```
#include <boost/bind.hpp>
#include <iostream>
#include <vector>
#include <algorithm>

void add(int i, int j)
{
  std::cout << i + j << std::endl;
}

int main()
{
  std::vector<int> v;
  v.push_back(1);
  v.push_back(3);
  v.push_back(2);

  std::for_each(v.begin(), v.end(), boost::bind(add, 10, _1));
}
```

Functions like add() no longer need to be converted to a function object in order to be used with std::for_each(). With boost::bind(), the function can be used as is by passing it as the first parameter.

Because the add() function expects two parameters, they need to be passed to boost::bind() as well. The first one is the constant value 10, the second one is a weird looking _1.

_1 is called a placeholder and is defined by Boost.Bind. Besides _1, Boost.Bind also defines _2 and _3. With these placeholders, boost::bind() can be transformed into a unary, binary, or tertiary function. In the case of _1, boost::bind() is transformed into a unary function – a function which expects a single parameter. This is necessary because std::for_each() expects a unary function.

When the program is run, std::for_each() calls the unary function for each value of the container **v**. The value is passed to the unary function through the placeholder _1. The placeholder and the literal are passed to the `add()` function. Through this mechanism, `std::for_each()` only sees the unary function defined by `boost::bind()`. `boost::bind()` itself simply calls a different function and passes values such as literals or placeholders as parameters.

Example 3.4 defines a binary function with the help of `boost::bind()`. Example 3.4 uses the algorithm `std::sort()` which expects a binary function as the third parameter.

Example 3.4

```cpp
#include <boost/bind.hpp>
#include <vector>
#include <algorithm>

bool compare(int i, int j)
{
  return i > j;
}

int main()
{
  std::vector<int> v;
  v.push_back(1);
  v.push_back(3);
  v.push_back(2);

  std::sort(v.begin(), v.end(), boost::bind(compare, _1, _2));
}
```

Because it uses two placeholders, _1 and _2, `boost::bind()` is a binary function. The `std::sort()` algorithm calls this function with two values from the container **v** and uses the return value to sort the container accordingly. The container is sorted in descending order using `compare()`.

However, because `compare()` is already a binary function, `boost::bind()` is actually superfluous.

Example 3.5

```cpp
#include <boost/bind.hpp>
#include <vector>
#include <algorithm>

bool compare(int i, int j)
{
  return i > j;
}

int main()
{
  std::vector<int> v;
  v.push_back(1);
  v.push_back(3);
  v.push_back(2);

  std::sort(v.begin(), v.end(), compare);
}
```

Using `boost::bind()` can still make sense. For example, if the container needs to be sorted in ascending order, and the function `compare()` can't be changed, `boost::bind()` can be used.

Example 3.6

```
#include <boost/bind.hpp>
#include <vector>
#include <algorithm>

bool compare(int i, int j)
{
  return i > j;
}

int main()
{
  std::vector<int> v;
  v.push_back(1);
  v.push_back(3);
  v.push_back(2);

  std::sort(v.begin(), v.end(), boost::bind(compare, _2, _1));
}
```

Example 3.6 only changed the order of the placeholders: _2 is passed as the first parameter to `compare()` while _1 is passed as the second parameter. This effectively changes the sort order.

Boost.Ref

The library Boost.Ref[4] is typically used in conjunction with Boost.Bind. It provides two functions – `boost::ref()` and `boost::cref()` – defined in `boost/ref.hpp`.

Boost.Ref is important when functions with a reference parameter are used with `boost::bind()`. As `boost::bind()` copies parameters, references need to be handled explicitly.

---

[4] http://www.boost.org/doc/html/ref.html

Example 3.7

```cpp
#include <boost/bind.hpp>
#include <iostream>
#include <vector>
#include <algorithm>

void add(int i, int j, std::ostream &os)
{
  os << i + j << std::endl;
}

int main()
{
  std::vector<int> v;
  v.push_back(1);
  v.push_back(3);
  v.push_back(2);

  std::for_each(v.begin(), v.end(), boost::bind(add, 10, _1,
    boost::ref(std::cout)));
}
```

Example 3.7 uses the add() function from the previous section. This time, however, the function expects a reference to a stream object in order to print the sum. As parameters to boost::bind() are passed by value, **std::cout** cannot be used directly because boost::bind() would try to make a copy of it.

With the template function boost::ref(), streams such as **std::cout** can be passed by reference, which makes it possible to compile the example successfully.

In order to pass constant objects by reference, the template function boost::cref() can be used.

Boost.Function

Boost.Function[5] provides a class called boost::function to encapsulate function pointers. It is defined in boost/function.hpp and is used as shown in Example 3.8.

Example 3.8

```cpp
#include <boost/function.hpp>
#include <iostream>
#include <cstdlib>
#include <cstring>

int main()
{
  boost::function<int (const char*)> f = std::atoi;
  std::cout << f("1609") << std::endl;
  f = std::strlen;
  std::cout << f("1609") << std::endl;
}
```

---

[5] http://www.boost.org/libs/function/

`boost::function` makes it possible to define a pointer to a function with a specific signature. Example 3.8 defines a pointer **f** which can point to functions that expect a parameter of type `const char*` and return a value of type `int`. Once defined, functions with matching signatures can be assigned to the pointer. Example 3.8 first assigns the function `std::atoi()` to **f** before **f** is reassigned to `std::strlen()`.

Please note that data types do not need to match exactly. Even though `std::strlen()` uses `std::size_t` as its return type, it can still be assigned to **f**. Because **f** is a function pointer, the assigned function can be called using `operator()`. Depending on what function is currently assigned, either `std::atoi()` or `std::strlen()` is called. If **f** is called without having a function assigned, an exception of type `boost::bad_function_call` is thrown (see Example 3.9).

Example 3.9

```
#include <boost/function.hpp>
#include <iostream>

int main()
{
  try
  {
    boost::function<int (const char*)> f;
    f("");
  }
  catch (boost::bad_function_call &ex)
  {
    std::cout << ex.what() << std::endl;
  }
}
```

Note that assigning the value 0 to a function pointer of type `boost::function` releases any currently assigned function. Calling it after releasing also results in a `boost::bad_function_call` exception being thrown. In order to check whether or not a function pointer is currently assigned to a function, the member function `empty()` or `operator bool` can be called.

Example 3.10

```
#include <boost/function.hpp>
#include <iostream>

struct world
{
  void hello(std::ostream &os)
  {
    os << "Hello, world!" << std::endl;
  }
};

int main()
{
  boost::function<void (world*, std::ostream&)> f = &world::hello;
  world w;
  f(&w, boost::ref(std::cout));
}
```

It is also possible to assign class member functions to objects of type `boost::function` (see Example 3.10).

When calling such a function, the first parameter passed indicates the particular object for which the function is called. Therefore, the first parameter after the open parenthesis inside the template definition must be a pointer to that particular class. The following parameters denote the signature of the corresponding member function.

The program also uses `boost::ref()` from Boost.Ref, which provides an easy way of passing references to a function.

Boost.Lambda

Unnamed functions – called lambda functions – currently exist in various programming languages, but not in C++. It is likely that C++0x will introduce lambda functions to C++. For example, lambda functions are already supported by Visual C++ 2010. With Boost.Lambda[6], lambda functions can be used in C++ programs today, no matter which C++ compiler is used.

The general goal of lambda functions is to make the source code more compact and thus more comprehensible. Consider Example 3.11, which is the same as Example 3.1 from the first section of this chapter.

Example 3.11

```
#include <iostream>
#include <vector>
#include <algorithm>

void print(int i)
{
  std::cout << i << std::endl;
}

int main()
{
  std::vector<int> v;
  v.push_back(1);
  v.push_back(3);
  v.push_back(2);

  std::for_each(v.begin(), v.end(), print);
}
```

This program takes the values of the container **v** and writes them to the standard output stream with `print()`. Because `print()` only writes an int, the implementation of the function is fairly simple. Strictly speaking, it is so simple that it would be convenient if one could define it on the same line where `std::for_each()` is called; thus saving the need for an additional function. The additional benefit is more compact code because the algorithm and the function for the data output are not locally separated. With Boost.Lambda this becomes possible (see Example 3.12).

---

[6] http://www.boost.org/libs/lambda/

Example 3.12

```
#include <boost/lambda/lambda.hpp>
#include <iostream>
#include <vector>
#include <algorithm>

int main()
{
  std::vector<int> v;
  v.push_back(1);
  v.push_back(3);
  v.push_back(2);

  std::for_each(v.begin(), v.end(), std::cout << boost::lambda::_1 << "\n");
}
```

Boost.Lambda provides several constructs to define unnamed functions. Code is placed where executed. The extra hassle of defining another function with a single line of code is skipped. As with the original example, the program writes all values of the container **v** to the standard output stream.

Similar to Boost.Bind, Boost.Lambda also defines three placeholders called _1, _2 and _3. Unlike Boost.Bind, these placeholders are defined in a separate namespace. Hence, the first placeholder in the example is referenced via **boost::lambda::_1**. In order to satisfy the compiler, the corresponding header file boost/lambda/lambda.hpp needs to be included.

Even though the position of the code as a third parameter to std::for_each() seems odd, Boost.Lambda allows for writing regular C++ code. Thanks to the placeholder, the values of the container **f** can be passed to **std::cout** via << to write them to the standard output stream.

While Boost.Lambda is quite powerful, there are some drawbacks. To insert a line break into the output, "\n" must be used instead of std::endl. Otherwise the code won't compile. Because the type expected by the unary std::endl template function is different from the lambda function std::cout << boost::lambda::_1, std::endl cannot be used in this case.

The header file boost/lambda/if.hpp defines several constructs to allow if statements within lambda functions. The most basic construct is the function boost::lambda::if_then(), which expects two parameters. The first parameter evaluates a condition. If the condition is true, the second parameter is executed. Each parameter can be a lambda function itself as shown in Example 3.13.

Example 3.13

```cpp
#include <boost/lambda/lambda.hpp>
#include <boost/lambda/if.hpp>
#include <iostream>
#include <vector>
#include <algorithm>

int main()
{
  std::vector<int> v;
  v.push_back(1);
  v.push_back(3);
  v.push_back(2);

  std::for_each(v.begin(), v.end(),
    boost::lambda::if_then(boost::lambda::_1 > 1,
    std::cout << boost::lambda::_1 << "\n"));
}
```

In addition to `boost::lambda::if_then()`, Boost.Lambda provides the functions `boost::lambda::if_then_else()` and `boost::lambda::if_then_else_return()`, each of which expects three parameters. Additional functions for loops, cast operators, and even for `throw`, which allows lambda functions to throw exceptions, are provided as well.

Even though complex lambda functions in C++ can be built, you need to consider aspects such as readability and maintainability. Because you need to learn and understand additional functions, like `boost::lambda::if_then()`, instead of using known C++ keywords, like `if` and `else`, the benefit of lambda functions usually decreases with their complexity. Most of the time, it is better to define a discrete function using familiar C++ constructs.

If you have access to a compiler that supports lambda functions, you don't need to use Boost.Lambda. Example 3.14, which does the same thing as Example 3.13, can be compiled with Visual C++ 2010 and shows how lambda functions will probably look like when the next version of the C++ standard becomes official.

Example 3.14

```cpp
#include <iostream>
#include <vector>
#include <algorithm>

int main()
{
  std::vector<int> v;
  v.push_back(1);
  v.push_back(3);
  v.push_back(2);

  std::for_each(v.begin(), v.end(),
    [] (int i) { if (i > 1) std::cout << i << std::endl; });
}
```

Exercises

1. Simplify the following program by converting the function object `divide_by` to a function and by replacing the `for` loop used to output the data with a standard C++ algorithm:

    Example 3.15

    ```cpp
    #include <algorithm>
    #include <functional>
    #include <vector>
    #include <iostream>

    class divide_by
      : public std::binary_function<int, int, int>
    {
    public:
      int operator()(int n, int div) const
      {
        return n / div;
      }
    };

    int main()
    {
      std::vector<int> numbers;
      numbers.push_back(10);
      numbers.push_back(20);
      numbers.push_back(30);

      std::transform(numbers.begin(), numbers.end(), numbers.begin(),
        std::bind2nd(divide_by(), 2));

      for (std::vector<int>::iterator it = numbers.begin();
        it != numbers.end(); ++it)
        std::cout << *it << std::endl;
    }
    ```

2. Simplify the following program by replacing both `for` loops with standard C++ algorithms:

Example 3.16

```
#include <string>
#include <vector>
#include <iostream>

int main()
{
  std::vector<std::string> strings;
  strings.push_back("Boost");
  strings.push_back("C++");
  strings.push_back("Libraries");

  std::vector<int> sizes;

  for (std::vector<std::string>::iterator it = strings.begin();
    it != strings.end(); ++it)
    sizes.push_back(it->size());

  for (std::vector<int>::iterator it = sizes.begin();
    it != sizes.end(); ++it)
    std::cout << *it << std::endl;
}
```

3. Simplify the following program by modifying the type of the variable **processors** and replacing the `for` loop with a standard C++ algorithm:

Example 3.17

```
#include <vector>
#include <iostream>
#include <cstdlib>
#include <cstring>

int main()
{
  std::vector<int(*)(const char*)> processors;
  processors.push_back(std::atoi);
  processors.push_back(
    reinterpret_cast<int(*)(const char*)>(std::strlen));

  const char data[] = "1.23";

  for (std::vector<int(*)(const char*)>::iterator it =
    processors.begin(); it != processors.end(); ++it)
    std::cout << (*it)(data) << std::endl;
}
```

4

Event Handling

General

Many developers think about graphical user interfaces when they hear the term "event handling." At the click of a button, a function is executed. The click is the event, and the function the event handler.

This pattern is certainly not limited to graphical user interfaces. In general, arbitrary objects can call dedicated functions based on specific events. The library Boost.Signals2[1] provides an easy way to apply this pattern in C++.

Strictly speaking, Boost.Function could also be used for event handling. One crucial difference between Boost.Function and Boost.Signals2, however, is the ability of Boost.Signals2 to associate more than one event handler with a single event. Therefore, Boost.Signals2 supports event-driven development much better and should be the first choice whenever events must be handled.

Boost.Signals2 is the successor of the library Boost.Signals[2], which is not discussed in this book. The main difference between the two libraries is that Boost.Signals2 supports multithreading. Because some of the interfaces have been improved as well, Boost.Signals2 should be preferred. Nonetheless, because the libraries are similar, you should be able to use Boost.Signals without many problems after reading this chapter.

Signals

While the name of the library may seem to be a bit misleading at first, it's actually not. Boost.Signals2 implements the signal/slot pattern: When a signal is fired, a corresponding slot is executed. In principle, one can substitute the words "signal" and "slot" with "event" and "event handler". However, because signals can be fired at any time, while an event implies that something has changed, the library's name is based on the signal/slot pattern.

---

[1] http://www.boost.org/libs/signals2/
[2] http://www.boost.org/libs/signals/

Consequently, Boost.Signals2 does not offer classes that resemble events. Instead, it provides a class called `boost::signals2::signal`, defined in `boost/signals2/signal.hpp`. Alternatively, the header file `boost/signals2.hpp` can be included. It defines all of the classes and functions available in Boost.Signals2. Boost.Signals2 defines `boost::signals2::signal` and other classes as well as all functions in the namespace `boost::signals2`.

Example 4.1

```
#include <boost/signals2.hpp>
#include <iostream>

void func()
{
  std::cout << "Hello, world!" << std::endl;
}

int main()
{
  boost::signals2::signal<void ()> s;
  s.connect(func);
  s();
}
```

`boost::signals2::signal` is a class template that expects the signature of a function, used as an event handler, as a template parameter. In Example 4.1, only functions with a signature of `void ()` can be associated with the signal **s**.

The function `func()` is associated with the signal **s** through `connect()`. Because `func()` conforms to the required signature `void ()`, the association is successfully established and `func()` is called whenever the signal **s** is triggered. The signal is triggered by calling **s** like a regular function. The signature of this function corresponds to the one passed as the template parameter. The brackets are empty because `void ()` does not expect any parameters. Calling **s** results in a trigger, which in turn executes the `func()` function that was previously associated with `connect()`.

The same example can also be implemented with Boost.Function.

Example 4.2

```
#include <boost/function.hpp>
#include <iostream>

void func()
{
  std::cout << "Hello, world!" << std::endl;
}

int main()
{
  boost::function<void ()> f;
  f = func;
  f();
}
```

In Example 4.2, `func()` is also executed when **f** is called. While Boost.Function can only be used in a scenario like Example 4.2, Boost.Signals2 provides far more variety, for example, it can associate multiple functions with a particular signal (see Example 4.3).

Example 4.3

```
#include <boost/signals2.hpp>
#include <iostream>

void func1()
{
  std::cout << "Hello" << std::flush;
}

void func2()
{
  std::cout << ", world!" << std::endl;
}

int main()
{
  boost::signals2::signal<void ()> s;
  s.connect(func1);
  s.connect(func2);
  s();
}
```

`boost::signals2::signal` allows you to assign multiple functions to a particular signal by calling `connect()` repeatedly. Whenever the signal is triggered, the functions are executed in the order they were associated with `connect()`. The order can also be explicitly specified with the help of an overloaded version of `connect()` that expects a value of type `int` as an additional parameter (Example 4.4). As in Example 4.3, in Example 4.4 `func1()` runs before `func2()`.

Example 4.4

```
#include <boost/signals2.hpp>
#include <iostream>

void func1()
{
  std::cout << "Hello" << std::flush;
}

void func2()
{
  std::cout << ", world!" << std::endl;
}

int main()
{
  boost::signals2::signal<void ()> s;
  s.connect(1, func2);
  s.connect(0, func1);
  s();
}
```

To release an associated function from a signal, call disconnect(). Example 4.5 only prints Hello because the association with func2() was released before the signal was triggered.

Example 4.5

```cpp
#include <boost/signals2.hpp>
#include <iostream>

void func1()
{
  std::cout << "Hello" << std::endl;
}

void func2()
{
  std::cout << ", world!" << std::endl;
}

int main()
{
  boost::signals2::signal<void ()> s;
  s.connect(func1);
  s.connect(func2);
  s.disconnect(func2);
  s();
}
```

Besides connect() and disconnect(), boost::signal provides a few more member functions (see Example 4.6).

Example 4.6

```cpp
#include <boost/signals2.hpp>
#include <iostream>

void func1()
{
  std::cout << "Hello" << std::flush;
}

void func2()
{
  std::cout << ", world!" << std::endl;
}

int main()
{
  boost::signals2::signal<void ()> s;
  s.connect(func1);
  s.connect(func2);
  std::cout << s.num_slots() << std::endl;
  if (!s.empty())
    s();
  s.disconnect_all_slots();
}
```

`num_slots()` returns the number of associated functions. If no function is associated, `num_slots()` returns 0. In this particular case, the member function `empty()` can be called instead. The member function `disconnect_all_slots()` does exactly what its name says: it releases all existing associations.

After having seen how functions are associated with signals as well as understanding what happens when a signal is triggered, one question remains: What happens to the return values of the functions? Example 4.7 answers this question.

Example 4.7

```
#include <boost/signals2.hpp>
#include <iostream>

int func1() { return 1; }
int func2() { return 2; }

int main()
{
  boost::signals2::signal<int ()> s;
  s.connect(func1);
  s.connect(func2);
  std::cout << *s() << std::endl;
}
```

Both `func1()` and `func2()` now have a return value of type `int`. **s** processes both return values and somehow writes them to the standard output stream. However, what happens exactly?

Example 4.7 will actually write 2 to the standard output stream. Both return values were correctly accepted by **s**, but except for the last one, were ignored. By default, only the last return value of all associated functions is returned.

Please note that `s()` does not directly return the result of the last function called. An object of type `boost::optional` is returned, which when dereferenced returns the number 2. Because triggering a signal that is not associated with any functions does not yield any return value, in this case `boost::optional` allows Boost.Signals2 to return an empty object.

It is possible to customize a signal so that the individual return values are processed accordingly. To do this, a "combiner" must be passed to `boost::signals2::signal` as a second parameter.

A combiner is a class with an overloaded `operator()`. This operator is automatically called with two iterators, which are used to access the functions associated with the particular signal. When the iterators are dereferenced, the functions are called and their return values become available in the combiner. A common algorithm from the C++ standard, such as `std::min_element()`, can then be used to calculate and return the smallest value.

Example 4.8

```cpp
#include <boost/signals2.hpp>
#include <iostream>
#include <algorithm>
#include <vector>

int func1() { return 1; }
int func2() { return 2; }

template <typename T>
struct min_element
{
  typedef T result_type;

  template <typename InputIterator>
  T operator()(InputIterator first, InputIterator last) const
  {
    std::vector<T> v(first, last);
    return *std::min_element(v.begin(), v.end());
  }
};

int main()
{
  boost::signals2::signal<int (), min_element<int> > s;
  s.connect(func1);
  s.connect(func2);
  std::cout << s() << std::endl;
}
```

The default combiner used by boost::signals2::signal is boost::signals2::optional_last_value. The combiner returns objects of type boost::optional. If a combiner is defined by a user, any data type can be used for the return value though. For instance, the combiner min_element in Example 4.8 returns the data type passed as a template parameter to min_element.

Unfortunately, it is not possible to pass an algorithm such as std::min_element() as a template parameter directly to boost::signals2::signal. boost::signals2::signal expects that the combiner defines a type called result_type, which denotes the type of the value returned by operator(). Since this type is not defined by standard C++ algorithms, the compiler would report an error.

Please note that it is not possible to pass the iterators **first** and **last** directly to std::min_element() as this algorithm expects forward iterators, while combiners work with input iterators. That's why a vector is used to store all return values before determining the smallest value with std::min_element().

Example 4.9 modifies the combiner to store all return values in a container rather than evaluating them. It stores all the return values in a vector which is then returned by s().

Example 4.9

```cpp
#include <boost/signals2.hpp>
#include <iostream>
#include <vector>
#include <algorithm>

int func1() { return 1; }
int func2() { return 2; }

template <typename T>
struct min_element
{
  typedef T result_type;

  template <typename InputIterator>
  T operator()(InputIterator first, InputIterator last) const
  {
    return T(first, last);
  }
};

int main()
{
  boost::signals2::signal<int (), min_element<std::vector<int> > > s;
  s.connect(func1);
  s.connect(func2);
  std::vector<int> v = s();
  std::cout << *std::min_element(v.begin(), v.end()) << std::endl;
}
```

Connections

Functions can be managed with the aid of the connect() and disconnect() member functions provided by boost::signals2::signal. Because connect() returns an object of type boost::signals2::connection, associations can also be managed differently (see Example 4.10).

Example 4.10

```cpp
#include <boost/signals2.hpp>
#include <iostream>

void func()
{
  std::cout << "Hello, world!" << std::endl;
}

int main()
{
  boost::signals2::signal<void ()> s;
  boost::signals2::connection c = s.connect(func);
  s();
  c.disconnect();
}
```

The `disconnect()` member function of `boost::signals2::signal` requires a function pointer to be passed in. This can be avoided if `disconnect()` is called on the `boost::signals2::connection` object.

To block a function for a short time without removing the association from the signal, `boost::signals2::shared_connection_block` can be used.

Example 4.11

```cpp
#include <boost/signals2.hpp>
#include <iostream>

void func()
{
  std::cout << "Hello, world!" << std::endl;
}

int main()
{
  boost::signals2::signal<void ()> s;
  boost::signals2::connection c = s.connect(func);
  s();
  boost::signals2::shared_connection_block b(c);
  s();
  b.unblock();
  s();
}
```

Example 4.11 executes `func()` twice. Even though the signal **s** is triggered three times, `func()` is not called for the second time because an object of type `boost::signals2::shared_connection_block` was created to block the call. Once the object goes out of scope, the block is automatically removed. A block can also be removed explicitly by calling `unblock()`. Because it is called before the last trigger, the final call to `func()` is executed again.

Besides `unblock()`, `boost::signals2::shared_connection_block` provides the additional member functions `block()` and `blocking()`. The former is used to block a connection after a call to `unblock()`, while the latter makes it possible to check whether or not a connection is currently blocked.

Please note that `boost::signals2::shared_connection_block` carries the word "shared" for a reason: multiple objects of type `boost::signals2::shared_connection_block` can be initialized with the same connection.

Example 4.12 accesses **s** twice, but `func()` is only called the second time. The program writes `Hello, world!` to the standard output stream only once.

Because `false` is passed to the constructor as the second parameter, the first object of type `boost::signals2::shared_connection_block` does not block the connection to the signal **s**. Hence, calling `blocking()` on the object **b1** returns `false`.

Example 4.12

```
#include <boost/signals2.hpp>
#include <iostream>

void func()
{
  std::cout << "Hello, world!" << std::endl;
}

int main()
{
  boost::signals2::signal<void ()> s;
  boost::signals2::connection c = s.connect(func);
  boost::signals2::shared_connection_block b1(c, false);
  {
    boost::signals2::shared_connection_block b2(c);
    std::cout << b1.blocking() << std::endl;
    s();
  }
  s();
}
```

Nevertheless, func() is not executed when **s** is accessed first because the access happens only after a second object of type boost::signals2::shared_connection_block has been instantiated. By not passing a second parameter to the constructor, the connection is blocked by the object. When **s** is accessed for the second time, func() is executed because the block was automatically removed once **b2** went out of scope.

Example 4.13

```
#include <boost/signals2.hpp>
#include <boost/bind.hpp>
#include <iostream>
#include <memory>

class world
{
  public:
    void hello() const
    {
      std::cout << "Hello, world!" << std::endl;
    }
};

int main()
{
  boost::signals2::signal<void ()> s;
  {
    std::auto_ptr<world> w(new world());
    s.connect(boost::bind(&world::hello, w.get()));
  }
  std::cout << s.num_slots() << std::endl;
  s();
}
```

Boost.Signals2 can release a connection once the object whose member function is associated with a signal is destroyed.

Example 4.13 associates the member function of an object with a signal with the help of Boost.Bind. The object is destroyed before the signal is triggered, which is a problem. Instead of passing the actual object **w**, only a pointer was passed to boost::bind(). By the time s() is called, the object referenced by the pointer no longer exists.

It is possible to modify the program so that the connection is automatically released once the object **w** is destroyed (see Example 4.14).

Example 4.14

```
#include <boost/signals2.hpp>
#include <boost/shared_ptr.hpp>
#include <iostream>

class world
{
  public:
    void hello() const
    {
      std::cout << "Hello, world!" << std::endl;
    }
};

int main()
{
  boost::signals2::signal<void ()> s;
  {
    boost::shared_ptr<world> w(new world());
    s.connect(boost::signals2::signal<void ()>::slot_type(
      &world::hello, w.get()).track(w));
  }
  std::cout << s.num_slots() << std::endl;
  s();
}
```

Now num_slots() returns 0. The program does not try to call a member function on an object that doesn't exist when the signal is triggered. The change was to tie the object of type world to a smart pointer of type boost::shared_ptr which is passed to track(). This member function is called on the slot that was passed to connect() to request tracking the corresponding object.

A function or member function associated with a signal is called a "slot." The data type to specify a slot was not used in the previous examples because passing a pointer to a function or member function to connect() was sufficient. The corresponding slot was created and associated with the signal automatically.

In Example 4.14, however, the smart pointer is associated with the slot by calling track(). Because the data type of the slot depends on the signal, boost::signals2::signal provides a type slot_type to access the required data type. slot_type behaves just like boost::bind, making it possible to pass both parameters to describe the slot directly. track() can then be called to associate the slot created with a smart pointer of type boost::shared_ptr. The object is then tracked by the smart pointer, which causes the slot to be automatically removed once the tracked object is destroyed.

To manage objects with different smart pointers, slots provide a member function called `track_foreign()`. While `track()` expects a smart pointer of type `boost::shared_ptr`, `track_foreign()` allows you to, for example, use a smart pointer of type `std::shared_ptr`. Using `track_foreign()` is a bit more complicated because smart pointers outside of the Boost libraries need to be introduced to Boost.Signals2 first.

The consumer of a particular event can access an object of type `boost::signals2::signal` to create new associations or release existing ones.

Example 4.15

```cpp
#include <boost/signals2.hpp>
#include <iostream>

boost::signals2::signal<void ()> s;

void func()
{
  std::cout << "Hello, world!" << std::endl;
}

void connect()
{
  s.connect(func);
}

int main()
{
  s.connect(connect);
  s();
}
```

Example 4.15 accesses **s** inside the `connect()` function to associate `func()` with the signal. Since `connect()` is called when the signal is triggered, the question is whether `func()` will also be called.

The program does not output anything, which means that `func()` is never called. While Boost.Signals2 supports associating functions to signals when a signal is triggered, the new associations will only be used when the signal is triggered again.

Example 4.16

```cpp
#include <boost/signals2.hpp>
#include <iostream>

boost::signals2::signal<void ()> s;

void func()
{
  std::cout << "Hello, world!" << std::endl;
}

void disconnect()
{
  s.disconnect(func);
}

int main()
{
  s.connect(disconnect);
  s.connect(func);
  s();
}
```

Example 4.16 does not create a new association, it releases an existing one. Just like Example 4.15, it does not write anything to the standard output stream and does not call func() either.

This behavior can be explained quite simply. Imagine that a temporary copy of all slots is created whenever a signal is triggered. Newly created associations are not added to the temporary copy and therefore can only be called the next time the signal is triggered. Released associations, on the other hand, are still part of the temporary copy, but will be checked by the combiner when dereferenced to avoid calling a member function on an object which has been destroyed already.

Multithreading

Almost all classes provided by Boost.Signals2 are thread-safe and can be used in multithreaded applications. For example, objects of type boost::signals2::signal and boost::signals2::connection can be accessed from different threads.

On the other hand, boost::signals2::shared_connection_block is not thread-safe. This limitation is insignificant because multiple objects of type boost::signals2::shared_connection_block can be created in different threads and can use the same connection object.

Example 4.17 uses functions of the Windows API to create and manage threads, and thus can only be run on Windows. However, it can be ported easily to different operating systems because Boost.Signals2 is platform independent.

Example 4.17

```cpp
#include <windows.h>
#include <boost/signals2.hpp>
#include <iostream>

boost::signals2::signal<void (int)> s;
CRITICAL_SECTION cs;

void print(int i)
{
  EnterCriticalSection(&cs);
  std::cout << i << std::endl;
  LeaveCriticalSection(&cs);
}

DWORD WINAPI loop(LPVOID)
{
  for (int i = 0; i < 100; ++i)
    s(i);
  return 0;
}

int main()
{
  s.connect(print);

  InitializeCriticalSection(&cs);

  HANDLE threads[2];
  threads[0] = CreateThread(0, 0, loop, 0, 0, 0);
  threads[1] = CreateThread(0, 0, loop, 0, 0, 0);
  WaitForMultipleObjects(2, threads, TRUE, INFINITE);

  DeleteCriticalSection(&cs);
}
```

Example 4.17 creates two threads that execute the loop() function, which accesses s one hundred times to call the associated print() function. Boost.Signals2 explicitly supports simultaneous access from different threads to objects of type boost::signals2::signal.

Example 4.17 displays numbers from 0 to 99. Because i is incremented in two threads and written to the standard output stream in print(), not only is every number displayed twice, they also overlap. Because boost::signals2::signal can be accessed from different threads, the program does not crash.

However, Example 4.17 still requires synchronization. Because two threads access s, the associated print() function runs parallel in two threads. Access to objects that are not thread-safe, such as **std::cout**, needs to be synchronized. Example 4.17 uses functions from the Windows API to create a critical section to guarantee that at any given time only one thread uses **std::cout**.

For single-threaded applications, support for multithreading can be disabled in Boost.Signals2.

Example 4.18

```
#include <boost/signals2.hpp>
#include <iostream>

boost::signals2::signal<void ()> s;

void func()
{
  std::cout << "Hello, world!" << std::endl;
}

int main()
{
  typedef boost::signals2::keywords::mutex_type<
    boost::signals2::dummy_mutex> dummy_mutex;
  boost::signals2::signal_type<void (), dummy_mutex>::type s;
  s.connect(func);
  s();
}
```

Out of the many template parameters supported by boost::signals2::signal, the last one defines the type of mutex used for synchronization. Fortunately, Boost.Signals2 offers a simpler way to disable synchronization than passing the complete list of parameters.

The boost::signals2::keywords namespace contains classes that make it possible to pass template parameters by name. boost::signals2::keywords::mutex_type can be used to pass the mutex type as the second template parameter to boost::signals2::signal_type. Please note that boost::signals2::signal_type, not boost::signals2::signal, must be used in this case. The data type equivalent to boost::signals2::signal, which is required to define the signal **s**, is retrieved via boost::signals2::signal_type::type.

Boost.Signals2 provides an empty mutex implementation called boost::signals2::dummy_mutex. If a signal is defined with this class, it will no longer support multithreading.

Exercises

1. Create a program by defining a class called button that represents a clickable button within a graphical user interface. Add two member functions, add_handler() and remove_handler(), both of which expect a function name as a parameter, to the class. If a click() member function is called, the registered functions should be executed sequentially.

   Test your code by creating an instance of the button class and writing a message to the standard output stream within the event handler. Call the click() function to simulate a mouse click on the button.

5

String Handling

General

In the C++ standard, strings are handled by the class `std::string`, which provides many member functions to manipulate strings. Among these are member functions to search a string for a specific character and member functions to return a substring. Even though `std::string` provides more than 100 member functions, which makes it one of the more bloated classes in the C++ standard, many developers still need additional functionality. For example, while Java and .NET provide functions to convert a string to uppercase, there is no equivalent available in `std::string`. The Boost C++ Libraries presented in this chapter try to close this gap.

Locales

Before the Boost C++ Libraries are introduced, lets take a brief look at locales. Many functions outlined in this chapter expect a locale as an additional parameter.

Locales are used in the C++ standard to encapsulate cultural conventions such as the currency symbol, date and time formats, the symbol used to separate the integer portion of a number from the fractional one (radix character), and the symbol used for grouping numbers with more than three digits (thousands separator).

In terms of string handling, the locale defines the sort order of the characters used by a particular culture. For instance, whether an alphabet contains mutated vowels and what place those vowels take in an alphabet depends on the culture.

If a function is called that converts a given string to uppercase, the individual steps taken depend on the particular locale. In the German language, it is obvious that the letter "ä" is converted to "Ä"; however, this does not necessarily hold true for other languages or cultures.

When working with `std::string`, locales can be neglected because none of the member functions depends on a particular culture. However, to work with the Boost C++ Libraries in this chapter, this knowledge is mandatory.

The C++ standard defines a class called `std::locale` in the header file `locale`. Every C++ program automatically has one instance of this class – the global locale, which cannot be directly accessed. Instead, a separate object of `std::locale` must be created via the default constructor, which will be initialized with the same properties as the global locale.

Example 5.1

```
#include <locale>
#include <iostream>

int main()
{
  std::locale loc;
  std::cout << loc.name() << std::endl;
}
```

Example 5.1 will output `C` on the standard output stream which is the name of the classic locale. This locale contains descriptions used by default in programs developed with the C language.

This also happens to be the default global locale for every C++ program. It contains descriptions used by the American culture. For example, the dollar sign is used as the currency symbol, the radix character is a period, and displaying a date causes the month to be written in English.

The global locale can be changed using the static function `global()` of the `std::locale` class (see Example 5.2).

Example 5.2

```
#include <locale>
#include <iostream>

int main()
{
  std::locale::global(std::locale("German"));
  std::locale loc;
  std::cout << loc.name() << std::endl;
}
```

The static function `global()` expects a new object of type `std::locale` as its sole parameter. Using a different constructor of the class, which expects a character string of type `const char*`, a locale object for a particular culture can be created. However, names of locales are not standardized except for the C locale which is named "C". Therefore, the implementation of the C++ standard library determines what names are actually accepted. In case of Visual C++ 2010, the definitions for German can be selected using the language string "German" as outlined in the Visual Studio documentation[1].

Example 5.2 will output `German_Germany.1252`. Specifying "German" as the language string selects the definitions for the German primary language and sublanguage as well as the character map 1252.

---

[1] http://msdn.microsoft.com/en-us/library/39cwe7zf.aspx

To set the sublanguage to a different location where German is spoken, such as Switzerland, a different language string can be used.

Example 5.3

```
#include <locale>
#include <iostream>

int main()
{
  std::locale::global(std::locale("German_Switzerland"));
  std::locale loc;
  std::cout << loc.name() << std::endl;
}
```

Example 5.3 will output `German_Switzerland.1252`.

Example 5.4

```
#include <locale>
#include <iostream>
#include <cstring>

int main()
{
  std::cout << std::strcoll("ä", "z") << std::endl;
  std::locale::global(std::locale("German"));
  std::cout << std::strcoll("ä", "z") << std::endl;
}
```

Example 5.4 shows how locales affect string handling. It uses the function `std::strcoll()`, defined in the header file `cstring`, to compare whether the first string is lexicographically less than the second one. In other words, which of the two strings would be found first in a dictionary.

The output of the sample program is `1` and `-1`. Even though the function is called with the same parameters, the results are different. The reason is quite simple – when calling `std::strcoll()` the first time, the global C locale is used. However, when called the second time, the global locale has been changed to incorporate definitions for the German culture. The order of the two characters "ä" and "z" is different for these locales as indicated by the output.

Many C functions and C++ streams access locales. Although functions of the `std::string` class work independently from locales, many of the functions outlined in the following sections don't.

Boost.StringAlgorithms

The library Boost.StringAlgorithms[2] provides many free-standing functions for string manipulation. Strings can be of type `std::string`, `std::wstring`, or any other instance of the class template `std::basic_string`.

---

[2] http://www.boost.org/doc/html/string_algo.html

The functions are categorized within different header files. For example, functions converting from uppercase to lowercase are defined in `boost/algorithm/string/case_conv.hpp`. Because Boost.StringAlgorithms consists of more than 20 different categories and as many header files, `boost/algorithm/string.hpp` acts as the common header including all other header files for convenience. All of the following examples will use this combined header.

As mentioned in the previous section, many of the functions in Boost.StringAlgorithms expect an object of type `std::locale` as an additional parameter. However, this parameter is optional. If it is not provided, the global locale is used.

Example 5.5

```
#include <boost/algorithm/string.hpp>
#include <locale>
#include <iostream>
#include <clocale>

int main()
{
  std::setlocale(LC_ALL, "German");
  std::string s = "Boris Schäling";
  std::cout << boost::algorithm::to_upper_copy(s) << std::endl;
  std::cout << boost::algorithm::to_upper_copy(s, std::locale("German")) <<
    std::endl;
}
```

The function `boost::algorithm::to_upper_copy()` converts a string to uppercase, and `boost::algorithm::to_lower_copy()` converts a string to lowercase. Both functions return a copy of the input string, converted to the specified case. To convert the string in place, use the functions `boost::algorithm::to_upper()` or `boost::algorithm::to_lower()`.

Example 5.5 converts the string "Boris Schäling" to uppercase using `boost::algorithm::to_upper_copy()`. The first call uses the global locale while the second call explicitly states the locale for the German culture.

Using the German locale results in a correctly converted string because there is a corresponding uppercase character "Ä" for the lowercase "ä". In the C locale, "ä" is an unknown character and thus is not converted. To yield correct results, either pass the correct locale explicitly or modify the global locale before calling `boost::algorithm::to_upper_copy()`.

Note that the program uses `std::setlocale()` – defined in the header file `clocale` – to set the locale for any C function. Internally, **std::cout** uses C functions to display data on the screen. By setting the correct locale, vowels such as "ä" and "Ä" are displayed correctly.

Example 5.6

```
#include <boost/algorithm/string.hpp>
#include <locale>
#include <iostream>

int main()
{
  std::locale::global(std::locale("German"));
  std::string s = "Boris Schäling";
  std::cout << boost::algorithm::to_upper_copy(s) << std::endl;
  std::cout << boost::algorithm::to_upper_copy(s, std::locale("German")) <<
    std::endl;
}
```

Example 5.6 sets the global locale to German, which causes the first call to `boost::al-gorithm::to_upper_copy()` to use the corresponding definitions for converting "ä" to "Ä".

Please note that `std::setlocale()` is not called in Example 5.6. By setting the global locale with the static function `std::locale::global()`, the C locale is automatically set as well. In practice, C++ programs almost always set the global locale with `std::locale::global()` rather than calling `std::setlocale()` as seen in Example 5.6.

Example 5.7

```
#include <boost/algorithm/string.hpp>
#include <locale>
#include <iostream>

int main()
{
  std::locale::global(std::locale("German"));
  std::string s = "Boris Schäling";
  std::cout << boost::algorithm::erase_first_copy(s, "i") << std::endl;
  std::cout << boost::algorithm::erase_nth_copy(s, "i", 0) << std::endl;
  std::cout << boost::algorithm::erase_last_copy(s, "i") << std::endl;
  std::cout << boost::algorithm::erase_all_copy(s, "i") << std::endl;
  std::cout << boost::algorithm::erase_head_copy(s, 5) << std::endl;
  std::cout << boost::algorithm::erase_tail_copy(s, 8) << std::endl;
}
```

Boost.StringAlgorithms provides several functions to delete individual characters from a string. For example, `boost::algorithm::erase_all_copy()` will remove all occurrences of a particular character from a string. To remove only the first occurrence of the character, use `boost::algorithm::erase_first_copy()` instead. To shorten a string by a specific number of characters on either end, use the functions `boost::algorithm::erase_head_copy()` and `boost::algorithm::erase_tail_copy()`.

Example 5.8

```
#include <boost/algorithm/string.hpp>
#include <locale>
#include <iostream>

int main()
{
  std::locale::global(std::locale("German"));
  std::string s = "Boris Schäling";
  boost::iterator_range<std::string::iterator> r =
    boost::algorithm::find_first(s, "Boris");
  std::cout << r << std::endl;
  r = boost::algorithm::find_first(s, "xyz");
  std::cout << r << std::endl;
}
```

Functions such as boost::algorithm::find_first(), boost::algorithm::find_last(), boost::algorithm::find_nth(), boost::algorithm::find_head() and boost::algorithm::find_tail() are available to find strings within strings.

All of these functions return a pair of iterators of type boost::iterator_range. This class originates from the Boost C++ Library Boost.Range[3], which implements a range concept based on the iterator concept. Because the operator << is overloaded for boost::iterator_range, the result of the individual search algorithm can be written directly to the standard output stream. Example 5.8 prints Boris for the first result and an empty string for the second one.

Example 5.9

```
#include <boost/algorithm/string.hpp>
#include <locale>
#include <iostream>
#include <vector>

int main()
{
  std::locale::global(std::locale("German"));
  std::vector<std::string> v;
  v.push_back("Boris");
  v.push_back("Schäling");
  std::cout << boost::algorithm::join(v, " ") << std::endl;
}
```

A container of strings is passed as the first parameter to the function boost::algorithm::join(), which concatenates them separated by the second parameter. Example 5.9 will output Boris Schäling.

---

[3] http://www.boost.org/libs/range/

Example 5.10

```cpp
#include <boost/algorithm/string.hpp>
#include <locale>
#include <iostream>

int main()
{
  std::locale::global(std::locale("German"));
  std::string s = "Boris Schäling";
  std::cout << boost::algorithm::replace_first_copy(s, "B", "D") <<
    std::endl;
  std::cout << boost::algorithm::replace_nth_copy(s, "B", 0, "D") <<
    std::endl;
  std::cout << boost::algorithm::replace_last_copy(s, "B", "D") <<
    std::endl;
  std::cout << boost::algorithm::replace_all_copy(s, "B", "D") <<
    std::endl;
  std::cout << boost::algorithm::replace_head_copy(s, 5, "Doris") <<
    std::endl;
  std::cout << boost::algorithm::replace_tail_copy(s, 8, "Becker") <<
    std::endl;
}
```

Like the functions for searching strings or removing characters from strings, Boost.StringAlgorithms also provides functions for replacing substrings within a string. Among these functions are `boost::algorithm::replace_first_copy()`, `boost::algorithm::replace_nth_copy()`, `boost::algorithm::replace_last_copy()`, `boost::algorithm::replace_all_copy()`, `boost::algorithm::replace_head_copy()` and `boost::algorithm::replace_tail_copy()`. They can be applied the same way as the functions for searching and removing, except they expect an additional parameter – the replacement string (see Example 5.10).

Example 5.11

```cpp
#include <boost/algorithm/string.hpp>
#include <locale>
#include <iostream>

int main()
{
  std::locale::global(std::locale("German"));
  std::string s = "\t Boris Schäling \t";
  std::cout << "." << boost::algorithm::trim_left_copy(s) << "." <<
    std::endl;
  std::cout << "." <<boost::algorithm::trim_right_copy(s) << "." <<
    std::endl;
  std::cout << "." <<boost::algorithm::trim_copy(s) << "." <<
    std::endl;
}
```

In order to automatically remove spaces on either end of a string, use `boost::algorithm::trim_left_copy()`, `boost::algorithm::trim_right_copy()` and boost::algorithm::trim_copy() (see Example 5.11). The global locale determines which characters are considered to be space.

Boost.StringAlgorithms lets you provide a predicate as an additional parameter for different functions to determine which characters of the string the function is applied to. The predicated versions for trimming a string are called boost::algorithm::trim_right_copy_if(), boost::algorithm::trim_left_copy_if(), and boost::algorithm::trim_copy_if().

Example 5.12

```
#include <boost/algorithm/string.hpp>
#include <locale>
#include <iostream>

int main()
{
  std::locale::global(std::locale("German"));
  std::string s = "--Boris Schäling--";
  std::cout << "." << boost::algorithm::trim_left_copy_if(s,
    boost::algorithm::is_any_of("-")) << "." << std::endl;
  std::cout << "." <<boost::algorithm::trim_right_copy_if(s,
    boost::algorithm::is_any_of("-")) << "." << std::endl;
  std::cout << "." <<boost::algorithm::trim_copy_if(s,
    boost::algorithm::is_any_of("-")) << "." << std::endl;
}
```

Example 5.12 uses another function called boost::algorithm::is_any_of(), which is a helper function to create a predicate that checks whether a certain character – passed as parameter to is_any_of() – exists in a string. With boost::algorithm::is_any_of(), the characters for trimming a string can be specified. In Example 5.12 it is the hyphen.

Boost.StringAlgorithms provides many helper functions that return commonly used predicates.

Example 5.13

```
#include <boost/algorithm/string.hpp>
#include <locale>
#include <iostream>

int main()
{
  std::locale::global(std::locale("German"));
  std::string s = "123456789Boris Schäling123456789";
  std::cout << "." << boost::algorithm::trim_left_copy_if(s,
    boost::algorithm::is_digit()) << "." << std::endl;
  std::cout << "." <<boost::algorithm::trim_right_copy_if(s,
    boost::algorithm::is_digit()) << "." << std::endl;
  std::cout << "." <<boost::algorithm::trim_copy_if(s,
    boost::algorithm::is_digit()) << "." << std::endl;
}
```

The predicate returned by boost::algorithm::is_digit() tests whether a character is numeric. Helper functions are also provided to check whether a character is uppercase or lowercase:

`boost::algorithm::is_upper()` and `boost::algorithm::is_lower()`. All of these functions use the global locale by default unless you pass in a different locale as a parameter.

Besides the predicates that verify individual characters of a string, Boost.StringAlgorithms also offers functions which work with strings instead (see Example 5.14).

Example 5.14

```cpp
#include <boost/algorithm/string.hpp>
#include <locale>
#include <iostream>

int main()
{
  std::locale::global(std::locale("German"));
  std::string s = "Boris Schäling";
  std::cout << boost::algorithm::starts_with(s, "Boris") << std::endl;
  std::cout << boost::algorithm::ends_with(s, "Schäling") << std::endl;
  std::cout << boost::algorithm::contains(s, "is") << std::endl;
  std::cout << boost::algorithm::lexicographical_compare(s, "Boris") <<
    std::endl;
}
```

The functions `boost::algorithm::starts_with()`, `boost::algorithm::ends_with()`, `boost::algorithm::contains()`, and `boost::algorithm::lexicographical_com-pare()` all compare two individual strings.

Example 5.15 introduces a function that splits a string into smaller parts.

Example 5.15

```cpp
#include <boost/algorithm/string.hpp>
#include <locale>
#include <iostream>
#include <vector>

int main()
{
  std::locale::global(std::locale("German"));
  std::string s = "Boris Schäling";
  std::vector<std::string> v;
  boost::algorithm::split(v, s, boost::algorithm::is_space());
  std::cout << v.size() << std::endl;
}
```

With `boost::algorithm::split()`, a given string can be split based on a delimiter. The substrings are stored in a container. The function requires as its third argument a predicate that tests each character and checks whether the string should be split at the given position. The sample program uses the helper function `boost::algorithm::is_space()` to create a predicate which splits the string at every space character.

Many of the functions introduced in this section have versions that ignore the case of the string. These versions typically have the same name except for a leading "i". For example, the equivalent to boost::algorithm::erase_all_copy() is boost::algorithm::ierase_all_copy().

Finally, many functions of Boost.StringAlgorithms also support regular expressions. Example 5.16 uses the function boost::algorithm::find_regex() to search for a regular expression.

Example 5.16

```
#include <boost/algorithm/string.hpp>
#include <boost/algorithm/string/regex.hpp>
#include <locale>
#include <iostream>

int main()
{
  std::locale::global(std::locale("German"));
  std::string s = "Boris Schäling";
  boost::iterator_range<std::string::iterator> r =
    boost::algorithm::find_regex(s, boost::regex("\\w\\s\\w"));
  std::cout << r << std::endl;
}
```

In order to use the regular expression, the program accesses a class called boost::regex which is provided by Boost.Regex. This library is presented in the following section.

Boost.Regex

The library Boost.Regex[4] allows you to use regular expressions in C++. Regular expressions are a powerful feature of many languages that supports searching for string patterns. Boost.Regex is expected to be included in the next revision of the C++ standard.

The two most important classes in Boost.Regex are boost::regex and boost::smatch, both defined in boost/regex.hpp. The former defines a regular expression, and the latter saves the search results.

Boost.Regex provides three different functions to search for regular expressions.

Example 5.17

```
#include <boost/regex.hpp>
#include <locale>
#include <iostream>

int main()
{
  std::locale::global(std::locale("German"));
  std::string s = "Boris Schäling";
  boost::regex expr("\\w+\\s\\w+");
  std::cout << boost::regex_match(s, expr) << std::endl;
}
```

---

[4] http://www.boost.org/libs/regex/

`boost::regex_match()` (see Example 5.17) compares a string with a regular expression. It will return `true` only if the expression matches the complete string.

`boost::regex_search()` searches a string for a regular expression.

Example 5.18

```
#include <boost/regex.hpp>
#include <locale>
#include <iostream>

int main()
{
  std::locale::global(std::locale("German"));
  std::string s = "Boris Schäling";
  boost::regex expr("(\\w+)\\s(\\w+)");
  boost::smatch what;
  if (boost::regex_search(s, what, expr))
  {
    std::cout << what[0] << std::endl;
    std::cout << what[1] << " " << what[2] << std::endl;
  }
}
```

`boost::regex_search()` expects a reference to an object of type `boost::smatch` as an additional parameter, which is used to store the results. `boost::regex_search()` only searches for groups. That's why Example 5.18 returns two strings based on the two groups found in the regular expression.

The result storage class `boost::smatch` is actually a container holding elements of type `boost::sub_match` which can be accessed through an interface similar to the one of `std::vector`. For example, elements can be accessed via `operator[]`.

The class `boost::sub_match` stores iterators to the specific positions in a string corresponding to the groups of a regular expression. Because `boost::sub_match` is derived from `std::pair`, the individual iterators referencing a particular substring can be accessed with **first** and **second**. However, to write a substring to the standard output stream, these iterators do not necessarily need to be accessed as seen in Example 5.18. Using the overloaded operator `<<`, the substring can be written directly to the standard output stream.

Please note that because iterators are used to point to matched strings, `boost::sub_match` does not copy them. This implies that they are accessible only as long as the corresponding string, which is referenced by the iterators, exists.

Furthermore, please note that the first element of the container `boost::smatch` stores iterators referencing the string that matches the entire regular expression. The first substring that matches the first group is accessible at index 1.

The third function offered by Boost.Regex is `boost::regex_replace()` (see Example 5.19).

Example 5.19

```
#include <boost/regex.hpp>
#include <locale>
#include <iostream>

int main()
{
  std::locale::global(std::locale("German"));
  std::string s = " Boris Schäling ";
  boost::regex expr("\\s");
  std::string fmt("_");
  std::cout << boost::regex_replace(s, expr, fmt) << std::endl;
}
```

In addition to the search string and the regular expression, boost::regex_replace() needs a format that defines how substrings that match individual groups of the regular expression should be replaced. In case the regular expression does not contain any groups, the corresponding substrings are replaced one-to-one using the given format. Thus, Example 5.19 will output _Boris_Schäling_.

boost::regex_replace() always searches through the entire string for the regular expression. Thus, the program actually replaces all three spaces with underscores.

Example 5.20

```
#include <boost/regex.hpp>
#include <locale>
#include <iostream>

int main()
{
  std::locale::global(std::locale("German"));
  std::string s = "Boris Schäling";
  boost::regex expr("(\\w+)\\s(\\w+)");
  std::string fmt("\\2 \\1");
  std::cout << boost::regex_replace(s, expr, fmt) << std::endl;
}
```

The format can access substrings returned by groups of the regular expression. Example 5.20 uses this technique to swap the first with the last name, displaying Schäling Boris as a result.

There are different standards for regular expressions and formats. Each of the three functions takes an additional parameter that allows you to select a specific standard. You can also specify whether or not special characters should be interpreted in a specific format or whether the format should replace the complete string matching the regular expression.

Example 5.21

```
#include <boost/regex.hpp>
#include <locale>
#include <iostream>

int main()
{
  std::locale::global(std::locale("German"));
  std::string s = "Boris Schäling";
  boost::regex expr("(\\w+)\\s(\\w+)");
  std::string fmt("\\2 \\1");
  std::cout << boost::regex_replace(s, expr, fmt,
    boost::regex_constants::format_literal) << std::endl;
}
```

Example 5.21 passes the flag `boost::regex_constants::format_literal` as the fourth parameter to `boost::regex_replace()` to suppress handling of special characters in the format. Because the complete string that matches the regular expression is replaced with the format, the output of Example 5.21 is \2 \1.

As indicated at the end of the previous section, regular expressions can also be used with Boost.StringAlgorithms. Boost.StringAlgorithms uses Boost.Regex to provide functions such as `boost::algorithm::find_regex()`, `boost::algorithm::replace_regex()`, `boost::algorithm::erase_regex()`, and `boost::algorithm::split_regex()`. Because Boost.Regex is expected to become part of the upcoming revision of the C++ standard, it would be advisable to be proficient in applying regular expressions without Boost.StringAlgorithms.

Boost.Tokenizer

The library Boost.Tokenizer[5] allows you to iterate over partial expressions in a string by interpreting certain characters as separators.

Example 5.22

```
#include <boost/tokenizer.hpp>
#include <string>
#include <iostream>

int main()
{
  typedef boost::tokenizer<boost::char_separator<char> > tokenizer;
  std::string s = "Boost C++ libraries";
  tokenizer tok(s);
  for (tokenizer::iterator it = tok.begin(); it != tok.end(); ++it)
    std::cout << *it << std::endl;
}
```

---

[5] http://www.boost.org/libs/tokenizer/

Boost.Tokenizer defines a class template called `boost::tokenizer` in `boost/tokenizer.hpp`. It expects a class as a template parameter which identifies coherent expressions. Example 5.22 uses the class `boost::char_separator`, which interprets spaces and punctuation marks as separators.

A tokenizer must be initialized with a string of type `std::string`. Using the member functions `begin()` and `end()`, the tokenizer can be accessed just like a container. Partial expressions of the string used to initialize the tokenizer are available via iterators. How partial expressions are evaluated depends on the kind of class passed as the template parameter.

Because `boost::char_separator` interprets spaces and punctuation marks as separators by default, the example displays `Boost`, `C`, `+`, `+`, and `libraries`. In order to identify these characters, `boost::char_separator` utilizes both `std::isspace()` and `std::ispunct()`. Boost.Tokenizer distinguishes between separators that should be displayed and separators that should be suppressed. By default, spaces are suppressed while punctuation marks are displayed. Hence the two plus signs are displayed accordingly.

If you do not want punctuation marks to be interpreted as separators, the `boost::char_separator` object can be initialized accordingly before being passed to the tokenizer. Example 5.23 does exactly that.

Example 5.23

```
#include <boost/tokenizer.hpp>
#include <string>
#include <iostream>

int main()
{
  typedef boost::tokenizer<boost::char_separator<char> > tokenizer;
  std::string s = "Boost C++ libraries";
  boost::char_separator<char> sep(" ");
  tokenizer tok(s, sep);
  for (tokenizer::iterator it = tok.begin(); it != tok.end(); ++it)
    std::cout << *it << std::endl;
}
```

The constructor of `boost::char_separator` expects a total of three parameters, but only the first one must be supplied. The first parameter describes the individual separators that are suppressed. Example 5.23, like Example 5.22, treats spaces as separators.

The second parameter specifies the separators that should be displayed. If this parameter is omitted, no separators are displayed at all, and the program will now display `Boost`, `C++` and `libraries`.

If a plus sign is passed as the second parameter, Example 5.24 behaves like Example 5.22.

The third parameter determines whether or not empty partial expressions are displayed. If two separators are found back-to-back, the corresponding partial expression is empty. By default, these empty expressions are not displayed. Using the third parameter, the default behavior can be changed.

Example 5.24

```
#include <boost/tokenizer.hpp>
#include <string>
#include <iostream>

int main()
{
  typedef boost::tokenizer<boost::char_separator<char> > tokenizer;
  std::string s = "Boost C++ libraries";
  boost::char_separator<char> sep(" ", "+");
  tokenizer tok(s, sep);
  for (tokenizer::iterator it = tok.begin(); it != tok.end(); ++it)
    std::cout << *it << std::endl;
}
```

Example 5.25 displays two additional empty partial expressions. The first one is found between the two plus signs, while the second one is found between the second plus sign and the following space.

Example 5.25

```
#include <boost/tokenizer.hpp>
#include <string>
#include <iostream>

int main()
{
  typedef boost::tokenizer<boost::char_separator<char> > tokenizer;
  std::string s = "Boost C++ libraries";
  boost::char_separator<char> sep(" ", "+", boost::keep_empty_tokens);
  tokenizer tok(s, sep);
  for (tokenizer::iterator it = tok.begin(); it != tok.end(); ++it)
    std::cout << *it << std::endl;
}
```

A tokenizer can also be used with different string types.

Example 5.26

```
#include <boost/tokenizer.hpp>
#include <string>
#include <iostream>

int main()
{
  typedef boost::tokenizer<boost::char_separator<wchar_t>,
    std::wstring::const_iterator, std::wstring> tokenizer;
  std::wstring s = L"Boost C++ libraries";
  boost::char_separator<wchar_t> sep(L" ");
  tokenizer tok(s, sep);
  for (tokenizer::iterator it = tok.begin(); it != tok.end(); ++it)
    std::wcout << *it << std::endl;
}
```

Example 5.26 iterates over a string of type `std::wstring`. In order to allow this type of string, the tokenizer must be initialized with additional template parameters. The same applies to the class `boost::char_separator`; it must also be initialized with `wchar_t`.

Besides `boost::char_separator`, Boost.Tokenizer provides two additional classes to identify partial expressions.

Example 5.27

```
#include <boost/tokenizer.hpp>
#include <string>
#include <iostream>

int main()
{
  typedef boost::tokenizer<boost::escaped_list_separator<char> > tokenizer;
  std::string s = "Boost,\"C++ libraries\"";
  tokenizer tok(s);
  for (tokenizer::iterator it = tok.begin(); it != tok.end(); ++it)
    std::cout << *it << std::endl;
}
```

`boost::escaped_list_separator` is used to read multiple values separated by comma. This format is commonly known as CSV (comma separated values). It also considers double quotes as well as escape sequences. Therefore the output of Example 5.27 is `Boost` and `C++ libraries`.

The second class provided is `boost::offset_separator`, which must be instantiated. The corresponding object must be passed to the constructor of `boost::tokenizer` as a second parameter.

Example 5.28

```
#include <boost/tokenizer.hpp>
#include <string>
#include <iostream>

int main()
{
  typedef boost::tokenizer<boost::offset_separator> tokenizer;
  std::string s = "Boost C++ libraries";
  int offsets[] = { 5, 5, 9 };
  boost::offset_separator sep(offsets, offsets + 3);
  tokenizer tok(s, sep);
  for (tokenizer::iterator it = tok.begin(); it != tok.end(); ++it)
    std::cout << *it << std::endl;
}
```

`boost::offset_separator` specifies the locations within the string where individual partial expressions end. Example 5.28 specifies that the first partial expression ends after 5 characters, the second ends after additional 5 characters and the third and last ends after the following 9 characters. The output will be `Boost`, `C++` and `libraries`.

Boost.Format

Boost.Format[6] offers a replacement for the function `std::printf()` defined in the header file `cstdio`. `std::printf()` originates from the C standard and allows formatted data output. However, it is neither type-safe nor expandable. In C++ applications, Boost.Format is usually preferred when you need formatted output.

The library Boost.Format provides a class called `boost::format` which is defined in `boost/format.hpp`. Similar to `std::printf()`, a string containing special characters to control formatting is passed to the constructor of `boost::format`. The data that replaces these special characters in the output is linked via the operator `%` as shown in Example 5.29.

Example 5.29

```
#include <boost/format.hpp>
#include <iostream>

int main()
{
  std::cout << boost::format("%1%.%2%.%3%") % 16 % 9 % 2011 << std::endl;
}
```

Boost.Format uses numbers placed between two percent signs as placeholders, which are later linked to the actual data with `%`. Example 5.29 uses the numbers 16, 9, and 2011 to create a date string in the form `16.9.2011`.

Example 5.30

```
#include <boost/format.hpp>
#include <iostream>

int main()
{
  std::cout << boost::format("%2%/%1%/%3%") % 16 % 9 % 2011 << std::endl;
}
```

To make the month appear in front of the day, which is common in the United States, the place-holders can simply be swapped. Example 5.30 does this, displaying `9/16/2011`.

Example 5.31

```
#include <boost/format.hpp>
#include <iostream>

int main()
{
  std::cout << boost::format("%1% %2% %1%") %
    boost::io::group(std::showpos, 99) % 100 << std::endl;
}
```

---

[6] http://www.boost.org/libs/format/

To format data using the C++ manipulators, Boost.Format provides a function called `boost::io::group()`.

Example 5.31 displays `+99  100  +99` as a result. Because the manipulator `std::showpos()` has been linked to the number `99` via `boost::io::group()`, the plus sign is automatically added whenever `99` is displayed.

If the plus sign should only be shown for the first output of `99`, the format placeholder needs to be customized.

Example 5.32

```
#include <boost/format.hpp>
#include <iostream>

int main()
{
   std::cout << boost::format("%|1$+| %2% %1%") % 99 % 100 << std::endl;
}
```

In Example 5.32, the placeholder `%1%` has been replaced with `%|1$+|`. Customization of a format does not just add two additional pipe signs. The reference to the data is also placed between the pipe signs and uses `1$` instead of `1%`. This is required to modify the output to be `+99  100  99`.

Even though references to data are generally optional, they must be specified either for all placeholders or for none. Example 5.33 only provides references for the second and third placeholder but omits them for the first one, which generates an error at run time.

Example 5.33

```
#include <boost/format.hpp>
#include <iostream>

int main()
{
  try
  {
    std::cout << boost::format("%|+| %2% %1%") % 99 % 100 << std::endl;
  }
  catch (boost::io::format_error &ex)
  {
    std::cout << ex.what() << std::endl;
  }
}
```

Example 5.33 will throw an exception of type `boost::io::format_error`. Strictly speaking, Boost.Format throws `boost::io::bad_format_string`. However, because the different exception classes are all derived from `boost::io::format_error`, it is usually easier to catch exceptions of this type.

Example 5.34 shows how to write the program without using references in the format string.

Example 5.34

```
#include <boost/format.hpp>
#include <iostream>

int main()
{
  std::cout << boost::format("%|+| %|| %||") % 99 % 100 % 99 << std::endl;
}
```

The pipe signs for the second and third placeholder can safely be omitted in this case because they do not specify the format in this case. The resulting syntax then closely resembles std::printf().

Example 5.35

```
#include <boost/format.hpp>
#include <iostream>

int main()
{
  std::cout << boost::format("%+d %d %d") % 99 % 100 % 99 << std::endl;
}
```

While the format may look like that used by std::printf(), Boost.Format provides the advantage of type safety. The letter "d" within the format string does not indicate the output of a number. Instead, it applies the manipulator std::dec() to the internal stream object used by boost::format. This makes it possible to specify format strings which would make no sense for std::printf() and would result in a crash.

Example 5.36

```
#include <boost/format.hpp>
#include <iostream>

int main()
{
  std::cout << boost::format("%+s %s %s") % 99 % 100 % 99 << std::endl;
}
```

While std::printf() uses the letter "s" only for strings of type const char*, Example 5.36 works perfectly. Boost.Format does not necessarily expect a string. Instead, it applies the appropriate manipulators to configure the internal stream. But even then it's still possible to write numbers to the stream internally used by Boost.Format.

Exercises

1. Create a program that extracts and displays data such as the first and last name, birthday and account balance from the following XML stream:

   ```
   <person>
     <name>Karl-Heinz Huber</name>
     <dob>1970-9-30</dob>
     <account>2,900.64 USD</account>
   </person>
   ```

   The first name should be displayed separated from the last name. The birthday should be shown using the typical format of "day.month.year", while the account balance should omit any decimal place. Test your program with different XML streams that contain additional spaces, a second first name, a negative number for the account balance, and so forth.

2. Create a program that formats and displays data records such as the following: **Munich Hamburg 92.12 8:25 9:45**. This record describes a flight from Munich to Hamburg that costs 92.12 Euro, departs at 8:25 AM, and arrives at 9:45 AM. It should be displayed as:

   Munich   -> Hamburg   92.12 EUR (08:25-09:45)

   The city should be placed in a 10-character wide field and left-aligned, while the price should be in a 7-digit wide field and right-aligned. The currency should be displayed after the price. The departure and arrival times should be shown in parentheses, without spaces, and separated by a hyphen. For times prior to 10 AM/PM, a leading 0 should be added. Test your program with different data records, for example with a city name that has more than 10 characters.

6

Multithreading

General

Threads are contexts in which functions are executed. A program with multiple threads can execute functions concurrently. This is important if you want to be sure a function that takes a long time to do a particular calculation does not block another function from executing. Threads allow the concurrent execution of two functions without requiring one to wait for the other.

When a program starts, by default it contains only one thread. This thread executes the main() function. Functions called from main() are executed sequentially in the context of this thread. Such a program is called a single threaded application.

In contrast, programs that create new threads are called multithreaded applications. Not only can they execute multiple functions at the same time, they can take advantage of computers that ship with multi-core CPUs. Because multiple cores allow functions to execute concurrently, they put a burden on developers to use the available processing capacity. While threads have always been used when functions had to execute concurrently, developers are now being forced to carefully structure their applications to benefit from CPUs that support concurrency better than before. Thus, knowledge of multithreaded programming has become more and more important in the age of multi-core systems.

This chapter introduces the Boost C++ Library Boost.Thread[1], which makes it possible to develop platform independent multithreaded applications in C++.

Thread Management

The most important class in this library is boost::thread, defined in boost/thread.hpp. This class is used to create a new thread. Example 6.1 is a simple example to create a thread.

---

[1] http://www.boost.org/libs/thread/

Example 6.1

```cpp
#include <boost/thread.hpp>
#include <iostream>

void wait(int seconds)
{
  boost::this_thread::sleep(boost::posix_time::seconds(seconds));
}

void thread()
{
  for (int i = 0; i < 5; ++i)
  {
    wait(1);
    std::cout << i << std::endl;
  }
}

int main()
{
  boost::thread t(thread);
  t.join();
}
```

The name of the function that the new thread should execute is passed to the constructor of boost::thread. Once the variable t in Example 6.1 is created, the function thread() starts immediately executing in its own thread. At this point, thread() executes concurrently with the main() function.

To keep the program from terminating, boost::thread::join() is called on the newly created thread. boost::thread::join() is a blocking call, which blocks the current thread until the thread for which boost::thread::join() was called has terminated. This causes main() to wait until thread() returns.

As seen in Example 6.1, a particular thread can be accessed using a variable – t in this example – to wait for its termination. However, the thread will continue to execute even if t goes out of scope and is destroyed. A thread is always bound to a variable of type boost::thread in the beginning, but once created, the thread no longer depends on it. There is even a member function called boost::thread::detach() that allows a variable of type boost::thread to be decoupled from its corresponding thread. Of course, it's not possible to call member functions like join() afterwards because the variable no longer represents a valid thread.

Anything that can be done inside a function can also be done inside a thread. Ultimately, a thread is no different from a function, except that it is executed concurrently to another function. In the example above, five numbers are written to the standard output stream in a loop. To slow down the output, every iteration of the loop calls the wait() function to stall execution for one second. wait() uses a function called boost::this_thread::sleep(), which is also provided by Boost.Thread and resides in the namespace boost::this_thread.

boost::this_thread::sleep() expects either a period of time or a specific point in time indicating how long or until when the current thread should be stalled. By passing an object of type boost::posix_time::seconds, a period of time is set. boost::posix_time::seconds comes from Boost.DateTime, which is used by Boost.Thread to manage and process time data.

While Example 6.1 shows how to wait for a different thread, Example 6.2 shows how a thread can be interrupted with "interruption points".

Example 6.2

```
#include <boost/thread.hpp>
#include <iostream>

void wait(int seconds)
{
  boost::this_thread::sleep(boost::posix_time::seconds(seconds));
}

void thread()
{
  try
  {
    for (int i = 0; i < 5; ++i)
    {
      wait(1);
      std::cout << i << std::endl;
    }
  }
  catch (boost::thread_interrupted&)
  {
  }
}

int main()
{
  boost::thread t(thread);
  wait(3);
  t.interrupt();
  t.join();
}
```

Calling boost::thread::interrupt() on a thread object interrupts the corresponding thread. In this context, interrupt means that an exception of type boost::thread_interrupted is thrown in the thread. However, this only happens when the thread reaches an interruption point.

Simply calling boost::thread::interrupt() does not have an effect if the given thread does not contain an interruption point. Whenever a thread reaches an interruption point it will check whether boost::thread::interrupt() has been called. If it has been called, an exception of type boost::thread_interrupted will be thrown.

Boost.Thread defines a series of interruption points such as the boost::this_thread::sleep() function. Because boost::this_thread::sleep() is called five times in Example 6.2, the thread checks five times whether or not it has been interrupted. Between the calls to boost::this_thread::sleep(), the thread can not be interrupted.

Once the program is executed, it will only print three numbers to the standard output stream. This happens because boost::thread::interrupt() is called after three seconds in main(). Thus, the corresponding thread is interrupted and throws a boost::thread_interrupted exception. The exception is correctly caught inside the thread although the catch handler is empty. Because the thread() function returns after the handler, the thread terminates as well. This in turn will also terminate the program because main() was waiting for the thread to terminate.

Boost.Thread defines about ten interruption points, including boost::this_thread::sleep(). Thanks to these interruption points, threads can easily be interrupted in a timely manner. However, they may not always be the best choice because an interruption point must be reached first to check for the boost::thread_interrupted exception.

Example 6.3 introduces two more functions provided by Boost.Thread.

Example 6.3

```cpp
#include <boost/thread.hpp>
#include <iostream>

int main()
{
  std::cout << boost::this_thread::get_id() << std::endl;
  std::cout << boost::thread::hardware_concurrency() << std::endl;
}
```

In the namespace boost::this_thread, free-standing functions are defined that apply to the current thread. One of these functions is boost::this_thread::sleep(), which we have seen before. Another one is boost::this_thread::get_id(), which returns a number to uniquely identify the current thread. It is also provided as a member function by the class boost::thread.

The static member function boost::thread::hardware_concurrency() returns the number of threads that could physically be executed at the same time based on the underlying number of CPUs or CPU cores. Calling this function on a dual-core machine returns a value of 2. This function provides a simple method to identify the theoretical maximum number of threads that should be used on a computer a program is executed on.

Synchronization

While using multiple threads can increase the performance of an application, it usually also increases complexity. If several functions execute at the same time, access to shared resources must be synchronized. This involves significant programming effort once the application reaches a certain size. This section introduces the classes provided by Boost.Thread to synchronize threads.

Example 6.4

```cpp
#include <boost/thread.hpp>
#include <iostream>

void wait(int seconds)
{
  boost::this_thread::sleep(boost::posix_time::seconds(seconds));
}

boost::mutex mutex;

void thread()
{
  for (int i = 0; i < 5; ++i)
  {
    wait(1);
    mutex.lock();
    std::cout << "Thread " << boost::this_thread::get_id() << ": " << i <<
      std::endl;
    mutex.unlock();
  }
}

int main()
{
  boost::thread t1(thread);
  boost::thread t2(thread);
  t1.join();
  t2.join();
}
```

Multithreaded programs use "mutexes" for synchronization. Boost.Thread provides different mutex classes with boost::mutex being the most simple one. The basic principle of a mutex is to prevent other threads from taking ownership while a particular thread owns the mutex. Once released, a different thread can take ownership. This causes threads to wait until another thread has finished processing and releases its ownership of the mutex.

Example 6.4 uses a global mutex of type boost::mutex called **mutex**. The thread() function takes ownership of this object by calling boost::mutex::lock(). This is done right before the function writes to the standard output stream. Once a message has been written, ownership is released by calling boost::mutex::unlock().

main() creates two threads, both executing the thread() function. Every thread counts to five and writes a message to the standard output stream in each iteration of the for loop. Unfortunately, the standard output stream is a global object which is shared among all threads. The C++ standard does not provide any guarantee that **std::cout** can be safely accessed from multiple threads. Thus, access to the standard output stream must be synchronized: At any given time, only one thread is allowed to access **std::cout**.

Because both threads try to acquire the mutex before writing to the standard output stream, it is guaranteed that only one thread at a time actually accesses **std::cout**. No matter which thread successfully calls lock(), all other threads need to wait until unlock() has been called.

Acquiring and releasing mutexes is a typical scheme and is supported by Boost.Thread through different data types. For example, instead of calling `lock()` and `unlock()` directly, the class `boost::lock_guard` can be used (see Example 6.5).

Example 6.5

```cpp
#include <boost/thread.hpp>
#include <iostream>

void wait(int seconds)
{
  boost::this_thread::sleep(boost::posix_time::seconds(seconds));
}

boost::mutex mutex;

void thread()
{
  for (int i = 0; i < 5; ++i)
  {
    wait(1);
    boost::lock_guard<boost::mutex> lock(mutex);
    std::cout << "Thread " << boost::this_thread::get_id() << ": " << i <<
      std::endl;
  }
}

int main()
{
  boost::thread t1(thread);
  boost::thread t2(thread);
  t1.join();
  t2.join();
}
```

`boost::lock_guard` automatically calls `lock()` and `unlock()` in its constructor and destructor, respectively. Access to the shared resource is as much synchronized as it was when both member functions were called explicitly. The class `boost::lock_guard` is yet another example of the RAII idiom presented in Chapter 2, *Smart Pointers.*

Besides `boost::mutex` and `boost::lock_guard`, Boost.Thread provides additional classes to support variants of synchronization. One of the essential ones is `boost::unique_lock` which, compared to `boost::lock_guard`, provides a number of helpful member functions.

Example 6.6 illustrates some of the features provided by `boost::unique_lock`. Certainly, using these features does not necessarily make sense for the given use case; `boost::lock_guard` in the previous example was already adequate. This example is rather meant to demonstrate the possibilities offered by `boost::unique_lock`.

Example 6.6

```cpp
#include <boost/thread.hpp>
#include <iostream>

void wait(int seconds)
{
  boost::this_thread::sleep(boost::posix_time::seconds(seconds));
}

boost::timed_mutex mutex;

void thread()
{
  for (int i = 0; i < 5; ++i)
  {
    wait(1);
    boost::unique_lock<boost::timed_mutex> lock(mutex, boost::try_to_lock);
    if (!lock.owns_lock())
    {
      lock.timed_lock(boost::get_system_time() +
        boost::posix_time::seconds(1));
    }
    std::cout << "Thread " << boost::this_thread::get_id() << ": " << i <<
      std::endl;
    boost::timed_mutex *m = lock.release();
    m->unlock();
  }
}

int main()
{
  boost::thread t1(thread);
  boost::thread t2(thread);
  t1.join();
  t2.join();
}
```

boost::unique_lock provides multiple constructors for acquiring a mutex. The first expects only a mutex, calls the boost::unique_lock::lock() member function, and waits until the mutex has been acquired. Thus, it behaves the same as the constructor of boost::lock_guard.

If a value of type boost::try_to_lock is passed as a second parameter, the constructor calls boost::unique_lock::try_lock() instead. This member function returns a value of type bool: true if the mutex could be acquired and false if it could not. Unlike boost::unique_lock::lock(), boost::unique_lock::try_lock() returns immediately and does not block until the mutex has been acquired.

Example 6.6 passes **boost::try_to_lock** as the second parameter to the constructor of boost::unique_lock. Whether or not the mutex has been acquired can be checked by calling boost::unique_lock::owns_lock(). If the mutex has not been acquired and false is returned, boost::unique_lock::timed_lock() is called to wait for a specified time to acquire the mutex. Example 6.6 waits for up to one second, which should be long enough time to acquire the mutex.

Example 6.6 shows the three fundamental ways of acquiring a mutex: `boost::unique_lock::lock()` waits until the mutex has been acquired. `boost::unique_lock::try_lock()` does not wait, but acquires the mutex if it is available at the time of the call and returns `false` otherwise. Finally, `boost::unique_lock::timed_lock()` tries to acquire the mutex within a given period of time. As with `boost::unique_lock::try_lock()`, success or failure is indicated by the return value of type `bool`.

While both `lock()` and `try_lock()` are provided by `boost::mutex`, `timed_lock()` is only supported by `boost::timed_mutex`, which is why that class is used in Example 6.6. Without `timed_lock()`, the mutex can be of type `boost::mutex` as seen in Example 6.5.

Just like `boost::lock_guard`, the destructor of `boost::unique_lock` releases the mutex. In addition, the mutex can be manually released with the member function `unlock()`. It is also possible to remove the association between `boost::unique_lock` and a mutex by calling `release()` as done in Example 6.6. In this case, however, the mutex must be released using the `unlock()` member function explicitly because this is no longer handled automatically by the destructor of `boost::unique_lock`.

`boost::unique_lock` is an "exclusive lock", which means that only one thread at a time can acquire the mutex. Other threads are required to wait until the mutex has been released again. In addition to exclusive locks there are non-exclusive ones. Boost.Thread provides a class called `boost::shared_lock` to support non-exclusive locks. This class must be used together with a mutex of type `boost::shared_mutex` as shown in Example 6.7.

Example 6.7

```
#include <boost/thread.hpp>
#include <iostream>
#include <vector>
#include <cstdlib>
#include <ctime>

void wait(int seconds)
{
  boost::this_thread::sleep(boost::posix_time::seconds(seconds));
}

boost::shared_mutex mutex;
std::vector<int> random_numbers;

void fill()
{
  std::srand(static_cast<unsigned int>(std::time(0)));
  for (int i = 0; i < 3; ++i)
  {
    boost::unique_lock<boost::shared_mutex> lock(mutex);
    random_numbers.push_back(std::rand() % 1000000);
    lock.unlock();
    wait(1);
  }
}
```

```
void print()
{
  for (int i = 0; i < 3; ++i)
  {
    wait(1);
    boost::shared_lock<boost::shared_mutex> lock(mutex);
    std::cout << random_numbers.back() << std::endl;
  }
}

int sum = 0;

void count()
{
  for (int i = 0; i < 3; ++i)
  {
    wait(1);
    boost::shared_lock<boost::shared_mutex> lock(mutex);
    sum += random_numbers.back();
  }
}

int main()
{
  boost::thread t1(fill);
  boost::thread t2(print);
  boost::thread t3(count);
  t1.join();
  t2.join();
  t3.join();
  std::cout << "Sum: " << sum << std::endl;
}
```

Non-exclusive locks of type `boost::shared_lock` can be used if threads only need read-only access to a specific resource. A thread modifying the resource needs write access and thus requires an exclusive lock. The reason for that should be obvious: threads with read-only access do not recognize other threads reading the same resource at the same time. Non-exclusive locks can therefore share a mutex.

In Example 6.7, both `print()` and `count()` only read **random_numbers**. The `print()` function writes the last value in **random_numbers** to the standard output stream, and the `count()` function adds it to the variable **sum**. Because neither function modifies **random_numbers**, both can access it at the same time using a non-exclusive lock of type `boost::shared_lock`.

Inside the `fill()` function, an exclusive lock of type `boost::unique_lock` is required because it inserts new random numbers into **random_numbers**. The mutex is explicitly released using the `unlock()` member function before `fill()` waits for one second. Unlike Example 6.6, `wait()` is called at the end of the `for` loop to guarantee that at least one random number exists in the container before it is accessed by either `print()` or `count()`. Both of these functions call the `wait()` function at the beginning of their `for` loops.

Looking at the individual calls to the `wait()` function from different locations, one potential issue becomes apparent: The order of the function calls is directly affected by the order in which the CPU actually executes the individual threads. Using "condition variables", the individual threads can be synchronized so that values added to **random_numbers** are immediately processed by a different thread (see Example 6.8).

Example 6.8

```cpp
#include <boost/thread.hpp>
#include <iostream>
#include <vector>
#include <cstdlib>
#include <ctime>

boost::mutex mutex;
boost::condition_variable_any cond;
std::vector<int> random_numbers;

void fill()
{
  std::srand(static_cast<unsigned int>(std::time(0)));
  for (int i = 0; i < 3; ++i)
  {
    boost::unique_lock<boost::mutex> lock(mutex);
    random_numbers.push_back(std::rand() % 1000000);
    cond.notify_all();
    cond.wait(mutex);
  }
}

void print()
{
  std::size_t next_size = 1;
  for (int i = 0; i < 3; ++i)
  {
    boost::unique_lock<boost::mutex> lock(mutex);
    while (random_numbers.size() != next_size)
      cond.wait(mutex);
    std::cout << random_numbers.back() << std::endl;
    ++next_size;
    cond.notify_all();
  }
}

int main()
{
  boost::thread t1(fill);
  boost::thread t2(print);
  t1.join();
  t2.join();
}
```

Example 6.8 removes the wait() and count() functions. Threads no longer wait for one second in every iteration; rather, they execute as fast as possible. In addition, no total is calculated; numbers are just written to the standard output stream.

To ensure correct processing of the random numbers, the individual threads are synchronized using a condition variable, which can be checked for certain conditions between multiple threads.

As before, the `fill()` function generates a random number with each iteration and places it in the **random_numbers** container. To block other threads from accessing the container at the same time, an exclusive lock is used. Instead of waiting for one second, this example uses a condition variable. Calling `notify_all()` will wake up every thread that has been waiting for this notification with `wait()`.

By looking at the `for` loop of the `print()` function, one can see that for the same condition variable, a member function called `wait()` is called. If the thread is woken up by a call to `noti-fy_all()`, it tries to acquire the mutex, which will only succeed after it has been successfully released in the `fill()` function.

The trick here is that calling `wait()` also releases the corresponding mutex which is passed as a parameter. After calling `notify_all()`, the `fill()` function releases the mutex by calling `wait()`. It then blocks and waits for some other thread to call `notify_all()`, which happens in the `print()` function once the random number has been written to the standard output stream.

Notice that the call to the `wait()` member function inside the `print()` function actually happens within a separate `while` loop. This is done to handle the scenario where a random number has already been placed in the container before the `wait()` member function is called for the first time in `print()`. By comparing the number of stored elements in **random_numbers** with the expected number of elements, this scenario is successfully handled and the random number is written to the standard output stream.

Thread Local Storage

Thread Local Storage (TLS) is a dedicated storage area that can only be accessed by one thread. TLS variables can be seen as global variables that are only visible to a particular thread and not the whole program.

Example 6.9

```
#include <boost/thread.hpp>
#include <iostream>

boost::mutex mutex;

void func()
{
  static bool done = false;
  boost::lock_guard<boost::mutex> lock(mutex);
  if (!done)
  {
    done = true;
    std::cout << "done" << std::endl;
  }
}

void thread()
{
  func();
  func();
}
```

```
int main()
{
  boost::thread t[3];

  for (int i = 0; i < 3; ++i)
    t[i] = boost::thread(thread);

  for (int i = 0; i < 3; ++i)
    t[i].join();
}
```

Example 6.9 executes a function `thread()` in three threads. `thread()` calls another function `func()` twice, and `func()` checks whether the boolean variable **done** is `false`. If it is, the variable is set to `true` and `done` is written to standard output.

done is a static variable that is shared by all threads. If the first thread set **done** to `true`, the second and third thread won't write `done` to standard output. Of course the second call of `func()` in any thread won't write `done` to standard output either. The example will print `done` only once.

Example 6.10

```
#include <boost/thread.hpp>
#include <iostream>

boost::mutex mutex;

void func()
{
  static boost::thread_specific_ptr<bool> tls;
  if (!tls.get())
  {
    tls.reset(new bool(true));
    boost::lock_guard<boost::mutex> lock(mutex);
    std::cout << "done" << std::endl;
  }
}

void thread()
{
  func();
  func();
}

int main()
{
  boost::thread t[3];

  for (int i = 0; i < 3; ++i)
    t[i] = boost::thread(thread);

  for (int i = 0; i < 3; ++i)
    t[i].join();
}
```

A static variable like **done** can be used to do a one-time initialization in a process. Once **done** has been set to true, neither the same nor another thread will print done again. To do a one-time initialization per thread, TLS variables can be used (see Example 6.10).

In Example 6.10, the static variable **done** has been replaced with a TLS variable, **tls**, which is based on the class template boost::thread_specific_ptr - instantiated with the data type bool. In principle, **tls** works just like **done**: It acts as a condition indicating whether or not something was already done. The crucial difference, however, is that the value stored by **tls** is only visible and available to the corresponding thread.

Once a variable of type boost::thread_specific_ptr is created, it can be set accordingly. However, it expects the address of a variable of type bool instead of the variable itself. Using the reset() member function, the corresponding address can be stored in **tls**. In the given example, a variable of type bool is dynamically allocated and its address, returned by new, is stored in **tls**. To avoid setting **tls** every time func() is called, it first checks whether an address is already stored via the get() member function. If an address is stored, we know it's the address of a boolean variable set to true.

The program prints done to standard output three times. Each thread prints done once, in the first call to func(). Because a TLS variable is used, each thread uses its own variable **tls**. When the first thread initializes **tls** with a pointer to a dynamically allocated boolean variable, **tls** in the second and third thread is still uninitialized. As TLS variables are not global per process, but global per thread, using **tls** in one thread does not change the variable in any other thread.

Exercises

1. Refactor the following program to calculate the total using two threads. Since many processors nowadays have at least two cores, the execution time should decrease by utilizing threads.

    Example 6.11

    ```
    #include <boost/date_time/posix_time/posix_time.hpp>
    #include <boost/cstdint.hpp>
    #include <iostream>

    int main()
    {
      boost::posix_time::ptime start =
        boost::posix_time::microsec_clock::local_time();

      boost::uint64_t sum = 0;
      for (int i = 0; i < 1000000000; ++i)
        sum += i;

      boost::posix_time::ptime end =
        boost::posix_time::microsec_clock::local_time();
      std::cout << end - start << std::endl;

      std::cout << sum << std::endl;
    }
    ```

2. Generalize the program from exercise 1 (Example 6.11) by using as many threads as the processor can physically execute at the same time. For example, if a processor contains four cores, a total of four threads should be used.

3. Change the following program (Example 6.12) to execute the `thread()` function in its own thread, which should be created in `main()`. The program should calculate the total and write it to the standard output stream twice. The implementations of `calculate()`, `print()` and `thread()` can be modified but the signatures must not be changed. In other words, neither function can accept any parameters or return a value.

Example 6.12

```cpp
#include <iostream>

int sum = 0;

void calculate()
{
    for (int i = 0; i < 1000; ++i)
        sum += i;
}

void print()
{
    std::cout << sum << std::endl;
}

void thread()
{
    calculate();
    print();
}

int main()
{
    thread();
}
```

Asynchronous Input and Output

General

This chapter introduces the library Boost.Asio[1] which handles asynchronous input and output. The name says it all: Asio stands for asynchronous input/output. This library makes it possible to process data asynchronously in a platform independent manner. Tasks are triggered and allowed to run asynchronously without blocking the program. Instead, Boost.Asio notifies a program once a task has completed. The main advantage of asynchronous tasks is that a program can perform a task while waiting for other tasks to complete.

Asynchronous tasks are of particular benefit in network programs. If data is sent over the Internet, it is important to know whether it was sent successfully. Without a library such as Boost.Asio, the return value of a function would need to be evaluated. However, this would require the program to wait until all data has been sent and either an acknowledgment or an error code becomes available. With Boost.Asio, the operation is split into two steps: the first step starts the data transmission as an asynchronous task. Once the transmission is complete, the program is notified about the result in a second step. The application does not need to block until the transmission has finished, but can execute other operations in the meantime.

I/O Services and I/O Objects

Programs that use Boost.Asio for asynchronous data processing are based on I/O services and I/O objects. I/O services abstract the operating system interfaces that process data asynchronously, and I/O objects initiate asynchronous operations. The reason there are two concepts is that I/O services look towards the operating system API, while I/O objects look towards developers and the tasks developers need to do.

---

[1] http://www.boost.org/libs/asio/

I/O services are available through the class boost::asio::io_service. This class is the central point of coordination and knows which I/O services are available on a given platform. Think of it as a registry that supports different asynchronous operations. Because different asynchronous operations use different underlying operating system interfaces, Boost.Asio ships several I/O services through boost::asio::io_service. If you only use the I/O objects that are shipped with Boost.Asio, you will never need to work with I/O services directly because boost::asio::io_service knows which I/O service to use for which I/O object.

While Boost.Asio provides only one class (boost::asio::io_service) to create an I/O service object, there are many different classes for I/O objects. Among these, the class boost::asio::ip::tcp::socket is used to send and receive data over a network, while the class boost::asio::deadline_timer provides a timer that either elapses at a particular time or after a certain period has elapsed. The timer in Example 7.1 is used because it does not require any prior knowledge about network programming.

Example 7.1

```
#include <boost/asio.hpp>
#include <iostream>

void handler(const boost::system::error_code &ec)
{
   std::cout << "5 s." << std::endl;
}

int main()
{
   boost::asio::io_service io_service;
   boost::asio::deadline_timer timer(io_service,
     boost::posix_time::seconds(5));
   timer.async_wait(handler);
   io_service.run();
}
```

The function main() first defines an I/O service object **io_service** that is used to initialize the I/O object **timer**. Just like boost::asio::deadline_timer, the constructors of all I/O objects expect an I/O service object as a first parameter. Because **timer** resembles an alarm, you can pass the constructor a second parameter that indicates either a point in time or a period after which the alarm should go off. Example 7.1 specifies a period of five seconds. The time starts elapsing once **timer** has been defined.

While it would be possible to call a function that returns after five seconds, with Boost.Asio an asynchronous operation can be started. This is done by calling async_wait() and passing the name of the function handler() as the sole parameter. Please note that the name of the function handler() is passed, but the function is not called.

The advantage of async_wait() is that the function call returns immediately instead of waiting five seconds. Once the alarm goes off, the function provided as the parameter is called. Thus the program can execute other operations after calling async_wait() instead of just blocking.

A member function such as `async_wait()` is described as non-blocking. I/O objects typically also provide blocking member functions in case the execution flow should be blocked until a certain operation is complete. Here the blocking member function `wait()` could have been called. Because it is a blocking call, it does not require a function name but rather returns at a specific time or after a certain period has expired.

Looking at the source code of Example 7.1, it can be seen that after the call to `async_wait()` a member function `run()` is called on the I/O service object. This call is mandatory because control needs to be taken over by the operating system in order to call the `handler()` function after five seconds. Remember that the I/O services within the I/O service object process data asynchronously as they call underlying operating system functions.

While `async_wait()` starts an asynchronous operation and returns immediately, `run()` blocks. Therefore, execution stops when `run()` is called. Ironically, many operating systems support asynchronous operations via a blocking function only. Example 7.2 shows why this limitation is typically not an issue.

Example 7.2

```cpp
#include <boost/asio.hpp>
#include <iostream>

void handler1(const boost::system::error_code &ec)
{
  std::cout << "5 s." << std::endl;
}

void handler2(const boost::system::error_code &ec)
{
  std::cout << "10 s." << std::endl;
}

int main()
{
  boost::asio::io_service io_service;
  boost::asio::deadline_timer timer1(io_service,
    boost::posix_time::seconds(5));
  timer1.async_wait(handler1);
  boost::asio::deadline_timer timer2(io_service,
    boost::posix_time::seconds(10));
  timer2.async_wait(handler2);
  io_service.run();
}
```

Example 7.2 uses two I/O objects of type `boost::asio::deadline_timer`. The first object represents an alarm going off after five seconds, while the second represents an alarm going off after ten seconds. After each time has elapsed, the functions `handler1()` and `handler2()` are called.

At the end of `main()`, the member function `run()` is called again on the I/O service object. This function blocks execution and passes control to the operating system, which takes over asynchronous processing. With the aid of the operating system, `handler1()` is called after five seconds, and `handler2()` is called after 10 seconds.

At first sight, it may come as a surprise that asynchronous processing requires calling a blocking member function run(). However, because the application needs to be prevented from terminating, this does actually not pose any issue. If run() did not block, main() would return and terminate the program. If the program should not be blocked, run() can be called in a new thread because it only blocks the current thread.

Once all asynchronous operations of the particular I/O service object have completed, run() returns. Thus both sample programs terminate once all the alarms have gone off.

Scalability and Multithreading

Developing a program based on a library like Boost.Asio differs from the usual C++ style. Functions that may take longer to return are no longer called in a sequential manner. Instead of calling blocking functions, Boost.Asio starts asynchronous operations. Functions which should be called after an operation finished are now called within the corresponding handler. The drawback of this approach is the physical separation of the sequentially executed functions which makes code more difficult to understand.

A library such as Boost.Asio is typically used to achieve greater efficiency. With no need to wait for a particular function to finish, a program can perform other tasks in between, e.g. starting another operation that may take a while to complete.

Scalability describes the ability of a program to effectively benefit from additional resources. Using Boost.Asio is already recommended if long-lasting operations should not block other operations. As today's computers are typically equipped with multi-core processors, using threads can increase the scalability of a program based on Boost.Asio even further.

If the member function run() is called on an object of type boost::asio::io_service, the associated handlers are invoked within the same thread. By using multiple threads, a program can call run() multiple times. Once an asynchronous operation is complete, the I/O service object will execute the handler in one of these threads. If a second operation is completed shortly after the first one, the I/O service object can execute the handler in a different thread without having to wait for the first handler to return.

Example 7.2 from the previous section is converted to a multithreaded program in Example 7.3. With the class boost::thread, defined in boost/thread.hpp and part of the library Boost.Thread, two threads are created in main(). Both threads call run() on the single I/O service object. This allows the I/O service object to use both threads for executing handler functions once individual asynchronous operations have been completed.

Both timers in the sample program are set to elapse after five seconds. As two threads are available, both handler1() and handler2() can execute concurrently. If the second timer elapses while the first handler is running, the second handler will run in the second thread. If the first handler has already returned, the I/O service object is free to choose either thread.

Example 7.3

```cpp
#include <boost/asio.hpp>
#include <boost/thread.hpp>
#include <iostream>

void handler1(const boost::system::error_code &ec)
{
  std::cout << "5 s." << std::endl;
}

void handler2(const boost::system::error_code &ec)
{
  std::cout << "5 s." << std::endl;
}

boost::asio::io_service io_service;

void run()
{
  io_service.run();
}

int main()
{
  boost::asio::deadline_timer timer1(io_service,
    boost::posix_time::seconds(5));
  timer1.async_wait(handler1);
  boost::asio::deadline_timer timer2(io_service,
    boost::posix_time::seconds(5));
  timer2.async_wait(handler2);
  boost::thread thread1(run);
  boost::thread thread2(run);
  thread1.join();
  thread2.join();
}
```

Threads can increase the performance of a program. Because threads are executed on processor cores, there is no sense in creating more threads than there are cores. This ensures that each thread is executed on its own core without competing with other threads for a core.

Please note that using threads does not always make sense. Running Example 7.3 can result in the messages being mixed in the the standard output stream because the two handlers, which may run in parallel, access a single shared resource, the standard output stream **std::cout**. Access must be synchronized to guarantee that each message is completely written before another thread writes to the standard output stream. Using threads in this scenario does not provide much benefit if the individual handlers cannot be executed in parallel.

Calling run() on a single I/O service object multiple times is the recommended way to improve scalability of a program based on Boost.Asio. There is an alternate method. Instead of binding multiple threads to a single I/O service object, multiple I/O service objects can be created. Then each of the I/O service objects can use one thread. If the number of I/O service objects matches the number of processor cores, each asynchronous operation can run on its own core.

Example 7.4

```cpp
#include <boost/asio.hpp>
#include <boost/thread.hpp>
#include <iostream>

void handler1(const boost::system::error_code &ec)
{
  std::cout << "5 s." << std::endl;
}

void handler2(const boost::system::error_code &ec)
{
  std::cout << "5 s." << std::endl;
}

boost::asio::io_service io_service1;
boost::asio::io_service io_service2;

void run1()
{
  io_service1.run();
}

void run2()
{
  io_service2.run();
}

int main()
{
  boost::asio::deadline_timer timer1(io_service1,
    boost::posix_time::seconds(5));
  timer1.async_wait(handler1);
  boost::asio::deadline_timer timer2(io_service2,
    boost::posix_time::seconds(5));
  timer2.async_wait(handler2);
  boost::thread thread1(run1);
  boost::thread thread2(run2);
  thread1.join();
  thread2.join();
}
```

Example 7.4 is a rewrite of Example 7.3 that uses two I/O service objects. The program is still based on two threads, but each thread is now bound to an individual I/O service object. Additionally, the two I/O objects, **timer1** and **timer2**, are now bound to different I/O service objects.

The program works the same as before. It can be beneficial under certain conditions to have multiple I/O service objects, each with its own thread and ideally running on its own processor core, because asynchronous operations, and their handlers can execute locally. If no distant data or function needs to be accessed, each I/O service object behaves like a small autonomous program. Local and distant in this case refers to resources such as cache and memory pages. Because specific knowledge about the hardware, operating system, compiler as well as potential bottlenecks is required before optimization strategies can be developed, multiple I/O service objects should only be used in scenarios that clearly benefit from them.

Network Programming

Even though Boost.Asio can process any kind of data asynchronously, it is mainly used for network programming. This is because Boost.Asio supported network functions long before additional I/O objects were added. Network functions are a perfect use for asynchronous operations because the transmission of data over a network may take a long time, which means acknowledgments and errors may not be available immediately.

Example 7.5

```
#include <boost/asio.hpp>
#include <boost/array.hpp>
#include <iostream>
#include <string>

boost::asio::io_service io_service;
boost::asio::ip::tcp::resolver resolver(io_service);
boost::asio::ip::tcp::socket sock(io_service);
boost::array<char, 4096> buffer;

void read_handler(const boost::system::error_code &ec,
  std::size_t bytes_transferred)
{
  if (!ec)
  {
    std::cout << std::string(buffer.data(), bytes_transferred) << std::endl;
    sock.async_read_some(boost::asio::buffer(buffer), read_handler);
  }
}

void connect_handler(const boost::system::error_code &ec)
{
  if (!ec)
  {
    boost::asio::write(sock, boost::asio::buffer(
      "GET / HTTP 1.1\r\nHost: www.highscore.de\r\n\r\n"));
    sock.async_read_some(boost::asio::buffer(buffer), read_handler);
  }
}

void resolve_handler(const boost::system::error_code &ec,
  boost::asio::ip::tcp::resolver::iterator it)
{
  if (!ec)
  {
    sock.async_connect(*it, connect_handler);
  }
}

int main()
{
  boost::asio::ip::tcp::resolver::query query("www.highscore.de", "80");
  resolver.async_resolve(query, resolve_handler);
  io_service.run();
}
```

Boost.Asio provides many I/O objects to develop network programs. Example 7.5 uses the class `boost::asio::ip::tcp::socket` to establish a connection to another computer and download the "Highscore" homepage, thus acting like a browser pointed to www.highscore.de[2].

The most obvious part of Example 7.5 is that three handlers are used. The functions `connect_handler()` and `read_handler()` are called once the connection has been established and when data is received, respectively. However, why is the function `resolve_handler()` required?

The Internet uses IP addresses to identify computers. IP addresses are essentially just a lengthy number that is hard to remember. It is much easier to remember names like www.highscore.de. In order to use such a name on the Internet, it must be translated to the corresponding IP address via a process called name resolution. This process is handled by a "name resolver", which explains the name of the corresponding I/O object: `boost::asio::ip::tcp::resolver`.

Name resolution requires an Internet connection. Dedicated computers, called DNS servers, act just like phone books and know what IP address is assigned to a computer. Because the process itself is transparent, it is only important to understand the concept behind it and why the I/O object `boost::asio::ip::tcp::resolver` is required. Because name resolution is a network operation that does not take place locally, it is implemented as an asynchronous operation. The function `resolve_handler()` is called once the name resolution has either succeeded or failed.

Because receiving data requires a successful connection, which in turn requires a successful name resolution, asynchronous operations are started within the individual handlers. `resolve_handler()` accesses the I/O object **sock** to create a connection using the resolved address provided by the iterator **it**. **sock** is also accessed inside of `connect_handler()` to send the HTTP request and to initiate the data reception. As all of these operations are asynchronous, the names of the individual handlers are passed as parameters. Depending on the corresponding handler, additional parameters are required such as the iterator **it**, which points to the resolved address or the buffer **buffer** which stores data received.

Once executed, the program creates an object **query** of type `boost::asio::ip::tcp::resolver::query`, which represents a query containing the name www.highscore.de and the port 80, which is commonly used on the web. This query is passed to the member function `async_resolve()` to resolve the name. Finally, `main()` calls `run()` on the I/O service object to transfer control of the asynchronous operations to the operating system.

Once name resolution is complete, `resolve_handler()` checks whether the name could be resolved. If successfully resolved, the object **ec**, which represents error codes, is set to 0. Only in this case, the socket is accessed to create a connection. The server address is provided via the second parameter of type `boost::asio::ip::tcp::resolver::iterator`.

After calling `async_connect()`, `connect_handler()` is called automatically. Inside the handler, **ec** is evaluated to check whether or not a connection has been established. In case a connection is available, the member function `async_read_some()` initiates the read operation. To store the received data, a buffer is provided as the first parameter. In Example 7.5, the buffer is of type `boost::array`, which is a class provided by Boost.Array and defined in `boost/array.hpp`.

---

[2] http://www.highscore.de/

The function read_handler() is called every time one or more bytes have been received and stored within the buffer. The exact number of bytes received is given via the parameter **bytes_transferred**, which is of type std::size_t. The handler should first evaluate the parameter **ec** to check for any reception error. If successfully received, the data is simply written to the standard output stream.

Please note that read_handler() calls async_read_some() again once data has been written to **std::cout**. This is necessary because there is no guarantee that the entire homepage has been received with just a single asynchronous operation. The alternating calls of async_read_some() and read_handler() only stop if the connection has been disrupted, e.g. when the web server has transmitted the entire homepage. In this case, an error is reported inside read_handler() which means that no data is written to the standard output stream, and async_read() is also not called. Example 7.5 will then terminate as no further asynchronous operations are outstanding.

While Example 7.5 was used to retrieve the homepage of www.highscore.de, Example 7.6 illustrates a simple web server. The crucial difference is that the program does not connect to other computers; instead it waits for incoming connections.

Example 7.6

```cpp
#include <boost/asio.hpp>
#include <string>

boost::asio::io_service io_service;
boost::asio::ip::tcp::endpoint endpoint(boost::asio::ip::tcp::v4(), 80);
boost::asio::ip::tcp::acceptor acceptor(io_service, endpoint);
boost::asio::ip::tcp::socket sock(io_service);
std::string data =
  "HTTP/1.1 200 OK\r\nContent-Length: 13\r\n\r\nHello, world!";

void write_handler(const boost::system::error_code &ec,
  std::size_t bytes_transferred)
{
}

void accept_handler(const boost::system::error_code &ec)
{
  if (!ec)
  {
    boost::asio::async_write(sock, boost::asio::buffer(data),
      write_handler);
  }
}

int main()
{
  acceptor.listen();
  acceptor.async_accept(sock, accept_handler);
  io_service.run();
}
```

The I/O object **acceptor** of type boost::asio::ip::tcp::acceptor is initialized with the protocol and the port and then waits for incoming connections from other computers. The initialization happens via the object **endpoint**, which is of type `boost::asio::ip::tcp::endpoint`, and configures the acceptor in the example to use port 80 to wait for incoming connections of version 4 of the Internet protocol. This is typically the port and protocol used on the web.

After initializing the acceptor, `main()` first calls the member function `listen()` to put the acceptor into receive mode before it waits for the initial connection with `async_accept()`. The socket used to send and receive data is passed as the first parameter.

Once a computer tries to establish a connection, `accept_handler()` is called automatically. If the connect request is successful, the free-standing function `boost::asio::async_write()` is invoked to send data stored in **data** through the socket. `boost::asio::ip::tcp::socket` also provides a member function called `async_write_some()` to send data, but it will invoke the associated handler whenever at least one byte has been sent. The handler would need to calculate how many bytes are left to send and invoke `async_write_some()` repeatedly until all bytes have been sent. This can be avoided by using `boost::asio::async_write()` since this asynchronous operation only terminates once all bytes in the buffer have been sent.

Once all of the data has been sent in Example 7.6, the empty function `write_handler()` is called. Since all asynchronous operations have finished, the program is terminated. The connection to the other computer is closed accordingly.

Developing Boost.Asio Extensions

Even though Boost.Asio mainly supports network functions, creating new I/O objects to perform other asynchronous operations is fairly easy. This section outlines the general layout of a Boost.Asio extension. While it is not mandatory, it provides a viable skeleton as a starting point for Boost.Asio extensions.

To add new asynchronous operations to Boost.Asio, three classes need to be implemented:

► A class derived from `boost::asio::basic_io_object` to represent the new I/O object. Developers using the new Boost.Asio extension will only see and use this I/O object.

► A class derived from `boost::asio::io_service::service` to represent an I/O service that is registered in the I/O service object and will be used by the I/O object. The difference between an I/O service and an I/O object is important. There is only one instance of an I/O service per I/O service object, although an I/O service object can be used by multiple I/O objects.

► A class not derived from any other class to represent the I/O service implementation. As there is only one instance of an I/O service per I/O service object at any given time, the service creates an instance of its implementation for every I/O object. This instance manages the internal data for an I/O object.

Instead of just providing the skeleton, the Boost.Asio extension developed in this section will resemble the available `boost::asio::deadline_timer` object. The difference between the two is that the period for the timer can be passed as a parameter to the member functions `wait()` or `async_wait()` instead of to the constructor.

Example 7.7

```
#include <boost/asio.hpp>
#include <cstddef>

template <typename Service>
class basic_timer
  : public boost::asio::basic_io_object<Service>
{
  public:
    explicit basic_timer(boost::asio::io_service &io_service)
      : boost::asio::basic_io_object<Service>(io_service)
    {
    }

    void wait(std::size_t seconds)
    {
      return this->service.wait(this->implementation, seconds);
    }

    template <typename Handler>
    void async_wait(std::size_t seconds, Handler handler)
    {
      this->service.async_wait(this->implementation, seconds, handler);
    }
};
```

An I/O object is usually implemented as a class template that is instantiated with a service – typically the service specifically developed for this I/O object. Whenever an I/O object is instantiated, the service is automatically registered by the parent class boost::asio::basic_io_object at the I/O service object, unless it was already registered before. This ensures that services used by any I/O object will only be registered once per I/O service object.

The corresponding service is accessible within the I/O object via the reference **service** and is typically accessed to forward member function calls to the service. Because services need to store data for every I/O object, an instance of the service implementation is automatically created for every I/O object which uses the service. This happens with the aid of the parent class boost::asio::basic_io_object. The service implementation is passed as a parameter to any member function call to let the service know which I/O object initiated the call. The service implementation is accessible via the member variable **implementation**.

In general, I/O objects are relatively simple. While the installation of the service as well as the creation of a service implementation is done by the parent class boost::asio::basic_io_object, member function calls are simply forwarded to the corresponding service, passing the actual service implementation of the I/O object as an argument.

Example 7.8

```cpp
#include <boost/asio.hpp>
#include <boost/thread.hpp>
#include <boost/bind.hpp>
#include <boost/scoped_ptr.hpp>
#include <boost/shared_ptr.hpp>
#include <boost/weak_ptr.hpp>
#include <boost/system/error_code.hpp>

template <typename TimerImplementation = timer_impl>
class basic_timer_service
  : public boost::asio::io_service::service
{
  public:
    static boost::asio::io_service::id id;

    explicit basic_timer_service(boost::asio::io_service &io_service)
      : boost::asio::io_service::service(io_service),
      async_work_(new boost::asio::io_service::work(async_io_service_)),
      async_thread_(boost::bind(&boost::asio::io_service::run,
        &async_io_service_))
    {
    }

    typedef boost::shared_ptr<TimerImplementation> implementation_type;

    void construct(implementation_type &impl)
    {
      impl.reset(new TimerImplementation());
    }

    void destroy(implementation_type &impl)
    {
      impl->destroy();
      impl.reset();
    }

    void wait(implementation_type &impl, std::size_t seconds)
    {
      boost::system::error_code ec;
      impl->wait(seconds, ec);
      boost::asio::detail::throw_error(ec);
    }

    template <typename Handler>
    class wait_operation
    {
      public:
        wait_operation(implementation_type &impl,
          boost::asio::io_service &io_service, std::size_t seconds,
          Handler handler)
          : impl_(impl),
          io_service_(io_service),
          work_(io_service),
          seconds_(seconds),
          handler_(handler)
        {
        }
```

```
      void operator()() const
      {
        implementation_type impl = impl_.lock();
        if (impl)
        {
            boost::system::error_code ec;
            impl->wait(seconds_, ec);
            this->io_service_.post(boost::asio::detail::bind_handler(
              handler_, ec));
        }
        else
        {
            this->io_service_.post(boost::asio::detail::bind_handler(
              handler_, boost::asio::error::operation_aborted));
        }
      }

    private:
      boost::weak_ptr<TimerImplementation> impl_;
      boost::asio::io_service &io_service_;
      boost::asio::io_service::work work_;
      std::size_t seconds_;
      Handler handler_;
    };

    template <typename Handler>
    void async_wait(implementation_type &impl, std::size_t seconds,
      Handler handler)
    {
      this->async_io_service_.post(wait_operation<Handler>(impl,
        this->get_io_service(), seconds, handler));
    }

  private:
    void shutdown_service()
    {
      async_work_.reset();
      async_io_service_.stop();
      async_thread_.join();
    }

    boost::asio::io_service async_io_service_;
    boost::scoped_ptr<boost::asio::io_service::work> async_work_;
    boost::thread async_thread_;
};

template <typename TimerImplementation>
boost::asio::io_service::id basic_timer_service<TimerImplementation>::id;
```

In order to be integrated with Boost.Asio, a service must fulfill a couple of requirements:

- It needs to be derived from `boost::asio::io_service::service`. The constructor must expect a reference to an I/O service object, which is forwarded to the constructor of `boost::asio::io_service::service`.

- A static public member variable **id** of type `boost::asio::io_service::id` must be defined by every service. Services are identified by an I/O service object through this ID.

- Two public member functions called `construct()` and `destruct()`, both expecting a parameter of type `implementation_type`, must be defined. `implementation_type` is typically a type definition for the service implementation. As shown in Example 7.8, an object of type `boost::shared_ptr` can be used to easily instantiate a service implementation in `construct()` and to destroy it in `destruct()`. Because both member functions are automatically called whenever an I/O object is created or destroyed, a service can easily create and destroy service implementations for each I/O object with `construct()` and `destruct()`.

- A member function called `shutdown_service()` must be defined, but it can be private. It replaces the destructor. Whatever you would normally put into the destructor, must be put into `shutdown_service()`.

Because I/O objects forward function calls to I/O services, appropriate member functions need to be defined. These member functions are typically called the same way the member functions of the I/O object are called (e.g., `wait()` and `async_wait()` in Example 7.8). While synchronous member functions such as `wait()` solely access the service implementation to call a blocking member function, the trick for asynchronous operations like `async_wait()` is to call the blocking member function within a thread.

In order to support asynchronous operations with the help of a thread, another I/O service object is typically used by the service internally. If you look at the implementation of the service, you'll notice the member variable **async_io_service_** of type `boost::asio::io_service`. The member function `run()` of this I/O service object is called within its own thread created with **async_thread_** of type `boost::thread` inside the constructor of the service. The third member variable, **async_work_** of type `boost::scoped_ptr<boost::asio::io_service::work>`, is required in order to keep `run()` from returning immediately, which otherwise could happen since there are no outstanding asynchronous operations when `run()` is called. Creating an object of type `boost::asio::io_service::work` and binding it to the I/O service object, which is also done in the constructor of the service, prevents `run()` from returning immediately.

A service can also be implemented without using another I/O service object – a thread would be sufficient. The reason a new I/O service object is used is simple: threads can communicate fairly easily with each other through I/O service objects. In the example, `async_wait()` creates a function object of type `wait_operation` and passes it to the internal I/O service object via the member function `post()`. The overloaded operator `operator()` of this function object is then called inside the thread that is used to execute `run()` of the internal I/O service object. `post()` offers a simple way of executing a function object within a different thread.

The overloaded operator `operator()` of `wait_operation` essentially performs the same work as `wait()`. It calls the blocking member function `wait()` of the service implementation. However, there is the possibility that the I/O object, including its service implementation, was destroyed while the thread executed the operator `operator()`. If the service implementation is destroyed in `destruct()`, the operator `operator()` should no longer access it. This is prevented by using a weak pointer (see Chapter 2, *Smart Pointers*). The weak pointer **impl_** returns a shared pointer to the service implementation if it still exists when `lock()` is called, otherwise it returns 0. In the latter case, `operator()` does not access the service implementation, but rather calls the handler with the error `boost::asio::error::operation_aborted`.

Example 7.9

```cpp
#include <boost/system/error_code.hpp>
#include <cstddef>
#include <windows.h>

class timer_impl
{
  public:
    timer_impl()
      : handle_(CreateEvent(NULL, FALSE, FALSE, NULL))
    {
    }

    ~timer_impl()
    {
      CloseHandle(handle_);
    }

    void destroy()
    {
      SetEvent(handle_);
    }

    void wait(std::size_t seconds, boost::system::error_code &ec)
    {
      DWORD res = WaitForSingleObject(handle_, seconds * 1000);
      if (res == WAIT_OBJECT_0)
        ec = boost::asio::error::operation_aborted;
      else
        ec = boost::system::error_code();
    }

private:
    HANDLE handle_;
};
```

In Example 7.9, the service implementation `timer_impl` uses Windows API functions and can only be compiled and used on Windows. Its purpose here is to show a potential implementation.

`timer_impl` exhibits two essential member functions: `wait()` is called to wait for one or more seconds, and `destroy()` is used to cancel a wait operation, which is mandatory because `wait()` is called inside its own thread for asynchronous operations. If the I/O object, including its service implementation, is destroyed, the blocking member function `wait()` should be canceled as soon as possible using `destroy()`.

Example 7.10

```cpp
#include <boost/asio.hpp>
#include <iostream>
#include "basic_timer.hpp"
#include "timer_impl.hpp"
#include "basic_timer_service.hpp"

void wait_handler(const boost::system::error_code &ec)
{
  std::cout << "5 s." << std::endl;
}

typedef basic_timer<basic_timer_service<> > timer;

int main()
{
  boost::asio::io_service io_service;
  timer t(io_service);
  t.async_wait(5, wait_handler);
  io_service.run();
}
```

Example 7.10 shows how to use this Boost.Asio extension. Compared to the program at the beginning of this chapter (Example 7.1), this Boost.Asio extension is used like `boost::asio::deadline_timer`. In practice, `boost::asio::deadline_timer` should be preferred since it is already shipped with Boost.Asio. The sole purpose of this extension is to show how Boost.Asio can be extended with new asynchronous operations.

Directory Monitor[3] is a real-world example of a Boost.Asio extension that provides an I/O object which can be used to monitor directories. If a file inside a monitored directory is created, modified, or deleted, a handler is called. The current version supports both Windows and Linux (kernel version 2.6.13 or higher).

Exercises

1. Modify the server in Example 7.6 (page 87) to prevent it from terminating after a single request has been processed. The server should be able to process an arbitrary number of requests.

2. Extend the client in Example 7.5 (page 85) to immediately parse the received HTML code for an URL. If an URL is found, the corresponding resource should be downloaded. For this exercise, the first URL found should be used. Ideally, the webpage as well as the resource should be saved in two files rather than writing both to the standard output stream.

3. Create a client/server application that can copy a file from one computer to another. Once the server is started, it should display the IP addresses of all local interfaces and wait for clients to connect. One of the available server IP addresses, and the name of a local file should be passed to the client as command line options. The client should transmit the file to the server, which saves it. While transmitting, the client should provide some visual indication of the progress to the user.

---

[3] http://www.highscore.de/boost/dir_monitor.zip

8

Interprocess Communication

General

Interprocess communication describes mechanisms to exchange data between programs running on the same computer. This does not include network communication. To exchange data between programs running on different computers connected through a network, see Chapter 7, *Asynchronous Input and Output*, which covers Boost.Asio.

This chapter presents the library Boost.Interprocess[1], which contains numerous classes that abstract operating system-specific interfaces for interprocess communication. Even though the concepts of interprocess communication are similar between different operating systems, the interfaces can vary greatly. Boost.Interprocess provides platform independent access.

While Boost.Asio can be used to exchange data between programs running on the same computer, Boost.Interprocess usually provides better performance. Boost.Interprocess calls operating system functions optimized for data exchange between programs running on the same computer and thus should be the first choice to exchange data without a network.

Shared Memory

Shared memory is typically the fastest form of interprocess communication. It provides a memory area that is shared between different processes. One process can write data to the area and another process can read it.

Such a memory area is represented in Boost.Interprocess by the class `boost::interprocess::shared_memory_object`. To use this class, include the header file `boost/interprocess/shared_memory_object.hpp`.

---

[1] http://www.boost.org/libs/interprocess/

Example 8.1

```cpp
#include <boost/interprocess/shared_memory_object.hpp>
#include <iostream>

int main()
{
  boost::interprocess::shared_memory_object shdmem(
    boost::interprocess::open_or_create, "Highscore",
    boost::interprocess::read_write);
  shdmem.truncate(1024);
  std::cout << shdmem.get_name() << std::endl;
  boost::interprocess::offset_t size;
  if (shdmem.get_size(size))
    std::cout << size << std::endl;
}
```

The constructor of `boost::interprocess::shared_memory_object` expects three parameters. The first specifies whether the shared memory should be created or just opened. Example 8.1 handles both cases. `boost::interprocess::open_or_create` opens shared memory if it already exists, otherwise shared memory is created.

Opening existing shared memory assumes that it has been created before. To uniquely identify shared memory, a name is assigned. The second parameter passed to the constructor of `boost::interprocess::shared_memory_object` specifies that name.

The third parameter determines how a process can access shared memory. In Example 8.1, `boost::interprocess::read_write` says the process has read/write access.

After creating an object of type `boost::interprocess::shared_memory_object`, a corresponding shared memory exists within the operating system. The size of this memory area is initially 0. To use the area, call `truncate()`, passing in the size of the shared memory in bytes. In Example 8.1, the shared memory provides space for 1,024 bytes. `truncate()` can only be called if the shared memory has been opened with `boost::interprocess::read_write`. If not, an exception of type `boost::interprocess::interprocess_exception` is thrown. `truncate()` can be called repeatedly to adjust the size of the shared memory.

After creating shared memory, member functions such as `get_name()` and `get_size()` can be used to query the name and the size. Because shared memory is used to exchange data between different processes, each process needs to map the shared memory into its address space, which is done via the class `boost::interprocess::mapped_region`.

It may come as a surprise that two classes are used to access shared memory. However, the class `boost::interprocess::mapped_region` can also be used to map other objects into the address space of a process. For example, Boost.Interprocess provides a class `boost::interprocess::file_mapping` which essentially represents a shared memory for a particular file. Thus, an object of type `boost::interprocess::file_mapping` corresponds to a file. Data written to such an object is automatically saved in the associated physical file. Because `boost::interprocess::file_mapping` does not load the file completely, but rather maps arbitrary parts into the address space through `boost::interprocess::mapped_region`, it is possible to process files that would otherwise be too big to be completely loaded into memory on 32-bit systems.

Example 8.2

```cpp
#include <boost/interprocess/shared_memory_object.hpp>
#include <boost/interprocess/mapped_region.hpp>
#include <iostream>

int main()
{
  boost::interprocess::shared_memory_object shdmem(
    boost::interprocess::open_or_create, "Highscore",
    boost::interprocess::read_write);
  shdmem.truncate(1024);
  boost::interprocess::mapped_region region(shdmem,
    boost::interprocess::read_write);
  std::cout << std::hex << "0x" << region.get_address() << std::endl;
  std::cout << std::dec << region.get_size() << std::endl;
  boost::interprocess::mapped_region region2(shdmem,
    boost::interprocess::read_only);
  std::cout << std::hex << "0x" << region2.get_address() << std::endl;
  std::cout << std::dec << region2.get_size() << std::endl;
}
```

In order to use the class boost::interprocess::mapped_region, the header file boost/interprocess/mapped_region.hpp needs to be included. An object of type boost::interprocess::shared_memory_object must be passed as the first parameter to the constructor of boost::interprocess::mapped_region. The second parameter determines whether the memory area can be accessed read-only or read-write.

Example 8.2 creates two objects of type boost::interprocess::mapped_region. The shared memory named Highscore is mapped twice into the address space of the process. The address as well as the size of the mapped memory area is written to the standard output stream using the member functions get_address() and get_size(). get_size() returns 1024 in both cases, but the return value of get_address() is different for each object.

Example 8.3

```cpp
#include <boost/interprocess/shared_memory_object.hpp>
#include <boost/interprocess/mapped_region.hpp>
#include <iostream>

int main()
{
  boost::interprocess::shared_memory_object shdmem(
    boost::interprocess::open_or_create, "Highscore",
    boost::interprocess::read_write);
  shdmem.truncate(1024);
  boost::interprocess::mapped_region region(shdmem,
    boost::interprocess::read_write);
  int *i1 = static_cast<int*>(region.get_address());
  *i1 = 99;
  boost::interprocess::mapped_region region2(shdmem,
    boost::interprocess::read_only);
  int *i2 = static_cast<int*>(region2.get_address());
  std::cout << *i2 << std::endl;
}
```

Example 8.3 uses the mapped memory area to write and read a number. **region** writes the number 99 to the beginning of the shared memory. **region2** then accesses the same location in shared memory to write the number to the standard output stream. Even though **region** and **region2** represent different memory areas within the process as seen by the return values of get_address() in the previous example, the program prints 99 because both memory areas access the same underlying shared memory.

Usually, multiple objects of type boost::interprocess::mapped_region are not used for the same shared memory in one program. After all it doesn't make much sense to map shared memory twice into the address space of a process. Example 8.3 is only provided to illustrate mapping of shared memory.

To delete a particular shared memory, boost::interprocess::shared_memory_object offers the static member function remove(), which takes the name of the shared memory to be deleted as a parameter.

Boost.Interprocess partially supports the RAII concept described in Chapter 2, *Smart Pointers*, through another class called boost::interprocess::remove_shared_memory_on_destroy. Its constructor expects the name of an existing shared memory. If an object of this class is destroyed, the shared memory is automatically deleted in the destructor.

Please note that the constructor of boost::interprocess::remove_shared_memory_on_destroy does not create or open the shared memory. Therefore, this class is not a typical representative of the RAII concept.

Example 8.4

```
#include <boost/interprocess/shared_memory_object.hpp>
#include <iostream>

int main()
{
  bool removed = boost::interprocess::shared_memory_object::remove(
    "Highscore");
  std::cout << removed << std::endl;
}
```

If remove() is not called at all, the shared memory continues to exist even if the program is terminated. Whether or not the shared memory is deleted depends on the underlying operating system. While many Unix operating systems, including Linux, automatically delete shared memory once the system is restarted, remove() must be called on Mac OS X. Mac OS X stores the shared memory as a persistent file, which means the shared memory will still exist after a restart.

On Windows, shared memory is also automatically deleted when the system reboots – at least since Boost 1.39.0. In older versions, shared memory on Windows behaved like shared memory on Mac OS X.

Windows provides a special kind of shared memory that is automatically deleted once the last process using it has been terminated. In order to use it, the class boost::interprocess::windows_shared_memory, which is defined in boost/interprocess/win-dows_shared_memory.hpp, must be accessed (see Example 8.5).

Example 8.5

```
#include <boost/interprocess/windows_shared_memory.hpp>
#include <boost/interprocess/mapped_region.hpp>
#include <iostream>

int main()
{
  boost::interprocess::windows_shared_memory shdmem(
    boost::interprocess::open_or_create, "Highscore",
    boost::interprocess::read_write, 1024);
  boost::interprocess::mapped_region region(shdmem,
    boost::interprocess::read_write);
  int *i1 = static_cast<int*>(region.get_address());
  *i1 = 99;
  boost::interprocess::mapped_region region2(shdmem,
    boost::interprocess::read_only);
  int *i2 = static_cast<int*>(region2.get_address());
  std::cout << *i2 << std::endl;
}
```

Please note that boost::interprocess::windows_shared_memory does not provide a member function truncate(). Instead, the size of the shared memory needs to be passed as the fourth parameter to the constructor.

Even though the class boost::interprocess::windows_shared_memory is not portable and can only be used on Windows, it is useful when data should be exchanged with an existing Windows program that uses this special kind of shared memory.

Managed Shared Memory

The previous section introduced the class boost::interprocess::shared_memory_object, which can be used to create and manage shared memory. In practice, this class is rarely used because it requires the program to read and write individual bytes from and to the shared memory. C++ style favors creating objects of classes and hiding the specifics of where and how data is stored in memory.

Boost.Interprocess provides a concept called managed shared memory through the class boost::interprocess::managed_shared_memory, defined in boost/interprocess/man-aged_shared_memory.hpp. This class lets you instantiate objects that have their memory located in shared memory, making the objects automatically available to any program that accesses the same shared memory.

Example 8.6

```cpp
#include <boost/interprocess/managed_shared_memory.hpp>
#include <iostream>

int main()
{
  boost::interprocess::shared_memory_object::remove("Highscore");
  boost::interprocess::managed_shared_memory managed_shm(
    boost::interprocess::open_or_create, "Highscore", 1024);
  int *i = managed_shm.construct<int>("Integer")(99);
  std::cout << *i << std::endl;
  std::pair<int*, std::size_t> p = managed_shm.find<int>("Integer");
  if (p.first)
    std::cout << *p.first << std::endl;
}
```

Example 8.6 opens the shared memory named Highscore with a size of 1,024 bytes. In case it does not exist, it will be automatically created.

In regular shared memory, individual bytes are directly accessed to read or write data. Managed shared memory uses member functions such as construct(), which expects a data type as a template parameter (in Example 8.6, int). The member function expects a name to denote the object created in the managed shared memory. Example 8.6 uses the name "Integer".

Because construct() returns a proxy object, parameters can be passed to it to initialize the created object. The syntax looks like a call to a constructor. This ensures that objects can not only be created in a managed shared memory, but can also be initialized as desired.

To access a particular object in a managed shared memory, the member function find() is used. By passing the name of the object to find, find() returns either a pointer to the object, or in case no object with the given name was found, 0.

As seen in Example 8.6, find() returns an object of type std::pair. The pointer to the object is provided as the member variable **first**. However, what is the member variable **second**?

In Example 8.7, an array with ten elements of type int is created by providing the value 10 enclosed by square brackets after the call to construct(). The same 10 is written to the standard output stream using the member variable **second**. Thanks to this member variable, objects returned by find() can be distinguished between single objects and arrays. For the former, **second** is set to 1, while for the latter it will specify the number of elements in the array.

Please note that all ten elements in the array are initialized with 99. It is not possible to initialize elements with different values.

Example 8.7

```
#include <boost/interprocess/managed_shared_memory.hpp>
#include <iostream>

int main()
{
  boost::interprocess::shared_memory_object::remove("Highscore");
  boost::interprocess::managed_shared_memory managed_shm(
    boost::interprocess::open_or_create, "Highscore", 1024);
  int *i = managed_shm.construct<int>("Integer")[10](99);
  std::cout << *i << std::endl;
  std::pair<int*, std::size_t> p = managed_shm.find<int>("Integer");
  if (p.first)
  {
    std::cout << *p.first << std::endl;
    std::cout << p.second << std::endl;
  }
}
```

construct() will fail if an object exists with the given name in the managed shared memory. In this case, construct() returns 0 and no initialization occurs. To use an existing shared memory, if one exists, use the member function find_or_construct(), which returns a pointer to an existing object or creates a new one.

Example 8.8

```
#include <boost/interprocess/managed_shared_memory.hpp>
#include <iostream>

int main()
{
  try
  {
    boost::interprocess::shared_memory_object::remove("Highscore");
    boost::interprocess::managed_shared_memory managed_shm(
      boost::interprocess::open_or_create, "Highscore", 1024);
    int *i = managed_shm.construct<int>("Integer")[4096](99);
  }
  catch (boost::interprocess::bad_alloc &ex)
  {
    std::cerr << ex.what() << std::endl;
  }
}
```

There are other cases that will cause construct() to fail. Example 8.8 tries to create an array of type int with 4,096 elements. The managed shared memory, however, only consists of 1,024 bytes. Therefore, the requested memory cannot be provided by the shared memory, which causes an exception of type boost::interprocess::bad_alloc to be thrown.

Once objects have been created in a managed shared memory, they can be deleted with the member function destroy().

Example 8.9

```cpp
#include <boost/interprocess/managed_shared_memory.hpp>
#include <iostream>

int main()
{
  boost::interprocess::shared_memory_object::remove("Highscore");
  boost::interprocess::managed_shared_memory managed_shm(
    boost::interprocess::open_or_create, "Highscore", 1024);
  int *i = managed_shm.find_or_construct<int>("Integer")(99);
  std::cout << *i << std::endl;
  managed_shm.destroy<int>("Integer");
  std::pair<int*, std::size_t> p = managed_shm.find<int>("Integer");
  std::cout << p.first << std::endl;
}
```

In Example 8.9, the name of the object to be deleted is passed as the only parameter to destroy(). If required, the return value of type bool can be checked to verify whether the given object was found and deleted successfully. Because an object will always be deleted if found, a return value of false indicates that no object with the given name was found.

Besides destroy(), the member function destroy_ptr() can be used to pass a pointer to an object in the managed shared memory. It can also be used to delete arrays.

Because managed shared memory makes it fairly easy to store objects shared between processes, it seems natural to use containers from the C++ standard library as well. However, these containers allocate required memory using new. In order to use these containers in managed shared memory, they need to be told to allocate memory in the shared memory.

Example 8.10

```cpp
#include <boost/interprocess/managed_shared_memory.hpp>
#include <boost/interprocess/allocators/allocator.hpp>
#include <boost/interprocess/containers/string.hpp>
#include <iostream>

int main()
{
  boost::interprocess::shared_memory_object::remove("Highscore");
  boost::interprocess::managed_shared_memory managed_shm(
    boost::interprocess::open_or_create, "Highscore", 1024);
  typedef boost::interprocess::allocator<char,
    boost::interprocess::managed_shared_memory::segment_manager>
    CharAllocator;
  typedef boost::interprocess::basic_string<char,
    std::char_traits<char>, CharAllocator> string;
  string *s = managed_shm.find_or_construct<string>("String")("Hello!",
    managed_shm.get_segment_manager());
  s->insert(5, ", world");
  std::cout << *s << std::endl;
}
```

Unfortunately, many implementations of the C++ standard library are not flexible enough to use the provided containers such as `std::string` or `std::list` with Boost.Interprocess. One example for such an implementation is the one that ships with Visual C++ 2010.

To allow developers to use the containers from the C++ standard, Boost.Interprocess provides a more flexible implementation in the namespace `boost::interprocess`. For example, `boost::interprocess::string` acts exactly like its C++ counterpart `std::string`, with the advantage that strings can be safely stored in a managed shared memory (Example 8.10).

To create a string that will allocate memory within the same managed shared memory it resides in, a corresponding data type must be defined. The new string data type must use an allocator provided by Boost.Interprocess instead of the default allocator provided by the C++ standard.

For this purpose, Boost.Interprocess provides the class `boost::interprocess::allocator` defined in `boost/interprocess/allocators/allocator.hpp`. With this class, an allocator can be created that internally uses the segment manager of the managed shared memory. The segment manager is responsible for managing the memory within a managed shared memory. Using the newly created allocator, a corresponding data type for the string can be defined. As indicated above, use `boost::interprocess::basic_string` rather than `std::basic_string`. The new data type – called `string` in Example 8.10 – is based on `boost::interprocess::basic_string` and accesses the segment manager via its allocator. To let the particular instance of `string`, created by a call to `find_or_construct()`, know which segment manager it should access, a pointer to the corresponding segment manager is passed as the second parameter to the constructor.

Alongside `boost::interprocess::string`, Boost.Interprocess provides implementations for many other containers known from the C++ standard. For example, `boost::interprocess::vector` and `boost::interprocess::map` are defined in `boost/interprocess/containers/vector.hpp` and `boost/interprocess/containers/map.hpp`, respectively.

Whenever the same managed shared memory is accessed from different processes, operations such as creating, finding, and destroying objects are automatically synchronized. If two programs try to create objects with different names in the managed shared memory, the access is serialized accordingly. To execute multiple operations at one time without being interrupted by operations from a different process, use the member function `atomic_func()` as in Example 8.11.

Example 8.11

```cpp
#include <boost/interprocess/managed_shared_memory.hpp>
#include <boost/bind.hpp>
#include <iostream>

void construct_objects(
  boost::interprocess::managed_shared_memory &managed_shm)
{
  managed_shm.construct<int>("Integer")(99);
  managed_shm.construct<float>("Float")(3.14);
}

int main()
{
  boost::interprocess::shared_memory_object::remove("Highscore");
  boost::interprocess::managed_shared_memory managed_shm(
    boost::interprocess::open_or_create, "Highscore", 1024);
  managed_shm.atomic_func(boost::bind(construct_objects,
    boost::ref(managed_shm)));
  std::cout << *managed_shm.find<int>("Integer").first << std::endl;
  std::cout << *managed_shm.find<float>("Float").first << std::endl;
}
```

atomic_func() expects as its single argument a function that takes no parameters and has no return value. The passed function will be called in a fashion that ensures exclusive access to the managed shared memory - but only for operations such as creating, finding, or deleting objects. If another process has a pointer to an object within the managed shared memory, it can access and modify this object using its pointer.

Boost.Interprocess can also be used to synchronize object access. As Boost.Interprocess does not know who can access the individual objects at what time, synchronization needs to be explicitly stated. The classes provided for synchronization are introduced in the following section.

Synchronization

Boost.Interprocess allows multiple processes to use a shared memory concurrently. As shared memory is by definition "shared" between processes, Boost.Interprocess needs to support some kind of synchronization.

Thinking about synchronization, the library Boost.Thread comes to mind. As can be seen in Chapter 6, *Multithreading*, Boost.Thread provides various concepts, such as mutexes and condition variables, to synchronize threads. Unfortunately, the classes from Boost.Thread can only be used to synchronize threads within the same process; they do not support synchronization of different processes. However, since the challenge in both cases is the same, the concepts are no different.

While synchronization objects such as mutexes and condition variables reside in the same address space in multithreaded applications, and therefore are available to all threads, the challenge with shared memory is that independent processes need to share these objects. For example, if one process creates a mutex, it somehow needs to be accessible from a different process.

Boost.Interprocess provides two kinds of synchronization objects: anonymous objects are directly stored in the shared memory, which makes them automatically available to all processes. Named objects are managed by the operating system and thus are not stored in the shared memory. They can be referenced from programs by name.

Example 8.12 creates and uses a named mutex using the class `boost::interprocess::named_mutex` defined in `boost/interprocess/sync/named_mutex.hpp`.

Example 8.12

```
#include <boost/interprocess/managed_shared_memory.hpp>
#include <boost/interprocess/sync/named_mutex.hpp>
#include <iostream>

int main()
{
  boost::interprocess::managed_shared_memory managed_shm(
    boost::interprocess::open_or_create, "shm", 1024);
  int *i = managed_shm.find_or_construct<int>("Integer")();
  boost::interprocess::named_mutex named_mtx(
    boost::interprocess::open_or_create, "mtx");
  named_mtx.lock();
  ++(*i);
  std::cout << *i << std::endl;
  named_mtx.unlock();
}
```

Besides a parameter specifying whether the mutex should be created or opened, the constructor of `boost::interprocess::named_mutex` expects a name for the mutex. Every process that knows the name can open the same mutex. To access the data in shared memory, the program needs to take ownership of the mutex by calling the member function `lock()`. Because mutexes can only be owned by one process at a time, another process may need to wait until the mutex has been released with `unlock()`. Once a process takes ownership of a mutex, it has exclusive access to the resource it guards. In Example 8.12 the resource is a variable of type `int`, which is incremented and written to the standard output stream.

If the sample program is started multiple times, each instance will print a value incremented by 1 compared to the previous value. Thanks to the mutex, access to the shared memory and the variable itself is synchronized between different processes.

Example 8.13 uses an anonymous mutex of type `boost::interprocess::interprocess_mutex`, which is defined in `boost/interprocess/sync/interprocess_mutex.hpp`. In order for it to be accessible for all processes, it is stored in the shared memory.

Example 8.13 behaves exactly like Example 8.12. The only difference is the mutex, which is now stored directly in shared memory. This can be done with the already known member functions `construct()` or `find_or_construct()` of the class `boost::interprocess::managed_shared_memory`.

Example 8.13

```
#include <boost/interprocess/managed_shared_memory.hpp>
#include <boost/interprocess/sync/interprocess_mutex.hpp>
#include <iostream>

int main()
{
  boost::interprocess::managed_shared_memory managed_shm(
    boost::interprocess::open_or_create, "shm", 1024);
  int *i = managed_shm.find_or_construct<int>("Integer")();
  boost::interprocess::interprocess_mutex *mtx = managed_shm
    .find_or_construct<boost::interprocess::interprocess_mutex>("mtx")();
  mtx->lock();
  ++(*i);
  std::cout << *i << std::endl;
  mtx->unlock();
}
```

Besides `lock()`, both `boost::interprocess::named_mutex` and `boost::interprocess::interprocess_mutex` provide the member functions `try_lock()` and `timed_lock()`. They behave exactly like their counterparts in Boost.Thread. If recursive mutexes are required, Boost.Interprocess provides two classes: `boost::interprocess::named_recursive_mutex` and `boost::interprocess::interprocess_recursive_mutex`.

While mutexes guarantee exclusive access to a shared resource, condition variables control who has exclusive access at what time. In general, the condition variables provided by Boost.Interprocess work like the ones provided by Boost.Thread. They have similar interfaces, which makes users of Boost.Thread feel immediately at home when using these variables in Boost.Interprocess.

Example 8.14 uses a condition variable of type `boost::interprocess::named_condition`, which is defined in `boost/interprocess/sync/named_condition.hpp`. Because it is a named variable, it does not need to be stored in shared memory.

The application uses a `while` loop to increment a variable of type `int` which is stored in shared memory. Although the variable is incremented with each iteration of the loop, it will only be written to the standard output stream with every second iteration – only odd numbers are written.

Every time, the variable is incremented by 1, the member function `wait()` of the condition variable **named_cnd** is called. A lock – in Example 8.14, the variable **lock** – is passed to this member function. The lock has the same meaning as it has in Boost.Thread. It is based on the RAII concept, taking ownership of a mutex inside the constructor and releasing it inside the destructor.

The lock is created before the `while` loop and takes ownership of the mutex for the entire execution of the program. However, if passed to `wait()` as a parameter, the lock is automatically released.

Condition variables are used to wait for a signal indicating that the wait is over. Synchronization is controlled by the member functions `wait()` and `notify_all()`. When a program calls `wait()`, ownership of the corresponding mutex is released when waiting starts. The program then waits until `notify_all()` is called on the same condition variable.

Example 8.14

```cpp
#include <boost/interprocess/managed_shared_memory.hpp>
#include <boost/interprocess/sync/named_mutex.hpp>
#include <boost/interprocess/sync/named_condition.hpp>
#include <boost/interprocess/sync/scoped_lock.hpp>
#include <iostream>

int main()
{
  boost::interprocess::managed_shared_memory managed_shm(
    boost::interprocess::open_or_create, "shm", 1024);
  int *i = managed_shm.find_or_construct<int>("Integer")(0);
  boost::interprocess::named_mutex named_mtx(
    boost::interprocess::open_or_create, "mtx");
  boost::interprocess::named_condition named_cnd(
    boost::interprocess::open_or_create, "cnd");
  boost::interprocess::scoped_lock<boost::interprocess::named_mutex> lock(
    named_mtx);
  while (*i < 10)
  {
    if (*i % 2 == 0)
    {
      ++(*i);
      named_cnd.notify_all();
      named_cnd.wait(lock);
    }
    else
    {
      std::cout << *i << std::endl;
      ++(*i);
      named_cnd.notify_all();
      named_cnd.wait(lock);
    }
  }
  named_cnd.notify_all();
  boost::interprocess::shared_memory_object::remove("shm");
  boost::interprocess::named_mutex::remove("mtx");
  boost::interprocess::named_condition::remove("cnd");
}
```

When started, Example 8.14 does not seem to do much. After the variable i is incremented from 0 to 1 within the while loop, the program waits for a signal by calling wait(). In order to fire the signal, a second instance of the program needs to be started.

The second instance tries to take ownership of the same mutex before entering the while loop. This succeeds since the first instance released the mutex by calling wait(). Because the variable has been incremented once, the second instance executes the else branch of the if expression and writes the current value to the standard output stream. Then the value is incremented by 1.

Now the second instance also calls wait(). However, before it does, it calls notify_all(), which ensures that the two instances cooperate correctly. The first instance is notified and tries to take ownership of the mutex again, which is still owned by the second instance. However, because the second instance calls wait() right after calling notify_all(), which automatically releases ownership, the first instance will take ownership at that point.

Both instances alternate, incrementing the variable in the shared memory. However, only one instance writes the value to the standard output stream. As soon as the variable reaches the value 10, the while loop is finished. In order to have the other instance not wait for a signal forever, notify_all() is called one more time after the loop. Before terminating, the shared memory, the mutex, and the condition variable are destroyed.

Example 8.15

```cpp
#include <boost/interprocess/managed_shared_memory.hpp>
#include <boost/interprocess/sync/interprocess_mutex.hpp>
#include <boost/interprocess/sync/interprocess_condition.hpp>
#include <boost/interprocess/sync/scoped_lock.hpp>
#include <iostream>

int main()
{
  try
  {
    boost::interprocess::managed_shared_memory managed_shm(
      boost::interprocess::open_or_create, "shm", 1024);
    int *i = managed_shm.find_or_construct<int>("Integer")(0);
    boost::interprocess::interprocess_mutex *mtx = managed_shm
      .find_or_construct<boost::interprocess::interprocess_mutex>("mtx")();
    boost::interprocess::interprocess_condition *cnd = managed_shm
      .find_or_construct<boost::interprocess::interprocess_condition>(
      "cnd")();
    boost::interprocess::scoped_lock<
      boost::interprocess::interprocess_mutex> lock(*mtx);
    while (*i < 10)
    {
      if (*i % 2 == 0)
      {
        ++(*i);
        cnd->notify_all();
        cnd->wait(lock);
      }
      else
      {
        std::cout << *i << std::endl;
        ++(*i);
        cnd->notify_all();
        cnd->wait(lock);
      }
    }
    cnd->notify_all();
  }
  catch (...)
  {
  }
  boost::interprocess::shared_memory_object::remove("shm");
}
```

Just as there are two types of mutexes – an anonymous type that must be stored in shared memory and a named type – there are also two types of condition variables. Example 8.15 is a rewrite of Example 8.14 using an anonymous condition variable.

Example 8.15 works exactly like Example 8.14 and thus needs to be started twice. The differences between the two examples are minimal. Whether anonymous or named condition variables are used is essentially irrelevant.

Besides mutexes and condition variables, Boost.Interprocess also supports semaphores and file locks. Semaphores are similar to condition variables except they do not distinguish between two states; instead, they are based on a counter. On the other hand, file locks behave like mutexes, except they are used for files on the hard drive, rather than objects in memory.

In the same way that Boost.Thread distinguishes between different types of mutexes and locks, Boost.Interprocess provides several mutexes and locks. For example, mutexes can be owned exclusively or non-exclusively. This is helpful if multiple processes need to read data simultaneously as an exclusive mutex is only required to write data. Different classes for locks are available to apply the RAII concept to individual mutexes.

Names should be unique unless anonymous synchronization objects are used. Even though mutexes and condition variables are objects based on different classes, this may not necessarily hold true for the operating system dependent interfaces wrapped by Boost.Interprocess. On Windows, the same operating system functions are used for both mutexes and condition variables. If the same name is used for both these objects, the program will not behave correctly on Windows.

Exercises

1. Create a client/server application that communicates via shared memory. The name of a file should be passed as a command line option to the client application. The file should then be sent to the server application via shared memory where it is saved locally in the same directory the server application was started in.

9

Filesystem

General

The library Boost.Filesystem[1] makes it easy to work with files and directories. It provides a class called `boost::filesystem::path` that processes paths. In addition, many free-standing functions are available to handle tasks like creating directories or checking whether a file exists.

Boost.Filesystem has been revised several times. This chapter introduces the current version, Boost.Filesystem 3, which is the default version since the Boost C++ Libraries 1.46. In order to use Boost.Filesystem 3 with versions 1.44 or 1.45, the macro `BOOST_FILESYSTEM_VERSION` must be defined as 3. Boost.Filesystem 3 is not available in versions prior to 1.44.

Paths

`boost::filesystem::path` is the central class in Boost.Filesystem for representing and processing paths. Definitions can be found in the namespace `boost::filesystem` and in the header file `boost/filesystem.hpp`. Paths can be built by passing a string to the constructor of `boost::filesystem::path` (see Example 9.1).

Example 9.1

```
#include <boost/filesystem.hpp>

int main()
{
  boost::filesystem::path p1("C:\\");
  boost::filesystem::path p2("C:\\Windows");
  boost::filesystem::path p3(L"C:\\Boost C++ \u5E93");
}
```

`boost::filesystem::path` can also be initialized with wide strings, which are based on the data type `wchar_t`. These strings are interpreted as Unicode and make it easy to create paths that

---

[1] http://www.boost.org/libs/filesystem/

contain characters from nearly any language. This is a crucial difference compared to Boost.Filesystem 2, which provided separate classes, such as `boost::filesystem::path` and `boost::filesystem::wpath`, for different string types.

None of the constructors of `boost::filesystem::path` validate paths or check whether the given file or directory exists. Thus, `boost::filesystem::path` can be instantiated even with meaningless paths.

Example 9.2

```
#include <boost/filesystem.hpp>

int main()
{
  boost::filesystem::path p1("...");
  boost::filesystem::path p2("\\");
  boost::filesystem::path p3("@:");
}
```

The reason Example 9.2 can be run without any problems is that paths are just strings. `boost::filesystem::path` only processes strings; the file system is not accessed.

Because `boost::filesystem::path` processes strings, the class provides several member functions to retrieve a path as a string.

Example 9.3

```
#include <boost/filesystem.hpp>
#include <iostream>

int main()
{
  boost::filesystem::path p("C:\\Windows\\System");

  std::wcout << p.native() << std::endl;

  std::cout << p.string() << std::endl;
  std::wcout << p.wstring() << std::endl;

  std::cout << p.generic_string() << std::endl;
  std::wcout << p.generic_wstring() << std::endl;
}
```

In general, Boost.Filesystem differentiates between native and generic paths. Native paths are operating system specific and must be used to call operating system functions. Generic paths are portable and independent of the operating system.

The member functions `native()`, `string()` and `wstring()` all return paths in the native format. When run on a Windows system, Example 9.3 writes `"C:\Windows\System"` to the standard output stream three times. The output uses the common path format on Windows. Because paths can contain spaces, the output is always enclosed in quotation marks.

The member functions `generic_string()` and `generic_wstring()` both return paths in a generic format. These are portable paths; the string is normalized based on rules of the POSIX standard. Generic paths are therefore identical to paths used on Linux. For example, the slash character / is used as the separator for directories. If Example 9.3 is run on Windows, both `generic_string()` and `generic_wstring()` write `"C:/Windows/System"` to the standard output stream.

The return value of member functions returning native paths depends on the operating system the program is executed on. The return value of member functions returning generic paths is independent of the operating system. Generic paths uniquely identify files and directories independently from the operating system and therefore make it easy to write platform independent code.

Because `boost::filesystem::path` can be initialized with different string types, several member functions are provided to retrieve paths in different string types. While `string()` and `generic_string()` return a string of type `std::string`, `wstring()` and `generic_wstring()` return a string of type `std::wstring`. Additional member functions, such as `u16string()` and `u32wstring()`, are available to retrieve paths in various Unicode encodings.

The return type of `native()` depends on the operating system the program was compiled for. On Windows a string of type `std::wstring` is returned. On Linux it is a string of type `std::string`.

The constructor of `boost::filesystem::path` supports both generic and platform dependent paths. The path "C:\\Windows\\System", which is used in the above example, is Windows-specific and not portable. It will only be recognized correctly by Boost.Filesystem if the program is run on Windows. When executed on a POSIX compliant operating system such as Linux, it will return `C:\Windows\System` for all member functions called. Since the backslash \ is not used as a separator on Linux in either the portable or the native format, Boost.Filesystem does not recognize this character as a separator for files and directories.

Example 9.4

```
#include <boost/filesystem.hpp>
#include <iostream>

int main()
{
  boost::filesystem::path p("/");
  std::cout << p.string() << std::endl;
  std::cout << p.generic_string() << std::endl;
}
```

Example 9.4 uses a portable path to initialize `boost::filesystem::path`.

Because `generic_string()` returns a portable path, its value will be the same as was used to initialize `boost::filesystem::path`: `"/"`. However, the member function `string()` returns different values depending on the operating system. On Windows, it will return `"\"`, and on Linux it will return `"/"`.

Example 9.5

```cpp
#include <boost/filesystem.hpp>
#include <iostream>

int main()
{
  boost::filesystem::path p("C:\\Windows\\System");
  std::cout << p.root_name() << std::endl;
  std::cout << p.root_directory() << std::endl;
  std::cout << p.root_path() << std::endl;
  std::cout << p.relative_path() << std::endl;
  std::cout << p.parent_path() << std::endl;
  std::cout << p.filename() << std::endl;
}
```

`boost::filesystem::path` provides several member functions to access certain components of a path. If Example 9.5 is executed on Windows, the string "C:\\Windows\\System" is interpreted as a platform dependent path. Consequently, `root_name()` returns `"C:"`, `root_directory()` returns `"/"`, `root_path()` returns `"C:\"`, `relative_path()` returns `"Windows\System"`, `parent_path()` returns `"C:\Windows"`, and `filename()` returns `"System"`.

All member functions return platform dependent paths because `boost::filesystem::path` stores paths in a platform dependent format internally. To retrieve paths in a portable format, member functions such as `generic_string()` need to be called explicitly.

If Example 9.5 is executed on Linux, the returned values are different. Most of the member functions return an empty string, except `relative_path()` and `filename()`, which return `"C:\Windows\System"`. This means that the string "C:\\Windows\\System" is interpreted as a file name on Linux, which is understandable given that it is neither a portable encoding of a path nor a platform dependent encoding on Linux. Therefore, Boost.Filesystem has no choice but to interpret it as a file name.

Boost.Filesystem provides additional member functions to verify whether a path contains a specific substring. These member functions are: `has_root_name()`, `has_root_directory()`, `has_root_path()`, `has_relative_path()`, `has_parent_path()` and `has_filename()`. Each member function returns a value of type `bool`.

Example 9.6

```cpp
#include <boost/filesystem.hpp>
#include <iostream>

int main()
{
  boost::filesystem::path p("photo.jpg");
  std::cout << p.stem() << std::endl;
  std::cout << p.extension() << std::endl;
}
```

There are two more member functions that can split a file name into its components. They should only be called if `has_filename()` returns `true`. Otherwise, they will return empty strings because there is nothing to split if there is no file name. Example 9.6 returns `"photo"` for `stem()` and `".jpg"` for `extension()`.

Example 9.7

```cpp
#include <boost/filesystem.hpp>
#include <iostream>

int main()
{
  boost::filesystem::path p("C:\\Windows\\System");
  for (boost::filesystem::path::iterator it = p.begin();
    it != p.end(); ++it)
    std::cout << *it << std::endl;
}
```

Instead of accessing the components of a path via member function calls, one can also iterate over the components. If executed on Windows, Example 9.7 will successively output `"C:"`, `"/"`, `"Windows"` and `"System"`. On Linux, the output will be `"C:\Windows\System"`.

While the previous examples introduced various member functions to access different components of a path, Example 9.8 uses a member function to modify a path.

Example 9.8

```cpp
#include <boost/filesystem.hpp>
#include <iostream>

int main()
{
  boost::filesystem::path p("C:\\");
  p /= "Windows\\System";
  std::cout << p.string() << std::endl;
}
```

Using `operator/=`, Example 9.8 appends one path to another. On Windows, the program outputs `"C:\Windows\System"`. On Linux, the output is `"C:\/Windows\System"`, since the slash / is used as a separator for files and directories. The slash is also the reason why `operator/=` has been overloaded; after all, the slash is part of the operator.

Besides `operator/=`, Boost.Filesystem provides the member functions `remove_filename()`, `replace_extension()`, `make_absolute()`, and `make_preferred()` to modify paths. The last member function mentioned is particularly designed for use on Windows.

Example 9.9

```
#include <boost/filesystem.hpp>
#include <iostream>

int main()
{
  boost::filesystem::path p("C:/Windows/System");
  std::cout << p.make_preferred() << std::endl;
}
```

Even though the backslash \ is used as the separator for files and directories by default, Windows still accepts the slash /. "C:/Windows/System" is therefore a valid native path. With make_preferred() such a path can be converted to the preferred notation on Windows. Example 9.9 writes "C:\Windows\System" to the standard output stream.

The member function make_preferred() has no effect on POSIX compliant operating systems such as Linux.

Please note that make_preferred() not only returns the converted path, but also modifies the object it has been called on. p contains "C:\Windows\System" after the call.

Files and Directories

The member functions presented with boost::filesystem::path simply process strings. They access individual components of a path, append paths to one another, and so on.

In order to work with physical files and directories on the hard drive, several free-standing functions are provided. They expect one or more parameters of type boost::filesystem::path and call operating system functions internally.

Prior to introducing the various functions, it is important to understand what happens in case of an error. All of the functions call operating system functions that may fail. Therefore, Boost.Filesystem provides two variants of the functions that behave differently in case of an error:

► The first variant throws an exception of type boost::filesystem::filesystem_error. This class is derived from boost::system::system_error and thus fits into the Boost.System framework.

► The second variant expects an object of type boost::system::error_code as an additional parameter. This object is passed by reference and can be examined after the function call. In case of a failure, the object stores the corresponding error code.

boost::system::system_error and boost::system::error_code are presented in the section called "Boost.System". In addition to the inherited interface from boost::system::system_error, boost::filesystem::filesystem_error provides two member functions called path1() and path2(), both returning an object of type boost::filesystem::path. Since there are functions which expect two parameters of type boost::filesystem::path, these two member functions provide an easy way to retrieve the corresponding paths in case of a failure.

Example 9.10

```cpp
#include <boost/filesystem.hpp>
#include <iostream>

int main()
{
  boost::filesystem::path p("C:\\");
  try
  {
    boost::filesystem::file_status s = boost::filesystem::status(p);
    std::cout << boost::filesystem::is_directory(s) << std::endl;
  }
  catch (boost::filesystem::filesystem_error &e)
  {
    std::cerr << e.what() << std::endl;
  }
}
```

Example 9.10 introduces boost::filesystem::status(), which queries the status of a file or directory. This function returns an object of type boost::filesystem::file_status, which can be passed to additional helper functions for evaluation. For example, boost::filesystem::is_directory() returns true if the status for a directory was queried. Besides boost::filesystem::is_directory(), other functions are available, including boost::filesystem::is_regular_file(), boost::filesystem::is_symlink(), and boost::filesystem::exists(), all of which return a value of type bool.

The function boost::filesystem::symlink_status() queries the status of a symbolic link. In this case, the status of the file referred to by the symbolic link is queried. On Windows, symbolic links are identified by the file extension lnk.

Example 9.11

```cpp
#include <boost/filesystem.hpp>
#include <iostream>

int main()
{
  boost::filesystem::path p("C:\\Windows\\win.ini");
  boost::system::error_code ec;
  boost::uintmax_t filesize = boost::filesystem::file_size(p, ec);
  if (!ec)
    std::cout << filesize << std::endl;
  else
    std::cout << ec << std::endl;
}
```

A different category of functions makes it possible to query attributes. The function boost::filesystem::file_size() returns the size of a file in bytes. The return value is of type boost::uintmax_t, which is a typedef for unsigned long long. The data type is provided by Boost.Integer. Example 9.11 uses an object of type boost::system::error_code, which needs to be evaluated explicitly to determine whether the call to boost::filesystem::file_size() was successful.

Example 9.12

```
#include <boost/filesystem.hpp>
#include <iostream>
#include <ctime>

int main()
{
  boost::filesystem::path p("C:\\Windows\\win.ini");
  try
  {
    std::time_t t = boost::filesystem::last_write_time(p);
    std::cout << std::ctime(&t) << std::endl;
  }
  catch (boost::filesystem::filesystem_error &e)
  {
    std::cerr << e.what() << std::endl;
  }
}
```

To determine the time a file was modified last, `boost::filesystem::last_write_time()` can be used (see Example 9.12).

Example 9.13

```
#include <boost/filesystem.hpp>
#include <iostream>

int main()
{
  boost::filesystem::path p("C:\\");
  try
  {
    boost::filesystem::space_info s = boost::filesystem::space(p);
    std::cout << s.capacity << std::endl;
    std::cout << s.free << std::endl;
    std::cout << s.available << std::endl;
  }
  catch (boost::filesystem::filesystem_error &e)
  {
    std::cerr << e.what() << std::endl;
  }
}
```

`boost::filesystem::space()` retrieves the total and remaining disk space. It returns an object of type `boost::filesystem::space_info` which provides three public member variables: **capacity**, **free**, and **available**, all of type `boost::uintmax_t`. The disk space is calculated in bytes.

While the functions presented so far leave files and directories untouched, there are several functions that can be used to create, rename, or delete files and directories.

Example 9.14

```cpp
#include <boost/filesystem.hpp>
#include <iostream>

int main()
{
  boost::filesystem::path p("C:\\Test");
  try
  {
    if (boost::filesystem::create_directory(p))
    {
      boost::filesystem::rename(p, "C:\\Test2");
      boost::filesystem::remove("C:\\Test2");
    }
  }
  catch (boost::filesystem::filesystem_error &e)
  {
    std::cerr << e.what() << std::endl;
  }
}
```

Example 9.14 should be self-explanatory. Looking closely, one can see that it's not always an object of type `boost::filesystem::path` that is passed to functions, but rather a simple string. This is possible because `boost::filesystem::path` provides a non-explicit constructor that will convert strings to objects of type `boost::filesystem::path`. This makes it easy to use Boost.Filesystem since it's not required to create paths explicitly.

Additional functions such as `create_symlink()` to create symbolic links or `copy_file()` and `copy_directory()` to copy files and directories are available as well.

Example 9.15

```cpp
#include <boost/filesystem.hpp>
#include <iostream>

int main()
{
  try
  {
    std::cout << boost::filesystem::absolute("photo.jpg") << std::endl;
  }
  catch (boost::filesystem::filesystem_error &e)
  {
    std::cerr << e.what() << std::endl;
  }
}
```

Example 9.15 presents a function that creates an absolute path based on a file name or section of a path. The path displayed depends on which directory the program is started in. For example, if the program was started in `C:\`, the output would be `"C:\photo.jpg"`.

Example 9.16

```cpp
#include <boost/filesystem.hpp>
#include <iostream>

int main()
{
  try
  {
    std::cout << boost::filesystem::absolute("photo.jpg", "D:\\") <<
      std::endl;
  }
  catch (boost::filesystem::filesystem_error &e)
  {
    std::cerr << e.what() << std::endl;
  }
}
```

To retrieve an absolute path relative to a different directory, a second parameter can be passed to boost::filesystem::absolute(). Example 9.16 displays "D:\photo.jpg".

The last example in this section, Example 9.17, introduces a useful helper function to retrieve the current working directory.

Example 9.17

```cpp
#include <windows.h>
#include <boost/filesystem.hpp>
#include <iostream>

int main()
{
  try
  {
    std::cout << boost::filesystem::current_path() << std::endl;
    SetCurrentDirectoryA("C:\\");
    std::cout << boost::filesystem::current_path() << std::endl;
  }
  catch (boost::filesystem::filesystem_error &e)
  {
    std::cerr << e.what() << std::endl;
  }
}
```

Example 9.17 can only be executed on Windows because it uses SetCurrentDirectoryA(), which is a function from the Windows API. This function modifies the current working directory so that each call to boost::filesystem::current_path() returns a different result.

boost::filesystem::current_path() can also be used to change the current working directory by passing the new directory as a parameter. To make Example 9.17 platform independent, the call to SetCurrentDirectoryA() can be replaced with a call to boost::filesystem::current_path().

Directory Iterators

Boost.Filesystem provides the iterator `boost::filesystem::directory_iterator` to iterate over files in a directory (Example 9.18).

Example 9.18

```
#include <boost/filesystem.hpp>
#include <iostream>

int main()
{
  boost::filesystem::path p = boost::filesystem::current_path();
  boost::filesystem::directory_iterator it(p);
  while (it != boost::filesystem::directory_iterator())
    std::cout << *it++ << std::endl;
}
```

`boost::filesystem::directory_iterator` is initialized with a path to retrieve an iterator pointing to the beginning of a directory. To retrieve the end of a directory, the class must be instantiated with the default constructor. Entries can be created or deleted while iterating without invalidating the iterator. However, whether changes become visible during the iteration is undefined. For example, the iterator might not point to newly created files. To ensure that all current entries are accessible, restart the iteration.

To recursively iterate over a directory and subdirectories, Boost.Filesystem provides the iterator `boost::filesystem::recursive_directory_iterator`.

File Streams

The C++ standard defines various file streams in the header file `fstream`. These streams do not accept parameters of type `boost::filesystem::path`. If Boost.Filesystem is included in Technical Report 2, file streams will be extended by corresponding constructors. In order to work with file streams and pass objects of type `boost::filesystem::path` today, the header file `boost/filesystem/fstream.hpp` can be used (see Example 9.19). It provides the required additions to file streams, which may be added to the C++ standard in the future.

Example 9.19

```
#include <boost/filesystem/fstream.hpp>
#include <iostream>

int main()
{
  boost::filesystem::path p("test.txt");
  boost::filesystem::ofstream ofs(p);
  ofs << "Hello, world!" << std::endl;
}
```

Not only the constructors but also the overloaded member functions `open()` accept parameters of type `boost::filesystem::path`.

Exercises

1. Develop a program that creates an absolute path for a file called `data.txt` that resides in the parent directory of the current working directory. For example, if the program is started in `C:\Program Files\Test\`, it should display `C:\Program Files\data.txt`.

10

Date and Time

General

The library Boost.DateTime[1] can be used to process time data such as calendar dates and times. In addition, Boost.DateTime provides extensions to account for time zones and supports formatted input and output of calendar dates and times. This chapter covers the individual components of Boost.DateTime.

Calendar Dates

Boost.DateTime only supports calendar dates based on the Gregorian calendar, which in general is not a problem since this is the most widely used calendar. If you arrange a meeting with someone from a different country for January 5, 2012, you don't need to say that the date is based on the Gregorian calendar.

The Gregorian calendar was introduced by Pope Gregory XIII in 1582. Strictly speaking, Boost.DateTime supports calendar dates for the years 1400 to 9999, which means that support goes back before the year 1582. Therefore, Boost.DateTime can be used for any calendar date after the year 1400 when converted to the Gregorian calendar. If earlier dates must be processed, a different library must be used.

All classes and functions to process calendar dates can be found in the namespace `boost::gregorian`, which is defined in `boost/date_time/gregorian/gregorian.hpp`. To create a date, use the class `boost::gregorian::date`.

---

[1] http://www.boost.org/libs/date_time/

Example 10.1

```
#include <boost/date_time/gregorian/gregorian.hpp>
#include <iostream>

int main()
{
  boost::gregorian::date d(2010, 1, 30);
  std::cout << d.year() << std::endl;
  std::cout << d.month() << std::endl;
  std::cout << d.day() << std::endl;
  std::cout << d.day_of_week() << std::endl;
  std::cout << d.end_of_month() << std::endl;
}
```

boost::gregorian::date provides several constructors to create dates. The most basic constructor takes a year, a month, and a day as arguments. If an invalid value is given, an exception of type boost::gregorian::bad_year, boost::gregorian::bad_month, or boost::gregorian::bad_day_of_month is thrown. All of these classes are derived from std::out_of_range.

As shown in Example 10.1, there are many member functions provided to access a date. While member functions such as year(), month(), and day() return the respective parts of a date, member functions like day_of_week() and end_of_month() calculate values.

While the constructor of boost::gregorian::date expects numeric values for year, month and day to set a date, the output of the sample program for the month is Jan and for the day of the week Sat. The return values of month() and day_of_week() are not regular numeric values, but values of type boost::gregorian::date::month_type and boost::gregorian::date::day_of_week_type. Boost.DateTime provides comprehensive support for formatted input and output to adjust the above output from, for example, Jan to 1.

The default constructor of boost::gregorian::date creates an invalid date. An invalid date can also be created explicitly by passing boost::date_time::not_a_date_time as the sole parameter to the constructor.

Besides calling a constructor directly, an object of type boost::gregorian::date can also be created via free-standing functions and member functions of other classes.

Example 10.2 uses the class boost::gregorian::day_clock, which returns the current date. The member function universal_day() returns a UTC date, which is independent of time zones and daylight savings. UTC is the international abbreviation for the universal time. boost::gregorian::day_clock also provides a member function called local_day() which takes local settings into account. To retrieve the current date within the local time zone, use local_day().

Example 10.2

```
#include <boost/date_time/gregorian/gregorian.hpp>
#include <iostream>

int main()
{
  boost::gregorian::date d = boost::gregorian::day_clock::universal_day();
  std::cout << d.year() << std::endl;
  std::cout << d.month() << std::endl;
  std::cout << d.day() << std::endl;

  d = boost::gregorian::date_from_iso_string("20100131");
  std::cout << d.year() << std::endl;
  std::cout << d.month() << std::endl;
  std::cout << d.day() << std::endl;
}
```

The namespace `boost::gregorian` contains free-standing functions to convert a date stored in a string to an object of type `boost::gregorian::date`. Example 10.2 converts a date in the ISO 8601 format with the function `boost::gregorian::date_from_iso_string()`. Other functions are available as well, including `boost::gregorian::from_simple_string()` and `boost::gregorian::from_us_string()`.

While `boost::gregorian::date` marks a specific point in time, `boost::gregorian::date_duration` denotes a duration.

Example 10.3

```
#include <boost/date_time/gregorian/gregorian.hpp>
#include <iostream>

int main()
{
  boost::gregorian::date d1(2008, 1, 31);
  boost::gregorian::date d2(2008, 8, 31);
  boost::gregorian::date_duration dd = d2 - d1;
  std::cout << dd.days() << std::endl;
}
```

Because `boost::gregorian::date` overloads `operator-`, two points in time can be subtracted (see Example 10.3). The return value is of type `boost::gregorian::date_duration` and marks the duration between the two dates.

The most important member function offered by `boost::gregorian::date_duration` is `days()`, which returns the number of days in the duration specified.

Objects of type `boost::gregorian::date_duration` can also be explicitly created by passing the number of days as a single parameter to the constructor. To create a duration that involves weeks, months, or years, use `boost::gregorian::weeks`, `boost::gregorian::months`, and `boost::gregorian::years`.

Example 10.4

```
#include <boost/date_time/gregorian/gregorian.hpp>
#include <iostream>

int main()
{
  boost::gregorian::date_duration dd(4);
  std::cout << dd.days() << std::endl;
  boost::gregorian::weeks ws(4);
  std::cout << ws.days() << std::endl;
  boost::gregorian::months ms(4);
  std::cout << ms.number_of_months() << std::endl;
  boost::gregorian::years ys(4);
  std::cout << ys.number_of_years() << std::endl;
}
```

Neither boost::gregorian::months nor boost::gregorian::years allow you to determine the number of days because months and years vary in length. Nonetheless, using these classes can still make sense, as shown in Example 10.5.

Example 10.5

```
#include <boost/date_time/gregorian/gregorian.hpp>
#include <iostream>

int main()
{
  boost::gregorian::date d(2009, 1, 31);
  boost::gregorian::months ms(1);
  boost::gregorian::date d2 = d + ms;
  std::cout << d2 << std::endl;
  boost::gregorian::date d3 = d2 - ms;
  std::cout << d3 << std::endl;
}
```

Example 10.5 adds one month to the given date of January 31, 2009 which results in d2 being February 28, 2009. In the next step, one month is subtracted and d3 becomes January 31, 2009 again. As shown, points in time as well as durations can be used in calculations. However, some specifics need to be taken into account. For example, starting at the last day of a month, boost::gregorian::months always arrives at the last day of another month, which can lead to surprises.

Example 10.6 is identical to Example 10.5, except d is initialized to be January 30, 2009. Even though this is not the last day in January, jumping forward by one month results in d2 becoming February 28, 2009, because there is no February 30. However, jumping backwards by one month again, results in d3 becoming January 31, 2009. Since February 28, 2009 is the last day in February, jumping backwards returns to the last day in January.

Example 10.6

```
#include <boost/date_time/gregorian/gregorian.hpp>
#include <iostream>

int main()
{
  boost::gregorian::date d(2009, 1, 30);
  boost::gregorian::months ms(1);
  boost::gregorian::date d2 = d + ms;
  std::cout << d2 << std::endl;
  boost::gregorian::date d3 = d2 - ms;
  std::cout << d3 << std::endl;
}
```

This behavior can be changed by revoking the definition of the macro BOOST_DATE_TIME_OP-TIONAL_GREGORIAN_TYPES. After that, the classes boost::gregorian::weeks, boost::gregorian::months, and boost::gregorian::years are no longer available. The only class left is boost::gregorian::date_duration, which simply jumps forwards and backwards by a specified number of days and does not give special consideration to the first and last day of the month.

While boost::gregorian::date_duration works with durations, boost::gregorian::date_period provides support for ranges between two dates.

Example 10.7

```
#include <boost/date_time/gregorian/gregorian.hpp>
#include <iostream>

int main()
{
  boost::gregorian::date d1(2009, 1, 30);
  boost::gregorian::date d2(2009, 10, 31);
  boost::gregorian::date_period dp(d1, d2);
  boost::gregorian::date_duration dd = dp.length();
  std::cout << dd.days() << std::endl;
}
```

Two parameters of type boost::gregorian::date specifying the beginning and end dates can be passed to the constructor of boost::gregorian::date_period. Alternatively, the beginning date and a duration of type boost::gregorian::date_duration can be specified. Please note that the day before the end date is actually the last day of the period. This is important in order to understand the output of Example 10.8.

Example 10.8

```
#include <boost/date_time/gregorian/gregorian.hpp>
#include <iostream>

int main()
{
  boost::gregorian::date d1(2009, 1, 30);
  boost::gregorian::date d2(2009, 10, 31);
  boost::gregorian::date_period dp(d1, d2);
  std::cout << dp.contains(d1) << std::endl;
  std::cout << dp.contains(d2) << std::endl;
}
```

Example 10.8 checks whether a specific date is within a period by calling contains(). Although **d2** was passed to the constructor of boost::gregorian::date_period to define the end of the period, it is not considered part of the period. Therefore, the member function contains() will return true when called with **d1**, but will return false when called with **d2**.

boost::gregorian::date_period provides additional member functions to, for example, move a period or calculate the intersection of two overlapping periods.

Besides classes for date, durations and periods, Boost.DateTime provides iterators and other useful free-standing functions as shown in Example 10.9.

Example 10.9

```
#include <boost/date_time/gregorian/gregorian.hpp>
#include <iostream>

int main()
{
  boost::gregorian::date d(2009, 1, 5);
  boost::gregorian::day_iterator it(d);
  std::cout << *++it << std::endl;
  std::cout << boost::date_time::next_weekday(*it,
    boost::gregorian::greg_weekday(boost::date_time::Friday)) << std::endl;
}
```

In order to jump forward or backward by a day from a specific date, the iterator boost::gregorian::day_iterator can be used. boost::gregorian::week_iterator, boost::gregorian::month_iterator, and boost::gregorian::year_iterator jump by weeks, months, or years, respectively.

Example 10.9 also uses the function boost::date_time::next_weekday(), which returns the date of the next weekday based on a given date. Example 10.9 displays 2009-Jan-09, which is the first Friday following January 6, 2009.

Location-independent Times

`boost::posix_time::ptime` defines a location-independent time. It uses the type `boost::gregorian::date`, but also stores a time. To use `boost::posix_time::ptime`, include the header file `boost/date_time/posix_time/posix_time.hpp`.

Example 10.10

```
#include <boost/date_time/posix_time/posix_time.hpp>
#include <boost/date_time/gregorian/gregorian.hpp>
#include <iostream>

int main()
{
  boost::posix_time::ptime pt(boost::gregorian::date(2009, 1, 5),
    boost::posix_time::time_duration(12, 0, 0));
  boost::gregorian::date d = pt.date();
  std::cout << d << std::endl;
  boost::posix_time::time_duration td = pt.time_of_day();
  std::cout << td << std::endl;
}
```

To initialize an object of type `boost::posix_time::ptime`, pass a date of type `boost::gregorian::date` and a duration of type `boost::posix_time::time_duration` as the first and second parameter to the constructor. The three parameters passed to the constructor of `boost::posix_time::time_duration` determine the time. Example 10.10 specifies 12 PM on January 5, 2009 as the point in time. To query date and time, use the member functions `date()` and `time_of_day()`.

Just as the default constructor of `boost::gregorian::date` creates an invalid date, a time of type `boost::posix_time::ptime` is also invalid if the default constructor is used. An invalid time can also be created explicitly by passing `boost::date_time::not_a_date_time` to the constructor. Similar to creating calendar dates of type `boost::gregorian::date` using free-standing functions or member functions of different objects, Boost.DateTime provides corresponding free-standing functions and member functions to create times.

Example 10.11

```
#include <boost/date_time/posix_time/posix_time.hpp>
#include <boost/date_time/gregorian/gregorian.hpp>
#include <iostream>

int main()
{
  boost::posix_time::ptime pt =
    boost::posix_time::second_clock::universal_time();
  std::cout << pt.date() << std::endl;
  std::cout << pt.time_of_day() << std::endl;

  pt = boost::posix_time::from_iso_string("20090105T120000");
  std::cout << pt.date() << std::endl;
  std::cout << pt.time_of_day() << std::endl;
}
```

The class boost::posix_time::second_clock returns the current time. The member function universal_time() returns the UTC time (see Example 10.11). local_time() returns the local time. If you need higher resolution, boost::posix_time::microsec_clock returns the current time including microseconds.

The free-standing function boost::posix_time::from_iso_string() converts a time stored in a string formatted using the ISO 8601 standard into an object of type boost::posix_time::ptime.

In addition to boost::posix_time::ptime, Boost.DateTime also provides the class boost::posix_time::time_duration, which specifies a duration. This class has been mentioned before because the constructor of boost::posix_time::ptime expects an object of type boost::posix_time::time_duration as the second argument. You can also use boost::posix_time::time_duration independently.

Example 10.12

```
#include <boost/date_time/posix_time/posix_time.hpp>
#include <iostream>

int main()
{
  boost::posix_time::time_duration td(16, 30, 0);
  std::cout << td.hours() << std::endl;
  std::cout << td.minutes() << std::endl;
  std::cout << td.seconds() << std::endl;
  std::cout << td.total_seconds() << std::endl;
}
```

hours(), minutes(), and seconds() return the respective parts of a time duration, while member functions such as total_seconds(), which returns the total number of seconds, provide additional information in a simple way (see Example 10.12).

Random values can legally be passed to boost::posix_time::time_duration because no upper limit, such as 24 hours, exists.

Example 10.13

```
#include <boost/date_time/posix_time/posix_time.hpp>
#include <iostream>

int main()
{
  boost::posix_time::ptime pt1(boost::gregorian::date(2009, 1, 05),
    boost::posix_time::time_duration(12, 0, 0));
  boost::posix_time::ptime pt2(boost::gregorian::date(2009, 1, 05),
    boost::posix_time::time_duration(18, 30, 0));
  boost::posix_time::time_duration td = pt2 - pt1;
  std::cout << td.hours() << std::endl;
  std::cout << td.minutes() << std::endl;
  std::cout << td.seconds() << std::endl;
}
```

As with calendar dates, calculations can also be performed with points in time and durations. If two times of type `boost::posix_time::ptime` are subtracted from each other, as in Example 10.13, the result is an object of type `boost::posix_time::time_duration` that specifies the duration between the two points in time.

Example 10.14

```
#include <boost/date_time/posix_time/posix_time.hpp>
#include <iostream>

int main()
{
  boost::posix_time::ptime pt1(boost::gregorian::date(2009, 1, 05),
    boost::posix_time::time_duration(12, 0, 0));
  boost::posix_time::time_duration td(6, 30, 0);
  boost::posix_time::ptime pt2 = pt1 + td;
  std::cout << pt2.time_of_day() << std::endl;
}
```

As shown in Example 10.14, a duration can be added to a time resulting in a new point in time. This example writes `18:30:00` to the standard output stream.

Boost.DateTime uses the same concepts for calendar dates and times. Just as there are classes for times and durations, there is also one for periods. For calendar dates, this class is `boost::gregorian::date_period`; for times it is `boost::posix_time::time_period`. The constructors of both classes expect two parameters: `boost::gregorian::date_period` expects two calendar dates while `boost::posix_time::time_period` expects two points in time.

Example 10.15

```
#include <boost/date_time/posix_time/posix_time.hpp>
#include <iostream>

int main()
{
  boost::posix_time::ptime pt1(boost::gregorian::date(2009, 1, 05),
    boost::posix_time::time_duration(12, 0, 0));
  boost::posix_time::ptime pt2(boost::gregorian::date(2009, 1, 05),
    boost::posix_time::time_duration(18, 30, 0));
  boost::posix_time::time_period tp(pt1, pt2);
  std::cout << tp.contains(pt1) << std::endl;
  std::cout << tp.contains(pt2) << std::endl;
}
```

In general `boost::posix_time::time_period` works exactly like `boost::gregorian::date_period`. It provides a member function, `contains()`, which returns `true` for every point in time within the period. Because the end time, which is passed to the constructor of `boost::posix_time::time_period`, is not part of the period, the second call to `contains()` in Example 10.15 returns `false`.

boost::posix_time::time_period provides additional member functions such as inter-section() and merge(), which respectively, calculate the intersection of two overlapping periods and merge two intersecting periods.

Finally, the iterator boost::posix_time::time_iterator iterates over points in time.

Example 10.16

```
#include <boost/date_time/local_time/local_time.hpp>
#include <iostream>

int main()
{
  boost::posix_time::ptime pt(boost::gregorian::date(2009, 1, 05),
    boost::posix_time::time_duration(12, 0, 0));
  boost::posix_time::time_iterator it(pt,
    boost::posix_time::time_duration(6, 30, 0));
  std::cout << *++it << std::endl;
  std::cout << *++it << std::endl;
}
```

Example 10.16 uses the iterator **it** to jump forward 6.5 hours from the time **pt**. Because the iterator is incremented twice, the output is 2009-Jan-05 18:30:00 and 2009-Jan-06 01:00:00.

Location-dependent Times

Unlike the location-independent times introduced in the previous section, location-dependent times account for time zones. Boost.DateTime provides the class boost::local_time::loc-al_date_time, defined in boost/date_time/local_time/local_time.hpp, which uses boost::local_time::posix_time_zone to store time zone related data.

Example 10.17

```
#include <boost/date_time/local_time/local_time.hpp>
#include <iostream>

int main()
{
  boost::local_time::time_zone_ptr tz(
    new boost::local_time::posix_time_zone("CET+1"));
  boost::posix_time::ptime pt(boost::gregorian::date(2009, 1, 5),
    boost::posix_time::time_duration(12, 0, 0));
  boost::local_time::local_date_time dt(pt, tz);
  std::cout << dt.utc_time() << std::endl;
  std::cout << dt << std::endl;
  std::cout << dt.local_time() << std::endl;
  std::cout << dt.zone_name() << std::endl;
}
```

The constructor of boost::local_time::local_date_time expects an object of type boost::posix_time::ptime as the first parameter and an object of type boost::loc-al_time::time_zone_ptr as the second. boost::local_time::time_zone_ptr is a type definition for `boost::shared_ptr<boost::local_time::posix_time_zone>`. In other words, no object of type `boost::local_time::posix_time_zone` is passed. Instead, a smart pointer referring to the object is passed. This allows multiple objects of type `boost::local_time::local_date_time` to share time zone data. When the last object is destroyed, the object representing the time zone will automatically be released.

To create an object of type `boost::local_time::posix_time_zone`, a string describing the time zone is passed to the constructor as the only parameter. Example 10.17 specifies Central Europe as the time zone (CET is the abbreviation for Central European Time). Since CET is one hour ahead of UTC, the deviation is represented as +1. Boost.DateTime is not able to interpret abbreviations for time zones and thus does not know the meaning of CET. Therefore, the deviation must always be provided in hours; use the value +0 if there is no deviation.

The program writes `2009-Jan-05 12:00:00`, `2009-Jan-05 13:00:00 CET`, `2009-Jan-05 13:00:00`, and `CET` to the standard output stream. Values used to initialize objects of type `boost::posix_time::ptime` and `boost::local_time::local_date_time` always relate to the UTC time zone by default. When an object of type `boost::local_time::local_date_time` is written to the standard output stream or a call to the member function `local_time()` is made, the deviation in hours is used to calculate the local time.

Example 10.18

```cpp
#include <boost/date_time/local_time/local_time.hpp>
#include <iostream>

int main()
{
  boost::local_time::time_zone_ptr tz(
    new boost::local_time::posix_time_zone("CET+1"));
  boost::posix_time::ptime pt(boost::gregorian::date(2009, 1, 5),
    boost::posix_time::time_duration(12, 0, 0));
  boost::local_time::local_date_time dt(pt, tz);
  std::cout << dt.local_time() << std::endl;
  boost::local_time::time_zone_ptr tz2(
    new boost::local_time::posix_time_zone("EET+2"));
  std::cout << dt.local_time_in(tz2).local_time() << std::endl;
}
```

With `local_time()` the deviation for the time zone is respected. In order to calculate the CET time, one hour needs to be added to the UTC time of 12 PM stored in **dt**, since CET is one hour ahead of UTC. That's why `local_time()` writes `2009-Jan-05 13:00:00` to the standard output stream.

In contrast, the member function `local_time_in()` interprets the time stored in **dt** as being in the time zone that is passed as a parameter. This means that 12 PM UTC equals 2 PM EET which stands for Eastern European Time and is two hours ahead of UTC.

Finally, location-dependent periods are provided by Boost.DateTime via the class `boost::local_time::local_time_period`.

Example 10.19

```
#include <boost/date_time/local_time/local_time.hpp>
#include <iostream>

int main()
{
  boost::local_time::time_zone_ptr tz(
    new boost::local_time::posix_time_zone("CET+0"));
  boost::posix_time::ptime pt1(boost::gregorian::date(2009, 1, 5),
    boost::posix_time::time_duration(12, 0, 0));
  boost::local_time::local_date_time dt1(pt1, tz);
  boost::posix_time::ptime pt2(boost::gregorian::date(2009, 1, 5),
    boost::posix_time::time_duration(18, 0, 0));
  boost::local_time::local_date_time dt2(pt2, tz);
  boost::local_time::local_time_period tp(dt1, dt2);
  std::cout << tp.contains(dt1) << std::endl;
  std::cout << tp.contains(dt2) << std::endl;
}
```

The constructor of boost::local_time::local_time_period in Example 10.19 expects two parameters of type boost::local_time::local_date_time. As with other data types provided for periods, the second parameter, which represents the end time, is not part of the period. With the help of member functions such as contains(), intersection(), merge(), and others, periods based on boost::local_time::local_time_period can be processed.

Formatted Input and Output

The sample programs described so far in this chapter write results in the format 2009-Jan-07. Boost.DateTime lets you display results in different formats. Calendar dates and times can be formatted using boost::date_time::date_facet and boost::date_time::time_facet.

Example 10.20

```
#include <boost/date_time/gregorian/gregorian.hpp>
#include <iostream>
#include <locale>

int main()
{
  boost::gregorian::date d(2009, 1, 7);
  boost::gregorian::date_facet *df = new boost::gregorian::date_facet(
    "%A, %d %B %Y");
  std::cout.imbue(std::locale(std::cout.getloc(), df));
  std::cout << d << std::endl;
}
```

Boost.DateTime uses the concept of locales from the C++ standard (see Chapter 5, *String Handling*, for a brief introduction). To format a calendar date, an object of type boost::date_time::date_facet must be created and installed within a locale. A string describing the new format is passed to the constructor of boost::date_time::date_facet.

Example 10.20 passes `%A, %d %B %Y`, which specifies that the day of the week is followed by the date with the month written in full: `Wednesday, 07 January 2009`.

Boost.DateTime provides numerous format flags, which consist of the percent sign followed by a character. The documentation of Boost.DateTime contains a complete overview of all supported flags. For example, %A specifies the name of the weekday.

If a program is used by people located in Germany or German-speaking countries, it is preferable to display both the weekday and the month in German rather than in English.

Example 10.21

```
#include <boost/date_time/gregorian/gregorian.hpp>
#include <iostream>
#include <locale>
#include <string>
#include <vector>

int main()
{
  std::locale::global(std::locale("German"));
  std::string months[12] = { "Januar", "Februar", "März", "April",
    "Mai", "Juni", "Juli", "August", "September", "Oktober",
    "November", "Dezember" };
  std::string weekdays[7] = { "Sonntag", "Montag", "Dienstag",
    "Mittwoch", "Donnerstag", "Freitag", "Samstag" };
  boost::gregorian::date d(2009, 1, 7);
  boost::gregorian::date_facet *df = new boost::gregorian::date_facet(
    "%A, %d. %B %Y");
  df->long_month_names(std::vector<std::string>(months, months + 12));
  df->long_weekday_names(std::vector<std::string>(weekdays, weekdays + 7));
  std::cout.imbue(std::locale(std::cout.getloc(), df));
  std::cout << d << std::endl;
}
```

The names for weekdays and months can be changed by passing vectors containing the desired names to the member functions `long_month_names()` and `long_weekday_names()` of the class `boost::date_time::date_facet`. Example 10.21 now writes `Mittwoch, 07. Januar 2009` to the standard output stream.

Boost.DateTime is flexible with regard to formatted input and output. Besides the output classes `boost::date_time::date_facet` and `boost::date_time::time_facet`, the classes `boost::date_time::date_input_facet` and `boost::date_time::time_input_facet` are available for formatted input. All four classes provide member functions to configure the input and output of different objects provided by Boost.DateTime. For example, it is possible to specify how periods of type `boost::gregorian::date_period` are input and output. To see all of the possibilities for formatted input and output, review the documentation for Boost.DateTime.

Exercises

1. Create a program that writes the weekdays for the next Christmas Eve, Christmas Day, and the following day to the standard output stream.

2. Calculate your age in days. The program should determine the current date for the computation automatically.

11

Serialization

General

The library Boost.Serialization[1] makes it possible to convert objects in a C++ program to a sequence of bytes that can be saved and loaded to restore the objects. There are different data formats available to define the rules for generating sequences of bytes. All of the formats supported by Boost.Serialization are only intended for use with this library. For example, the XML format developed for Boost.Serialization should not be used to exchange data with programs which do not use Boost.Serialization. The only advantage of the XML format is that it can make debugging easier since C++ objects are saved in a readable format.

Archive

The main concept of Boost.Serialization is the archive. An archive is a sequence of bytes that represent serialized C++ objects. Objects can be added to an archive to serialize them and later load them from the archive again. In order to restore previously saved C++ objects, the same data types are presumed.

Example 11.1 is a simple example.

Example 11.1

```cpp
#include <boost/archive/text_oarchive.hpp>
#include <iostream>

int main()
{
  boost::archive::text_oarchive oa(std::cout);
  int i = 1;
  oa << i;
}
```

---

[1] http://www.boost.org/libs/serialization/

Boost.Serialization provides multiple archive classes such as boost::archive::text_oarchive, which is defined in boost/archive/text_oarchive.hpp. This class makes it possible to serialize objects as a text stream. Example 11.1 writes "22 serialization::archive 9 1" to the standard output stream.

As can be seen, the object **oa** of type boost::archive::text_oarchive can be used like a stream to serialize a variable via <<. However, archives should not be considered as regular streams storing arbitrary data. To restore data later, it is necessary to use the same data types in the same order as when data was saved. Example 11.2 serializes and restores the variable of type int.

Example 11.2

```
#include <boost/archive/text_oarchive.hpp>
#include <boost/archive/text_iarchive.hpp>
#include <iostream>
#include <fstream>

void save()
{
  std::ofstream file("archiv.txt");
  boost::archive::text_oarchive oa(file);
  int i = 1;
  oa << i;
}

void load()
{
  std::ifstream file("archiv.txt");
  boost::archive::text_iarchive ia(file);
  int i = 0;
  ia >> i;
  std::cout << i << std::endl;
}

int main()
{
  save();
  load();
}
```

boost::archive::text_oarchive serializes data as a text stream, and boost::archive::text_iarchive restores data from such a text stream. To use the class, include the header file boost/archive/text_iarchive.hpp.

Constructors of archives expect an input or output stream as a parameter. The stream is used to serialize or to restore data. While Example 11.2 accesses a file, other streams such as a stringstream can be used as well. Example 11.3 writes 1 to the standard output stream using a stringstream to serialize data.

Example 11.3

```cpp
#include <boost/archive/text_oarchive.hpp>
#include <boost/archive/text_iarchive.hpp>
#include <iostream>
#include <sstream>

std::stringstream ss;

void save()
{
  boost::archive::text_oarchive oa(ss);
  int i = 1;
  oa << i;
}

void load()
{
  boost::archive::text_iarchive ia(ss);
  int i = 0;
  ia >> i;
  std::cout << i << std::endl;
}

int main()
{
  save();
  load();
}
```

So far, only primitive data types have been serialized. Example 11.4 shows how to serialize objects of user-defined data types.

Example 11.4

```cpp
#include <boost/archive/text_oarchive.hpp>
#include <boost/archive/text_iarchive.hpp>
#include <iostream>
#include <sstream>

std::stringstream ss;

class person
{
public:
  person() {}
  person(int age) : age_(age) {}
  int age() const { return age_; }

private:
  friend class boost::serialization::access;

  template <typename Archive>
  void serialize(Archive &ar, const unsigned int version)
  {
    ar & age_;
  }
```

```
  int age_;
};

void save()
{
  boost::archive::text_oarchive oa(ss);
  person p(31);
  oa << p;
}

void load()
{
  boost::archive::text_iarchive ia(ss);
  person p;
  ia >> p;
  std::cout << p.age() << std::endl;
}

int main()
{
  save();
  load();
}
```

In order to serialize objects of user-defined data types, a member function called `serialize()` must be defined. It is called when the object is serialized to or restored from a byte stream. Because `serialize()` is used for both serializing and restoring, Boost.Serialization supports the operator `&` in addition to `<<` and `>>`. With `&` there is no need to distinguish between serializing and restoring within `serialize()`.

`serialize()` is automatically called any time an object is serialized or restored. It should never be called explicitly and thus should be declared as private. If it is declared as private, the class `boost::serialization::access` must be declared as friend to allow Boost.Serialization to access the member function.

There may be situations that do not you allow to modify an existing class in order to add `serialize()`. For example, this is true for classes from the C++ standard library.

Example 11.5

```
#include <boost/archive/text_oarchive.hpp>
#include <boost/archive/text_iarchive.hpp>
#include <iostream>
#include <sstream>

std::stringstream ss;

class person
{
public:
  person() {}
  person(int age) : age_(age) {}
  int age() const { return age_; }
```

```
private:
  friend class boost::serialization::access;

  template <typename Archive>
  friend void serialize(Archive &ar, person &p, const unsigned int version);

  int age_;
};

template <typename Archive>
void serialize(Archive &ar, person &p, const unsigned int version)
{
  ar & p.age_;
}

void save()
{
  boost::archive::text_oarchive oa(ss);
  person p(31);
  oa << p;
}

void load()
{
  boost::archive::text_iarchive ia(ss);
  person p;
  ia >> p;
  std::cout << p.age() << std::endl;
}

int main()
{
  save();
  load();
}
```

In order to serialize data types that cannot be modified, the free-standing function `serialize()` can be defined as shown in Example 11.5. The function expects a reference to an object of the corresponding data type as its second argument.

If the data type to be serialized contains private member variables that cannot be accessed via public member functions, things get more complicated. In this case, the data type may need to be modified. For example, the `serialize()` function in Example 11.5 would not be able to access the member variable **age_** without the `friend` declaration.

Fortunately, Boost.Serialization provides `serialize()` functions for many classes from the C++ standard. To serialize objects based on C++ standard classes, additional header files need to be included.

Example 11.6

```cpp
#include <boost/archive/text_oarchive.hpp>
#include <boost/archive/text_iarchive.hpp>
#include <boost/serialization/string.hpp>
#include <iostream>
#include <sstream>
#include <string>

std::stringstream ss;

class person
{
public:
  person() {}
  person(int age, const std::string &name) : age_(age), name_(name) {}
  int age() const { return age_; }
  std::string name() const { return name_; }

private:
  friend class boost::serialization::access;

  template <typename Archive>
  friend void serialize(Archive &ar, person &p, const unsigned int version);

  int age_;
  std::string name_;
};

template <typename Archive>
void serialize(Archive &ar, person &p, const unsigned int version)
{
  ar & p.age_;
  ar & p.name_;
}

void save()
{
  boost::archive::text_oarchive oa(ss);
  person p(31, "Boris");
  oa << p;
}

void load()
{
  boost::archive::text_iarchive ia(ss);
  person p;
  ia >> p;
  std::cout << p.age() << std::endl;
  std::cout << p.name() << std::endl;
}

int main()
{
  save();
  load();
}
```

Example 11.6 extends the class person by adding a name of type std::string. In order to serialize this member variable, the header file boost/serialization/string.hpp must be included to provide the appropriate free-standing function serialize().

As mentioned before, Boost.Serialization defines serialize() functions for many classes from the C++ standard. These are defined in header files that carry the same name as the corresponding header files from the C++ standard. In order to serialize objects of type std::string, the header file boost/serialization/string.hpp must be included. To serialize an object of type std::vector, the header file boost/serialization/vector.hpp must be used instead. Therefore, it is fairly obvious which header file has to be included.

One parameter of serialize(), which has been ignored so far, is **version**. This parameter is relevant if archives should be forward compatible to support future versions of a program. Example 11.7 considers archives of the class person to be forward compatible. Since the original version of person did not contain a name, the new version of person should still be able to manage old archives that were created without a name.

Example 11.7

```cpp
#include <boost/archive/text_oarchive.hpp>
#include <boost/archive/text_iarchive.hpp>
#include <boost/serialization/string.hpp>
#include <iostream>
#include <sstream>
#include <string>

std::stringstream ss;

class person
{
public:
  person() {}
  person(int age, const std::string &name) : age_(age), name_(name) {}
  int age() const { return age_; }
  std::string name() const { return name_; }

private:
  friend class boost::serialization::access;

  template <typename Archive>
  friend void serialize(Archive &ar, person &p, const unsigned int version);

  int age_;
  std::string name_;
};

template <typename Archive>
void serialize(Archive &ar, person &p, const unsigned int version)
{
  ar & p.age_;
  if (version > 0)
    ar & p.name_;
}

BOOST_CLASS_VERSION(person, 1)
```

```
void save()
{
  boost::archive::text_oarchive oa(ss);
  person p(31, "Boris");
  oa << p;
}

void load()
{
  boost::archive::text_iarchive ia(ss);
  person p;
  ia >> p;
  std::cout << p.age() << std::endl;
  std::cout << p.name() << std::endl;
}

int main()
{
  save();
  load();
}
```

The macro BOOST_CLASS_VERSION is used to assign a version number to a class. The version number for the class person in the above program is set to 1. If BOOST_CLASS_VERSION is not used, the version number is 0 by default.

The version number is stored in the archive and is part of it. While the version number specified for a particular class via the BOOST_CLASS_VERSION macro is used during serialization, the parameter **version** of serialize() is set to the value stored in the archive when restoring. If the new version of person accesses an archive containing an object serialized with the old version, the member variable **name_** would not be restored because the old version did not have such a member variable. Because it is possible to load C++ objects from archives that were created with older versions of a program, Boost.Serialization is said to support forward compatible archives.

Pointers and References

Boost.Serialization can also serialize pointers and references. Because a pointer stores the address of an object, serializing the address does not make much sense. When serializing pointers and references, it is the referenced object which is serialized.

Example 11.8

```
#include <boost/archive/text_oarchive.hpp>
#include <boost/archive/text_iarchive.hpp>
#include <iostream>
#include <sstream>

std::stringstream ss;

class person
{
public:
  person() {}
```

```
  person(int age) : age_(age) {}
  int age() const { return age_; }

private:
  friend class boost::serialization::access;

  template <typename Archive>
  void serialize(Archive &ar, const unsigned int version)
  {
    ar & age_;
  }

  int age_;
};

void save()
{
  boost::archive::text_oarchive oa(ss);
  person *p = new person(31);
  oa << p;
  std::cout << std::hex << p << std::endl;
  delete p;
}

void load()
{
  boost::archive::text_iarchive ia(ss);
  person *p;
  ia >> p;
  std::cout << std::hex << p << std::endl;
  std::cout << p->age() << std::endl;
  delete p;
}

int main()
{
  save();
  load();
}
```

Example 11.8 creates a new object of type person with new and assigns it to the pointer **p**. The pointer - not *p - is then serialized. Boost.Serialization automatically serializes the object referenced by **p** and not the address of the object.

If the archive is restored, **p** does not necessarily contain the same address. A new object is created and its address is assigned to **p** instead. Boost.Serialization only guarantees that the object is equal to the one serialized, not that its address is the same.

Because modern C++ uses smart pointers in connection with dynamically allocated memory, Boost.Serialization provides also support for them.

Example 11.9

```cpp
#include <boost/archive/text_oarchive.hpp>
#include <boost/archive/text_iarchive.hpp>
#include <boost/serialization/scoped_ptr.hpp>
#include <boost/scoped_ptr.hpp>
#include <iostream>
#include <sstream>

std::stringstream ss;

class person
{
public:
  person() {}
  person(int age) : age_(age) {}
  int age() const { return age_; }

private:
  friend class boost::serialization::access;

  template <typename Archive>
  void serialize(Archive &ar, const unsigned int version)
  {
    ar & age_;
  }

  int age_;
};

void save()
{
  boost::archive::text_oarchive oa(ss);
  boost::scoped_ptr<person> p(new person(31));
  oa << p;
}

void load()
{
  boost::archive::text_iarchive ia(ss);
  boost::scoped_ptr<person> p;
  ia >> p;
  std::cout << p->age() << std::endl;
}

int main()
{
  save();
  load();
}
```

Example 11.9 uses the smart pointer boost::scoped_ptr to manage a dynamically allocated object of type person. To serialize such a pointer, the header file boost/serialization/scoped_ptr.hpp must be included. Boost.Serialization can also serialize references without any issue. Just like with pointers, the referenced object is serialized automatically.

To serialize a smart pointer of type boost::shared_ptr, use the header file boost/serializ-ation/shared_ptr.hpp.

Example 11.10 uses a reference instead of a pointer.

Example 11.10

```cpp
#include <boost/archive/text_oarchive.hpp>
#include <boost/archive/text_iarchive.hpp>
#include <iostream>
#include <sstream>

std::stringstream ss;

class person
{
public:
  person() {}
  person(int age) : age_(age) {}
  int age() const { return age_; }

private:
  friend class boost::serialization::access;

  template <typename Archive>
  void serialize(Archive &ar, const unsigned int version)
  {
    ar & age_;
  }

  int age_;
};

void save()
{
  boost::archive::text_oarchive oa(ss);
  person p(31);
  person &pp = p;
  oa << pp;
}

void load()
{
  boost::archive::text_iarchive ia(ss);
  person p;
  person &pp = p;
  ia >> pp;
  std::cout << pp.age() << std::endl;
}

int main()
{
  save();
  load();
}
```

Serialization of Class Hierarchy Objects

In order to serialize objects based on class hierarchies, child classes must access the function boost::serialization::base_object() inside the member function serialize(). This function guarantees that inherited member variables of base classes are correctly serialized. Example 11.11 uses a class called developer, which is derived from person.

Example 11.11

```
#include <boost/archive/text_oarchive.hpp>
#include <boost/archive/text_iarchive.hpp>
#include <boost/serialization/string.hpp>
#include <iostream>
#include <sstream>
#include <string>

std::stringstream ss;

class person
{
public:
  person() {}
  person(int age) : age_(age) {}
  int age() const { return age_; }

private:
  friend class boost::serialization::access;

  template <typename Archive>
  void serialize(Archive &ar, const unsigned int version)
  {
    ar & age_;
  }

  int age_;
};

class developer : public person
{
public:
  developer() {}
  developer(int age, const std::string &language)
    : person(age), language_(language) {}
  std::string language() const { return language_; }

private:
  friend class boost::serialization::access;

  template <typename Archive>
  void serialize(Archive &ar, const unsigned int version)
  {
    ar & boost::serialization::base_object<person>(*this);
    ar & language_;
  }

  std::string language_;
};
```

```
void save()
{
  boost::archive::text_oarchive oa(ss);
  developer d(31, "C++");
  oa << d;
}

void load()
{
  boost::archive::text_iarchive ia(ss);
  developer d;
  ia >> d;
  std::cout << d.age() << std::endl;
  std::cout << d.language() << std::endl;
}

int main()
{
  save();
  load();
}
```

Both `person` and `developer` define a private member function `serialize()` that makes it possible to serialize objects based on either class. Because `developer` is derived from `person`, `serialize()` must ensure that member variables inherited from `person` are serialized, too.

Inherited member variables are serialized by accessing the base class inside the member function `serialize()` of the child class and calling `boost::serialization::base_object()`. It is mandatory to use this function rather than, for example, `static_cast` because only `boost::serialization::base_object()` ensures correct serialization.

Addresses of dynamically created objects can be assigned to pointers of the corresponding base class type. Example 11.12 shows that Boost.Serialization can serialize them correctly as well.

Example 11.12

```
#include <boost/archive/text_oarchive.hpp>
#include <boost/archive/text_iarchive.hpp>
#include <boost/serialization/string.hpp>
#include <boost/serialization/export.hpp>
#include <iostream>
#include <sstream>
#include <string>

std::stringstream ss;

class person
{
public:
  person() {}
  person(int age) : age_(age) {}
  virtual int age() const { return age_; }

private:
  friend class boost::serialization::access;
```

```
  template <typename Archive>
  void serialize(Archive &ar, const unsigned int version)
  {
    ar & age_;
  }

  int age_;
};

class developer : public person
{
public:
  developer() {}
  developer(int age, const std::string &language)
    : person(age), language_(language) {}
  std::string language() const { return language_; }

private:
  friend class boost::serialization::access;

  template <typename Archive>
  void serialize(Archive &ar, const unsigned int version)
  {
    ar & boost::serialization::base_object<person>(*this);
    ar & language_;
  }

  std::string language_;
};

BOOST_CLASS_EXPORT(developer)

void save()
{
  boost::archive::text_oarchive oa(ss);
  person *p = new developer(31, "C++");
  oa << p;
  delete p;
}

void load()
{
  boost::archive::text_iarchive ia(ss);
  person *p;
  ia >> p;
  std::cout << p->age() << std::endl;
  delete p;
}

int main()
{
  save();
  load();
}
```

The program creates an object of type developer inside the function save() and assigns it to a pointer of type person*, which in turn is serialized via <<.

As mentioned in the previous section, the referenced object and not the pointer is serialized. In order to have Boost.Serialization recognize that an object of type developer must be serialized, even though the pointer is of type person*, the class developer needs to be declared. This is done using the macro BOOST_CLASS_EXPORT defined in boost/serialization/export.hpp. Because the type developer does not appear in the pointer definition, Boost.Serialization would not be able to serialize an object of type developer correctly without the macro.

The macro BOOST_CLASS_EXPORT must be used if objects of child classes are to be serialized using a pointer to their corresponding base class.

A disadvantage of BOOST_CLASS_EXPORT is that because of static registration, classes can be registered that may not be used for serialization at all. Boost.Serialization offers a solution for this scenario.

Example 11.13

```cpp
#include <boost/archive/text_oarchive.hpp>
#include <boost/archive/text_iarchive.hpp>
#include <boost/serialization/string.hpp>
#include <boost/serialization/export.hpp>
#include <iostream>
#include <sstream>
#include <string>

std::stringstream ss;

class person
{
public:
  person() {}
  person(int age) : age_(age) {}
  virtual int age() const { return age_; }

private:
  friend class boost::serialization::access;

  template <typename Archive>
  void serialize(Archive &ar, const unsigned int version)
  {
    ar & age_;
  }

  int age_;
};

class developer : public person
{
public:
  developer() {}
  developer(int age, const std::string &language)
    : person(age), language_(language) {}
  std::string language() const { return language_; }
```

```
private:
  friend class boost::serialization::access;

  template <typename Archive>
  void serialize(Archive &ar, const unsigned int version)
  {
    ar & boost::serialization::base_object<person>(*this);
    ar & language_;
  }

  std::string language_;
};

void save()
{
  boost::archive::text_oarchive oa(ss);
  oa.register_type<developer>();
  person *p = new developer(31, "C++");
  oa << p;
  delete p;
}

void load()
{
  boost::archive::text_iarchive ia(ss);
  ia.register_type<developer>();
  person *p;
  ia >> p;
  std::cout << p->age() << std::endl;
  delete p;
}

int main()
{
  save();
  load();
}
```

Instead of using the macro BOOST_CLASS_EXPORT, Example 11.13 calls the template member function register_type(). The type to be registered is passed as a template parameter.

Please note that register_type() must be called both in save() and load().

The advantage of register_type() is that only classes used for serialization must be registered. For example, when developing a library, one does not know which classes a developer may use for serialization later. While the macro BOOST_CLASS_EXPORT makes this easy, it may register types that are not going to be used for serialization.

Wrapper Functions for Optimization

This section introduces wrapper functions to optimize the serialization process. These functions mark objects to allow Boost.Serialization to apply certain optimization techniques.

Example 11.14

```
#include <boost/archive/text_oarchive.hpp>
#include <boost/archive/text_iarchive.hpp>
#include <boost/array.hpp>
#include <iostream>
#include <sstream>

std::stringstream ss;

void save()
{
  boost::archive::text_oarchive oa(ss);
  boost::array<int, 3> a = { 0, 1, 2 };
  oa << a;
}

void load()
{
  boost::archive::text_iarchive ia(ss);
  boost::array<int, 3> a;
  ia >> a;
  std::cout << a[0] << ", " << a[1] << ", " << a[2] << std::endl;
}

int main()
{
  save();
  load();
}
```

Example 11.14 uses Boost.Serialization without any wrapper function. It creates and writes "22 serialization::archive 9 0 0 3 0 1 2" to the string. Using the wrapper function `boost::serialization::make_array()`, the string can be shortened to "22 serialization::archive 9 0 1 2."

`boost::serialization::make_array()` expects the address and the length of an array. As the length is hard-coded, it does not need to be serialized as part of the array. The function can be used whenever classes such as `boost::array` or `std::vector` contain an array that can be serialized directly. Additional member variables, which would normally also be serialized, are skipped (see Example 11.15).

Example 11.15

```cpp
#include <boost/archive/text_oarchive.hpp>
#include <boost/archive/text_iarchive.hpp>
#include <boost/serialization/array.hpp>
#include <boost/array.hpp>
#include <iostream>
#include <sstream>

std::stringstream ss;

void save()
{
  boost::archive::text_oarchive oa(ss);
  boost::array<int, 3> a = { 0, 1, 2 };
  oa << boost::serialization::make_array(a.data(), a.size());
}

void load()
{
  boost::archive::text_iarchive ia(ss);
  boost::array<int, 3> a;
  ia >> boost::serialization::make_array(a.data(), a.size());
  std::cout << a[0] << ", " << a[1] << ", " << a[2] << std::endl;
}

int main()
{
  save();
  load();
}
```

Another wrapper function provided by Boost.Serialization is `boost::serialization::make_binary_object()`. Similar to `boost::serialization::make_array()`, it expects an address and a length. `boost::serialization::make_binary_object()` is used solely for binary data that has no underlying structure, while `boost::serialization::make_array()` is used for arrays.

Exercises

1. Develop a program that can serialize and restore an arbitrary number of records, each of which contains an employee's name, department, and unique identification number. The data should be serialized to a file. Records should be displayed on the screen after restoring them. Use sample records to test the program.

2. Extend the program by storing the birth date for each employee. The program should still be able to restore records serialized with the older version of the program created in the previous exercise.

12

Parser

General

Developers use parsers to read formats that allow flexible and therefore potentially complicated data structures. A good example of such a format is C++ code. The parser of your compiler needs to understand the various language constructs in all their possible combinations in order to translate C++ code to binary form.

The biggest challenge in developing parsers is that a huge number of rules may be needed to handle all the ways data can be structured. For example, C++ supports so many language constructs that it would take countless if expressions to recognize valid C++ code.

The library Boost.Spirit[1], which is introduced in this chapter, turns the tables on developing parsers. Instead of translating explicit rules from the C++ standard into code and validating C++ code using countless if expressions, Boost.Spirit lets you express rules using Extended Backus-Naur Form (EBNF). Once rules have been written down in this form, Boost.Spirit does the rest and can parse a C++ source file.

The basic idea of Boost.Spirit is similar to the idea behind regular expressions. Instead of using if expressions to search a text for a specific pattern, the pattern is specified as a regular expression. The search is then performed by a library such as Boost.Regex, so developers do not need to care about the details.

This chapter shows you how to use Boost.Spirit to read complicated formats for which regular expressions are no longer feasible. To fully introduce Boost.Spirit, which is a comprehensive library that introduces various concepts, a simple parser for the JSON format[2] is developed in this chapter. JSON is a format used by Ajax applications to exchange data similar to XML between applications that can run on different platforms.

There are two major versions of Boost.Spirit: Boost.Spirit 2.x is the latest version and is introduced in this chapter. Boost.Spirit 1.x is known as Spirit Classic and is still available to give developers

---

[1] http://www.boost.org/libs/spirit/
[2] http://www.json.org/

time to upgrade. Developers using Boost.Spirit for the first time should use version 2.x, not Spirit Classic.

Extended Backus-Naur Form

Backus-Naur Form, abbreviated as BNF, is a language to describe rules. It is used in many technical specifications because it supports precise descriptions of rules. The specifications for many Internet protocols (Request for Comments, or RFCs) contain rules in BNF in addition to annotations in text form.

Boost.Spirit supports the Extended Backus-Naur Form (EBNF). This extension makes it possible to describe rules in a shorter form than would be possible with BNF. The main advantage of EBNF is a shortened and thus simplified notation.

There are many variants of EBNF. The variant used by Boost.Spirit is called Parsing Expression Grammar (PEG). The advantage of this variant is that no ambiguities are possible.

Because Boost.Spirit expects rules to be expressed in EBNF, developers need to understand EBNF. Most of the time, developers already know EBNF and select Boost.Spirit in order to reuse rules that have already been specified in EBNF. Because you need to know EBNF for Boost.Spirit, we will start with a short introduction. If you know EBNF already and want to get a quick overview on the syntax used by Boost.Spirit, please refer to the introduction to PEG[3] in the Boost.Spirit documentation.

[1]   digit : : = "0" | "1" | "2" | "3" | "4" | "5" | "6" | "7" | "8" | "9"

EBNF denotes rules as production rules. Any number of production rules can be combined to describe a format. The above format consists of only one production rule. It defines a digit, which is a number between 0 and 9.

Definitions such as digit are called nonterminal symbols. Literals, like the numeric values 0 to 9 in the definition above, are called terminal symbols. Terminal symbols can be easily recognized because they are enclosed in quotes. Terminal symbols have no special meaning – they are simply characters.

All numeric values are connected by the pipe operator, which has the same meaning as the operator | | in C++: it denotes an alternative.

To summarize, production rule [1] defines a digit as any number between 0 and 9.

[2]   integer : : = ("+" | "-")? digit+

Production rule [2] defines a new nonterminal symbol integer, which consists of at least one digit, which optionally can be preceded by a plus or minus sign.

The definition of integer uses a couple of new operators. Parentheses are used to create partial expressions as in math. Other operators can then be applied to these expressions. For example, the question mark denotes that the partial expression can only be declared once or not at all. The plus sign following digit means that the preceding expression must be declared at least once.

---

[3] http://www.boost.org/libs/spirit/doc/html/spirit/abstracts/parsing_expression_grammar.html

Production rule [2] defines an arbitrary positive or negative integer. While a digit consists of exactly one digit, an integer can consist of an arbitrary number of digits, which can be preceded by a sign. Whereas 5 is a digit and an integer, +5 is only an integer. 169 and -8 are two more examples that only match the integer production rule.

More complex production rules can be created by defining and combining nonterminal symbols.

[3]   real : : =integer "." digit*

Production rule [3] defines the nonterminal symbol real, which represents floating-point numbers. This rule is based on the nonterminal symbols integer and digit, separated by a dot. The asterisk after digit specifies that there can be zero or more digits after the dot.

Floating-point numbers such as 1.2, -16.99 or even 3. satisfy the definition of real. However, production rule [3] does not allow floating-point numbers, like .9, that do not have a leading zero.

As mentioned in the beginning of this chapter, we want to use Boost.Spirit to develop a parser for the JSON format. To do this, the rules of the JSON format need to be expressed in EBNF.

[4]   object : : ="{" member ("," member)* "}"
[5]   member : : =string ":" value
[6]   string : : ="" character* ""
[7]   value : : =string | number | object | array | "true" | "false" |
                     "null"
[8]   number : : =integer | real
[9]   array : : ="[" value ("," value)* "]"
[10]   character : : ="a" | "b" | "c" | "d" | "e" | "f" | "g" | "h" | "i" | "j" | "k" | "l"
                     | "m" | "n" | "o" | "p" | "q" | "r" | "s" | "t" | "u" | "v" | "w"
                     | "x" | "y" | "z"

The JSON format is based on objects that contain key/value pairs in braces. While keys are simple strings, values can be strings, numbers, arrays, other objects, or the literals `true`, `false`, or `null`. Strings are character sequences enclosed by double quotes. Numbers can be integers or floating-point numbers. Arrays contain values separated by commas and are enclosed in brackets.

The definition above (production rules [4] through [10]) is not complete. First, the definition of character lacks capital letters as well as other printable characters. Second, JSON supports additional character sets such as Unicode and control characters. All of this can be ignored for now since Boost.Spirit defines frequently-used nonterminal symbols.

For example, it's not necessary to type endless character streams to define a nonterminal symbol for alphanumerics. In addition, a string will be defined for the JSON format as a consecutive stream of arbitrary characters, excluding double quotes. Since double quotes are used to terminate a string, all other characters can be used within a string. The reason this cannot be expressed with the production rules defined above is that in EBNF an exclusion requires the definition of a nonterminal symbol for all characters from which characters should be excluded.

Example 12.1

```
{
  "Boris Schaeling" :
  {
    "Male": true,
    "Programming Languages": [ "C++", "Java", "C#" ],
    "Age": 33
  }
}
```

Example 12.1 is a JSON format for which above definition applies. The global object is denoted by the outer braces and contains one key/value pair. The key is "Boris Schaeling", and the value is a new object with three more key/value pairs. While the keys are all strings, the values are the literal true, an array containing several strings and a number. With Boost.Spirit, it's now possible to reuse the above rules and create a parser which can read the above JSON format.

Grammar

Once the rules for the JSON format have been defined in EBNF, they need to be used with Boost.Spirit. Boost.Spirit lets you write EBNF rules as C++ code. This works because Boost.Spirit overloads many C++ operators, which are then used in EBNF rules.

The EBNF rules have to be modified slightly to create valid C++ code. For example, symbols, which are concatenated using space in EBNF, need to be concatenated with an operator in C++. In addition, operators like the asterisk (*), the question mark (?) and the plus sign (+), which are appended to symbols in EBNF, need to prepend symbols in code, since that's how unary operators work in C++.

Example 12.2

```
#include <boost/spirit/include/qi.hpp>

using namespace boost::spirit;

template <typename Iterator>
struct json : qi::grammar<Iterator>
{
  json()
    : json::base_type(object)
  {
    object = "{" >> member >> *("," >> member) >> "}";
    member = str >> ":" >> value;
    str = "\"" >> *~qi::lit('"') >> "\"";
    value = str | number | object | array | "true" | "false" | "null";
    number = qi::double_;
    array = "[" >> value >> *("," >> value) >> "]";
  }

  qi::rule<Iterator> object, member, str, value, number, array;
};

int main() {}
```

Example 12.2 shows how the EBNF rules for the JSON format are expressed in C++ code with Boost.Spirit.

To use the classes Boost.Spirit provides, include the header file `boost/spirit/include/qi.hpp`. The classes from Boost.Spirit will then be available in the namespace `boost::spirit::qi`.

Beginning with version 2.0, Boost.Spirit can be used for more than developing parsers. It's now also possible to develop generators, which do the opposite of parsers. While parsers extract data out of a text format, generators can be used to write data into a text format. That's why Boost.Spirit consists of two parts: Qi and Karma. Qi is used to develop parsers, and Karma is used to develop generators. Because in this chapter we are developing a parser, we will only use Qi. Therefore, it's only necessary to include the header file of Qi and to access code in the namespace `boost::spirit::qi`.

Because Boost.Spirit is a large library that not only contains components like Qi and Karma, but also contains Spirit Classic, lots of header files exist. To be less confusing and to improve compatibility with future releases, you should only include headers from the directory `boost/spirit/include/`. Boost.Spirit guarantees that this directory won't change in future versions.

If you want to develop a parser with Boost.Spirit, you need to create a grammar. A grammar defines the rules by which data is structured. Example 12.2 above defines a class `json`, which is derived from the class template `boost::spirit::qi::grammar`. The class `json` defines the entire grammar required to parse JSON formats.

`json` is a class template that must be instantiated with an iterator type. In the next example you are going to use the grammar to extract data from a string. The connection between a grammar and a string is established through iterators. For the greatest possible flexibility you should pass iterator types as template parameters.

The rules to describe the JSON format are defined in the constructor of `json`. This is done with the help of the class `boost::spirit::qi::rule`, which is also a class template that expects the iterator type as a parameter.

Now you can create as many objects of type `boost::spirit::qi::rule` as you need to define the required rules. We meet the nonterminal symbols object, member, string, value, number and array from the previous section again - they are all objects of type `boost::spirit:qi::rule`.

All of these objects are member variables of the class `json`. This is not a requirement, but it makes it easier when rules refer to each other recursively. As you have already seen from the EBNF examples in the previous section, recursive rules are no problem.

Let's look at the definition of the rules in the constructor of the `json` class. At first sight they should look very similar to the production rules of EBNF from the previous section. After all, the goal of Boost.Spirit is to reuse production rules from EBNF.

While the C++ code does look similar to EBNF rules, there are a few peculiarities. For example, all symbols are concatenated with the operator `>>`. Furthermore, EBNF operators like the asterisk are prepended and not appended to symbols. These changes are required to write valid C++ code. Other than these changes, Boost.Spirit tries hard to make it as easy as possible to move EBNF rules into C++ code.

Boost.Spirit provides two classes used in the constructor of json. These are boost::spirit::qi::double_ and boost::spirit::qi::lit. Boost.Spirit predefines some rules that are frequently used by developers. Arbitrary numbers – positive and negative integers and floating-point numbers – can be parsed with boost::spirit::qi::double_ without having to define nonterminal symbols like digit or real yourself.

The class boost::spirit::qi::lit can be used to create a parser for a single character. That's basically the same as if a single character is enclosed by single quotes. The reason boost::spirit::qi::lit has to be used in Example 12.2 is to handle cases that would be rejected as invalid C++ code. For example, if you apply the operators ~ and * to the double quote without boost::spirit::qi::lit, the code would read *~'"' which would be rejected as invalid C++ code by the compiler.

The operator ~ handles the exclusion case that was mentioned in the previous section. Prepending this operator to the double quote indicates that all characters should be accepted by the parser except the double quote.

After you have learned how to define rules to parse the JSON format, Example 12.3 shows how to use them.

Example 12.3

```cpp
#include <boost/spirit/include/qi.hpp>
#include <string>
#include <iostream>

using namespace boost::spirit;

template <typename Iterator>
struct json : qi::grammar<Iterator>
{
  json()
    : json::base_type(object)
  {
    object = "{" >> member >> *("," >> member) >> "}";
    member = str >> ":" >> value;
    str = "\"" >> *~qi::lit('"') >> "\"";
    value = str | number | object | array | "true" | "false" | "null";
    number = qi::double_;
    array = "[" >> value >> *("," >> value) >> "]";
  }

  qi::rule<Iterator> object, member, str, value, number, array;
};

int main()
{
  std::string s = "{\"Boris Schaeling\":{\"Male\":true,\"Programming "
                  "Languages\":[\"C++\",\"Java\",\"C#\"],\"Age\":33}}";
  json<std::string::iterator> json_parser;
  bool success = qi::parse(s.begin(), s.end(), json_parser);
  std::cout << (success ? "OK" : "Error") << std::endl;
}
```

Boost.Spirit provides the free-standing function `boost::spirit::qi::parse()` to parse strings. This function expects as its first two parameters iterators that point to the beginning and end of the string to be parsed. The third parameter is the parser to use.

You do not need to put strings in objects of type `std::string`. Just like `json`, the function `boost::spirit::qi::parse()` is a template that is instantiated with an iterator type. In Example 12.3, no template parameter is passed since the compiler can derive the type automatically from the first two parameters passed to `boost::spirit::qi::parse()`. Because Boost.Spirit does not depend on classes like `std::string` but on iterators, the class is much more flexible and can process strings of different types.

If you look closely at the string **s** in Example 12.3 example, you will notice that it does not contain any space. All valid characters in the JSON format follow each other directly. If you add a space, for example after the curly bracket at the very beginning of the string, `boost::spirit::qi::parse()` returns `false`. The function does not accept any separators.

Example 12.4 supports separators as well.

Example 12.4

```
#include <boost/spirit/include/qi.hpp>
#include <string>
#include <iostream>

using namespace boost::spirit;

template <typename Iterator, typename Skipper>
struct json : qi::grammar<Iterator, Skipper>
{
  json()
    : json::base_type(object)
  {
    object = "{" >> member >> *("," >> member) >> "}";
    member = str >> ":" >> value;
    str = "\"" >> *~qi::lit('"') >> "\"";
    value = str | number | object | array | "true" | "false" | "null";
    number = qi::double_;
    array = "[" >> value >> *("," >> value) >> "]";
  }

  qi::rule<Iterator, Skipper> object, member, str, value, number, array;
};

int main()
{
  std::string s = "{ \"Boris Schaeling\" : { \"Male\": true, "
                  "\"Programming Languages\": [ \"C++\", \"Java\", "
                  "\"C#\" ], \"Age\": 33 } }";
  json<std::string::iterator, ascii::space_type> json_parser;
  bool success = qi::phrase_parse(s.begin(), s.end(), json_parser,
    ascii::space);
  std::cout << (success ? "OK" : "Error") << std::endl;
}
```

If you like to be more flexible in parsing, call `boost::spirit::qi::phrase_parse()` instead of `boost::spirit::qi::parse()`. This function accepts a fourth parameter which is a "skipper." If you pass an object of type **boost::spirit::ascii::space** as a skipper – as was done in Example 12.4 – spaces will be skipped. That's why the sample program writes OK to the standard output stream. Now, spaces are allowed everywhere the operator `>>` is used.

The skipper used here is defined in the namespace `boost::spirit::ascii`. Boost.Spirit also defines skippers in other namespaces, like `boost::spirit::iso8859_1`, `boost::spirit::standard`, and `boost::spirit::standard_wide`. While skippers from the namespace `boost::spirit::ascii` are based on ASCII and skippers from the namespace `boost::spirit::iso8859_1` on ISO 8859-1, skippers defined in `boost::spirit::standard` and `boost::spirit::standard_wide` use functions like `std::isspace()` from the C++ standard to identify spaces. In Example 12.4 one could also use **boost::spirit::standard::space** and still get the output OK.

Please note that the class `json` got a second template parameter. The type of the skipper has to be passed to the grammar and to the rules in the grammar.

Actions

You now know how to define a grammar to create a new parser. You can use the parser to check whether a certain text conforms to the rules of the grammar. However, reading the format doesn't work, yet.

In order to process data that has been recognized by a rule, you need to define actions. Actions are functions that are bound to rules. When a parser finds a token that conforms to a rule, the action bound to the rule is invoked. The token is passed as a parameter to the action, which can then process the data.

Example 12.5

```cpp
#include <boost/spirit/include/qi.hpp>
#include <string>
#include <iostream>

using namespace boost::spirit;

void print(const std::string &s)
{
  std::cout << s << std::endl;
}

template <typename Iterator, typename Skipper>
struct json : qi::grammar<Iterator, Skipper>
{
  json()
    : json::base_type(object)
  {
    object = "{" >> member >> *("," >> member) >> "}";
    member = str[print] >> ":" >> value;
    str = qi::lexeme["\"" >> *~qi::lit('"') >> "\""];
    value = str | number | object | array | "true" | "false" | "null";
```

```
      number = qi::double_;
      array = "[" >> value >> *("," >> value) >> "]";
  }

  qi::rule<Iterator, Skipper> object, member, value, number, array;
  qi::rule<Iterator, std::string(), Skipper> str;
};

int main()
{
  std::string s = "{ \"Boris Schaeling\" : { \"Male\": true, "
                  "\"Programming Languages\": [ \"C++\", \"Java\", "
                  "\"C#\" ], \"Age\": 33 } }";
  json<std::string::iterator, ascii::space_type> json_parser;
  bool success = qi::phrase_parse(s.begin(), s.end(), json_parser,
    ascii::space);
  std::cout << (success ? "OK" : "Error") << std::endl;
}
```

In Example 12.5, the function `print()` is an action – actions are simply functions. You can also use function objects as actions, if you need to initialize actions or keep a state between repeated invocation of actions.

`print()` becomes an action by passing the function in brackets to a parser. That's how a function or function object is bound to a parser. This is all done in the constructor of `json`. `print()` is passed to the operator `[]` of **str**. Because **str** is used to parse the key within the **member** rule – that is, the key of the key/value pair – `print()` is called every time the parser recognizes a key.

We don't want `print()` to only be called when a key has been parsed. We want the key to be passed to `print()` so the function can write it to the standard output stream. Although `print()` has been defined to accept a parameter, you must also tell the rule **str** that the key should be passed to the action. That's why the definition of **str** was changed.

By default, user-defined parsers don't pass any value to actions. If a value should be passed, the data type of the parser has to be changed. In Example 12.5, `std::string()` is passed as a second template parameter to **str**. This is the signature of a function whose return value is `std::string`.

Whether you pass the signature as the second or third template parameter doesn't matter. Boost.Spirit tries to be as flexible as possible.

The parameter `std::string()` says that **str** returns a "synthesized" attribute of type `std::string`. The attribute is called synthesized because the parser automatically converts the recognized token into the desired data type. For example, the parser **boost::spirit::qi::double_** has a synthesized attribute of type `double`. Any number parsed is automatically converted to type `double`. That means that an action like `print()` will receive the data in the preferred type.

Example 12.5 writes `Boris Schaeling`, `Male`, `Programming Languages` and `Age` to the standard output stream. You must use the directive **boost::spirit::qi::lexeme** in the definition of **str**. Without this directive, spaces would be skipped, and the program would write `BorisSchaeling`, instead of `Boris Schaeling`, to the standard output stream.

Now you can bind as many actions to parsers as you like to extract and process data. Because the parser in this chapter has been defined to read the JSON format, it should ideally return a JSON object. In Example 12.6, we don't want to pick individual substrings anymore. Instead our JSON parser should return a JSON object just like the parser **boost::spirit::qi::double_**, which returns a double.

Example 12.6

```cpp
#include <boost/spirit/include/qi.hpp>
#include <boost/fusion/include/adapt_struct.hpp>
#include <boost/variant.hpp>
#include <boost/foreach.hpp>
#include <string>
#include <vector>
#include <iostream>

using namespace boost::spirit;

struct json_object;
struct json_array;

typedef boost::variant<std::string, double,
  boost::recursive_wrapper<json_object>,
  boost::recursive_wrapper<json_array> > json_value;

struct json_array
{
  std::vector<json_value> array;
};

BOOST_FUSION_ADAPT_STRUCT(
  json_array,
  (std::vector<json_value>, array)
)

struct json_member
{
  std::string key;
  json_value value;
};

BOOST_FUSION_ADAPT_STRUCT(
  json_member,
  (std::string, key)
  (json_value, value)
)

struct json_object
{
  std::vector<json_member> members;
};

BOOST_FUSION_ADAPT_STRUCT(
  json_object,
  (std::vector<json_member>, members)
)
```

```cpp
template <typename Iterator, typename Skipper>
struct json : qi::grammar<Iterator, json_object(), Skipper>
{
  json()
    : json::base_type(object)
  {
    object %= "{" >> member % "," >> "}";
    member %= str >> ":" >> value;
    str %= qi::lexeme["\"" >> *~qi::lit('"') >> "\""];
    value %= str | number | object | array | qi::string("true") |
      qi::string("false") | qi::string("null");
    number %= qi::double_;
    array %= "[" >> value % "," >> "]";
  }

  qi::rule<Iterator, json_object(), Skipper> object;
  qi::rule<Iterator, json_member(), Skipper> member;
  qi::rule<Iterator, std::string(), Skipper> str;
  qi::rule<Iterator, json_value(), Skipper> value;
  qi::rule<Iterator, double(), Skipper> number;
  qi::rule<Iterator, json_array(), Skipper> array;
};

struct output :
  public boost::static_visitor<>
{
  void operator()(const std::string &s) const
  {
    std::cout << s << std::endl;
  }

  void operator()(double d) const
  {
    std::cout << d << std::endl;
  }

  void operator()(const json_object &o) const
  {
    BOOST_FOREACH(json_member member, o.members)
    {
      std::cout << member.key << std::endl;
      boost::apply_visitor(output(), member.value);
    }
  }

  void operator()(const json_array &a) const
  {
    BOOST_FOREACH(json_value value, a.array)
    {
      boost::apply_visitor(output(), value);
    }
  }
};

int main()
{
  std::string s = "{ \"Boris Schaeling\" : { \"Male\": true, "
                  "\"Programming Languages\": [ \"C++\", \"Java\", "
                  "\"C#\" ], \"Age\": 33 } }";
```

```
json<std::string::iterator, ascii::space_type> json_parser;
json_object json_data;
bool success = qi::phrase_parse(s.begin(), s.end(), json_parser,
  ascii::space, json_data);
if (success)
{
  BOOST_FOREACH(json_member member, json_data.members)
  {
    std::cout << member.key << std::endl;
    boost::apply_visitor(output(), member.value);
  }
}
}
```

In order to make the JSON parser return a JSON object, an appropriate structure must be defined first. This is done with the help of the types `json_object`, `json_member`, `json_array`, and `json_value`. While the first three classes are structures, `json_value` is based on `boost::variant`.

The types are nested to make it possible to structure data as it's structured in JSON and described by the grammar. For example, a JSON object can store an arbitrary number of key/value pairs, which is modeled with a vector in the structure `json_object`.

There is a good reason to use the type `std::vector` in the structures, and `boost::variant` has also been used specifically to define `json_value`. Boost.Spirit can use these types automatically and even depends on them to a certain degree. For example, if a rule allows an arbitrary number of symbols, like key/value pairs in JSON, the parser stores the data in an object of type `std::vector`. If a rule identifies alternatives with different types, like values that can be associated with a key in JSON, the parser stores the data in an object of type `boost::variant`.

Even though Boost.Spirit gives types like `std::vector` and `boost::variant` preferential treatment, the structures still have to be converted into fusion tuples. This can be easily done with the macro `BOOST_FUSION_ADAPT_STRUCT`. This step can't be skipped.

Boost.Spirit is based on the library Boost.Fusion, which is a by-product of Boost.Spirit. It is an infrastructure library which can be used to build other libraries. Application developers typically won't use Boost.Fusion directly.

The main concept of Boost.Fusion is the tuple, which can bundle objects of different data types. This makes a tuple similar to a structure. After all, a structure is also a group of objects that can have different data types. With `BOOST_FUSION_ADAPT_STRUCT` any structure can be viewed as a tuple.

What does all of this have to do with Boost.Spirit? Rules that search for tokens actually return tuples. For example, the **member** rule in Example 12.6 searches for a key followed by a colon followed by a value. If this rule is applied successfully, an object for the key and an object for the value is returned. Because these objects can have different types – the key is always a string but the value can be different, for example a number – the return value of the rule can be expressed as a tuple.

Boost.Fusion is a library which provides many tools to process tuples. Among others, the library defines the macro `BOOST_FUSION_ADAPT_STRUCT` to turn a structure into a tuple. This macro is used several times in Example 12.6 since several structures are required to save a JSON object. The header file `boost/fusion/include/adapt_struct.hpp` must be included to use `BOOST_FUSION_ADAPT_STRUCT`.

After the various types have been defined and introduced as tuples, they are used in the grammar. For example, it's not just that a parser of type `json` should return an object of type `json_object`. The rules within the grammar should also save data in objects of types `json_member`, `json_array`, or `json_value`.

A signature is passed as an additional template parameter to the grammar and to the rules to define which synthesized attribute should be returned and passed to actions. For example, we pass the signature `json_value()` to the rule **value** because we want the rule to return a synthesized attribute of type `json_value`.

You could bind actions to the rules which would be called when data is parsed successfully. However, Boost.Spirit provides an operator which does automatically what we want the grammar to do (`%=`). For example, the object of type `json_value` which is returned by the rule **value** is automatically saved in an object of type `json_member` – after all that's where **value** is used. The attribute returned by **member** (an object of type `json_member`) is stored in an object of type `json_object` because **member** is used within the rule **object**. Since the structures have to conform to the rules, rules can automatically store data. That's all possible with the operator `%=`, which has been overloaded by Boost.Spirit.

Please note that two rules had to change slightly. The sequence of key/value pairs that are separated by commas is now expressed using `member % ","`. This is required because only this form is compatible with the data type `std::vector`, which should store the key/value pairs. Furthermore, the literals `true`, `false`, and `null` are used with **boost::spirit::qi::string** because only then will an attribute of type `std::string` be returned. Literals themselves don't return anything.

To retrieve JSON data in an object of type `json_object`, just instantiate this class and pass the object as the fifth parameter to `boost::spirit::qi::phrase_parse()`. This is equivalent to binding an action to **parser**, which expects a parameter of type `json_object`. The rest of the code in Example 12.6 simply writes the parsed data to the standard output stream.

Boost.Spirit provides a lot more than can be introduced in this book. While this chapter only explains how to use parsers, Boost.Spirit can also be used to create generators. For more information, look at the documentation for Boost.Spirit.

Exercises

1. Develop a calculator that can add and subtract arbitrary integers and floating-point numbers. The calculator should accept input such as `=-4+8 + 1.5` and then display `5.5` as a result.

13

Containers

General

This chapter introduces various Boost C++ Libraries that provide containers to complement the ones from the C++ standard. For example, it outlines the use of containers from Boost.Unordered, which were standardized in Technical Report 1, shows how to define containers with Boost.Multi-Index and explains when to use Boost.Bimap, a library developed with the help of Boost.MultiIndex. The first library introduced, however, is Boost.Array, which allows us to treat traditional arrays like containers from the C++ standard.

Boost.Array

The library Boost.Array[1] defines the class template `boost::array` in `boost/array.hpp`. With this class an array can be created that exhibits the same properties as a traditional array in C++. In addition, `boost::array` also conforms to the requirements of C++ containers, which makes handling such an array as easy as handling any other container. In principle, one can think of `boost::array` as the C++ container `std::vector`, except the number of elements in `boost::array` is constant.

---

[1] http://www.boost.org/libs/array/

Example 13.1

```
#include <boost/array.hpp>
#include <iostream>
#include <string>
#include <algorithm>

int main()
{
  typedef boost::array<std::string, 3> array;
  array a;

  a[0] = "Boris";
  a.at(1) = "Anton";
  *a.rbegin() = "Caesar";

  std::sort(a.begin(), a.end());

  for (array::const_iterator it = a.begin(); it != a.end(); ++it)
    std::cout << *it << std::endl;

  std::cout << a.size() << std::endl;
  std::cout << a.max_size() << std::endl;
}
```

As seen in Example 13.1, using boost::array is fairly simple and needs no additional explanation since the member functions called have the same meaning as their counterparts from std::vector.

However, there is one peculiarity, which is pointed out in Example 13.2. An array of type boost::array can be initialized just like a traditional C++ array. Because this container has been added to Technical Report 1, it can also be accessed using std::array, which is defined in the header file array in implementations of the C++ standard that support Technical Report 1.

Example 13.2

```
#include <boost/array.hpp>
#include <string>

int main()
{
  typedef boost::array<std::string, 3> array;
  array a = { "Boris", "Anton", "Caesar" };
}
```

Boost.Unordered

Boost.Unordered[2] complements the C++ containers std::set, std::multiset, std::map, and std::multimap with four additional classes: boost::unordered_set, boost::unordered_multiset, boost::unordered_map, and boost::unordered_multimap. These classes differ only slightly from the existing containers and have a similar interface. In many cases, either one of the classes can be used.

---

[2] http://www.boost.org/libs/unordered/

The difference between the containers from the C++ standard and those from Boost.Unordered is that containers from Boost.Unordered do not sort their elements and thus do not require elements to be sortable. Boost.Unordered makes sense when the order of stored elements is unimportant.

In order to find elements quickly, hash values are calculated. Hash values are numbers that uniquely identify elements in a container and can be compared faster than data types like strings. Because hash values need to be calculated, data types stored inside containers of Boost.Unordered must support calculating these IDs. While, for example, std::set requires elements to be sortable, boost::unordered_set requires elements to support the calculation of hash values. Despite this requirement, Boost.Unordered is usually preferred unless sorting of elements is required.

Example 13.3

```cpp
#include <boost/unordered_set.hpp>
#include <iostream>
#include <string>

int main()
{
  typedef boost::unordered_set<std::string> unordered_set;
  unordered_set set;

  set.insert("Boris");
  set.insert("Anton");
  set.insert("Caesar");

  for (unordered_set::iterator it = set.begin(); it != set.end(); ++it)
    std::cout << *it << std::endl;

  std::cout << set.size() << std::endl;
  std::cout << set.max_size() << std::endl;

  std::cout << (set.find("David") != set.end()) << std::endl;
  std::cout << set.count("Boris") << std::endl;
}
```

boost::unordered_set provides similar member functions to std::set. In fact, Example 13.3 could have used std::set without having to change the source code very much.

Example 13.4 uses boost::unordered_map to store the age of each person in addition to his or her name.

As with Example 13.3, there are no major differences between boost::unordered_map and std::map, and std::map could have been used without any issues.

Example 13.4

```
#include <boost/unordered_map.hpp>
#include <iostream>
#include <string>

int main()
{
  typedef boost::unordered_map<std::string, int> unordered_map;
  unordered_map map;

  map.insert(unordered_map::value_type("Boris", 31));
  map.insert(unordered_map::value_type("Anton", 35));
  map.insert(unordered_map::value_type("Caesar", 25));

  for (unordered_map::iterator it = map.begin(); it != map.end(); ++it)
    std::cout << it->first << ", " << it->second << std::endl;

  std::cout << map.size() << std::endl;
  std::cout << map.max_size() << std::endl;

  std::cout << (map.find("David") != map.end()) << std::endl;
  std::cout << map.count("Boris") << std::endl;
}
```

As mentioned above, Boost.Unordered requires elements stored in the container to support the calculation of hash values. Miscellaneous data types such as std::string are supported by default. For user-defined types, a corresponding hash function must be defined.

Example 13.5

```
#include <boost/unordered_set.hpp>
#include <string>

struct person
{
  std::string name;
  int age;

  person(const std::string &n, int a)
    : name(n), age(a) {}

  bool operator==(const person &p) const
  {
    return name == p.name && age == p.age;
  }
};

std::size_t hash_value(person const &p)
{
  std::size_t seed = 0;
  boost::hash_combine(seed, p.name);
  boost::hash_combine(seed, p.age);
  return seed;
}

int main()
```

```
{
  typedef boost::unordered_set<person> unordered_set;
  unordered_set set;

  set.insert(person("Boris", 31));
  set.insert(person("Anton", 35));
  set.insert(person("Caesar", 25));
}
```

Example 13.5 stores elements of type person in a container of type boost::unordered_set. Because the built-in hash function of boost::unordered_set does not recognize the class person, hash values cannot be calculated. Without providing an alternative hash function, the code would not compile.

The name of the hash function to be defined is hash_value(). It takes as its sole argument an object of the data type for which a hash value should be calculated. Because hash values are simple numbers, the return value of the function must be std::size_t.

Whenever a hash value needs to be calculated for an object, hash_value() is called automatically. The Boost C++ Libraries already define this function for various data types such as std::string. For user-defined types such as person, it needs to be defined manually.

Implementing the function hash_value() is usually fairly simple. The hash value is calculated by accessing the individual member variables sequentially using the function boost::hash_combine() from Boost.Hash. boost::hash_combine() is defined in boost/functional/hash.hpp. This header file is automatically included if Boost.Unordered is used because all containers calculate hash values based on Boost.Hash.

Besides defining hash_value(), user-defined types need to support comparing two objects via the == operator. Therefore, person implements operator==.

Boost.MultiIndex

The library Boost.MultiIndex[3] is much more complex than any of the libraries presented so far. While both Boost.Array and Boost.Unordered provide containers that can be used immediately, Boost.MultiIndex makes it possible to define new containers.

Unlike the containers from the C++ standard, a user-defined container based on Boost.MultiIndex doesn't provides only one interface to data in the container; it can support an arbitrary number of interfaces. For example, one can create a container that assigns values to keys similar to std::map, but can also use values as keys. Without the help of a library like Boost.MultiIndex, two containers of type std::map would be required, and they would need to be synchronized continuously to guarantee data integrity.

Example 13.6 defines a new container with Boost.MultiIndex, which makes it possible to store the name and age of people. Unlike std::map, the container can be searched for both name and age.

---

[3] http://www.boost.org/libs/multi_index/

Example 13.6

```cpp
#include <boost/multi_index_container.hpp>
#include <boost/multi_index/hashed_index.hpp>
#include <boost/multi_index/member.hpp>
#include <iostream>
#include <string>

struct person
{
  std::string name;
  int age;

  person(const std::string &n, int a) : name(n), age(a) {}
};

typedef boost::multi_index::multi_index_container<
  person,
  boost::multi_index::indexed_by<
    boost::multi_index::hashed_non_unique<
      boost::multi_index::member<
        person, std::string, &person::name
      >
    >,
    boost::multi_index::hashed_non_unique<
      boost::multi_index::member<
        person, int, &person::age
      >
    >
  >
> person_multi;

int main()
{
  person_multi persons;

  persons.insert(person("Boris", 31));
  persons.insert(person("Anton", 35));
  persons.insert(person("Caesar", 25));

  std::cout << persons.count("Boris") << std::endl;

  const person_multi::nth_index<1>::type &age_index = persons.get<1>();
  std::cout << age_index.count(25) << std::endl;
}
```

As mentioned before, Boost.MultiIndex does not provide specific containers. Instead it provides classes to define containers. Typically, the first step is to access different classes from Boost.Multi-Index and design a new container with `typedef`.

A class used for every container definition is `boost::multi_index::multi_index_container`, which is defined in `boost/multi_index_container.hpp`. `boost::multi_index::multi_index_container` is a class template that requires at least two parameters. The first parameter is the data type the container should store – in Example 13.6, a user-defined class called `person`. The second parameter is used to denote different indexes the container should provide.

The key advantage of containers based on Boost.MultiIndex is the ability to access data via different interfaces. When a new container is defined, the number and type of interfaces can be specified. Because the container in Example 13.6 should support searching for people by name or age, two interfaces have been defined. Boost.MultiIndex calls these interfaces indexes – that's where the library's name comes from.

Interfaces are defined with the help of the class `boost::multi_index::indexed_by`. Each interface is passed as a template parameter. Example 13.6 defines two interfaces of type `boost::multi_index::hashed_non_unique`, which are defined in `boost/multi_index/hashed_index.hpp`. These interfaces are used if the container should behave like one from Boost.Unordered and look up values using a hash value.

The class `boost::multi_index::hashed_non_unique` is a template as well and expects as its sole parameter a class able to calculate hash values. Because both interfaces of the container should look up persons, one interface calculates hash values for the name, while the other interface does so for the age.

Boost.MultiIndex offers the helper class template `boost::multi_index::member`, defined in `boost/multi_index/member.hpp`, to access a member variable. As seen in Example 13.6, several parameters have been specified to let `boost::multi_index::member` know which member variable of `person` should be accessed and which data type the member variable has.

Even though the definition of `person_multi` looks complicated at first, the class works like `boost::unordered_map` from Boost.Unordered. The important difference is that both the name and the age of a person can be used to search the container.

To access any MultiIndex container, an interface must be selected. If the object **persons** is directly accessed using `insert()` or `count()`, the first interface is used. In Example 13.6, this would be the hash container for the member variable **name**. If you need a different interface, you must explicitly select it.

Interfaces are numbered consecutively, starting at index 0 for the first interface. To access the second interface in Example 13.6, call the member function `get()` and pass in the index of the desired interface as the template parameter.

The return value of `get()` looks complicated. It accesses a class of the MultiIndex container called `nth_index` which, again, is a template. Thus, the index of the interface to be used must be specified as a template parameter. This index must be the same as the one passed to `get()`. The final step is to access the type definition named `type` of `nth_index` using `::`. The value of `type` represents the type of the corresponding interface.

Although the specifics of an interface do not need to be known, since they are automatically derived from `nth_index` and `type`, you should still understand what kind of interface is accessed. Given that interfaces are numbered consecutively in the container definition, this can be answered fairly easily, since the index is passed to `get()`, as well as `nth_index`. Thus, **age_index** is a hash interface that looks up persons by age.

Because data such as names and ages can be keys of the MultiIndex container, they can no longer be changed arbitrarily. If the age of a person is altered after the person has been looked up by name, an interface using age as a key would not be aware of the change and would not know that a new hash value needs to be calculated.

Just as the keys in a container of type `std::map` cannot be modified, neither can data stored within a MultiIndex container. Strictly speaking, all data stored in a MultiIndex container is constant. To avoid having to delete values from a MultiIndex container and insert new ones, since it is not possible to change them while they are stored in the container, Boost.MultiIndex provides a couple of useful member functions to change values directly. Because these member functions operate on the MultiIndex container itself, and no element in a container is modified directly, all interfaces will be notified and can calculate new hash values.

Example 13.7

```cpp
#include <boost/multi_index_container.hpp>
#include <boost/multi_index/hashed_index.hpp>
#include <boost/multi_index/member.hpp>
#include <iostream>
#include <string>

struct person
{
  std::string name;
  int age;

  person(const std::string &n, int a) : name(n), age(a) {}
};

typedef boost::multi_index::multi_index_container<
  person,
  boost::multi_index::indexed_by<
    boost::multi_index::hashed_non_unique<
      boost::multi_index::member<
        person, std::string, &person::name
      >
    >,
    boost::multi_index::hashed_non_unique<
      boost::multi_index::member<
        person, int, &person::age
      >
    >
  >
> person_multi;

void set_age(person &p)
{
  p.age = 32;
}

int main()
{
  person_multi persons;

  persons.insert(person("Boris", 31));
  persons.insert(person("Anton", 35));
  persons.insert(person("Caesar", 25));

  person_multi::iterator it = persons.find("Boris");
```

```
  persons.modify(it, set_age);

  const person_multi::nth_index<1>::type &age_index = persons.get<1>();
  std::cout << age_index.count(32) << std::endl;
}
```

Every interface offered by Boost.MultiIndex provides the member function modify(), which operates directly on the container. The object to be modified is identified through an iterator passed as the first parameter to modify(). The second parameter is a function or function object that expects as its sole parameter an object of the type stored in the container. In Example 13.7, this is an object of type person. This function, set_age() in the example, makes it possible to modify an object in the container.

So far, only one interface has been introduced: boost::multi_index::hashed_non_unique, which calculates a hash value that does not have to be unique. In order to guarantee that no value is stored twice, use boost::multi_index::hashed_unique. Please note that values cannot be stored if they don't satisfy the requirements of all interfaces of a particular container. If an interface does not allow you to store values multiple times, it does not matter whether another interface does allow it, as can be seen in Example 13.8.

Example 13.8

```
#include <boost/multi_index_container.hpp>
#include <boost/multi_index/hashed_index.hpp>
#include <boost/multi_index/member.hpp>
#include <iostream>
#include <string>

struct person
{
  std::string name;
  int age;

  person(const std::string &n, int a) : name(n), age(a) {}
};

typedef boost::multi_index::multi_index_container<
  person,
  boost::multi_index::indexed_by<
    boost::multi_index::hashed_non_unique<
      boost::multi_index::member<
        person, std::string, &person::name
      >
    >,
    boost::multi_index::hashed_unique<
      boost::multi_index::member<
        person, int, &person::age
      >
    >
  >
> person_multi;

int main()
{
  person_multi persons;
```

```
    persons.insert(person("Boris", 31));
    persons.insert(person("Anton", 31));
    persons.insert(person("Caesar", 25));

    const person_multi::nth_index<1>::type &age_index = persons.get<1>();
    std::cout << age_index.count(31) << std::endl;
}
```

The container in Example 13.8 uses `boost::multi_index::hashed_unique` as the second interface. That means no two persons with the same age can be stored in the container because the hash values would be the same.

The program tries to store a person called Anton who has the same age as the already stored person Boris. Because this violates the requirement of having unique hash values for the second interface, the object will not be stored in the container. Therefore, when searching for people of age 31, the application displays 1, and only Boris is stored and counted.

Example 13.9 introduces the three remaining interfaces of Boost.MultiIndex: `boost::multi_index::sequenced`, `boost::multi_index::ordered_non_unique`, and `boost::multi_index::random_access`.

Example 13.9

```
#include <boost/multi_index_container.hpp>
#include <boost/multi_index/sequenced_index.hpp>
#include <boost/multi_index/ordered_index.hpp>
#include <boost/multi_index/random_access_index.hpp>
#include <boost/multi_index/member.hpp>
#include <iostream>
#include <string>

struct person
{
  std::string name;
  int age;

  person(const std::string &n, int a) : name(n), age(a) {}
};

typedef boost::multi_index::multi_index_container<
  person,
  boost::multi_index::indexed_by<
    boost::multi_index::sequenced<>,
    boost::multi_index::ordered_non_unique<
      boost::multi_index::member<
        person, int, &person::age
      >
    >,
    boost::multi_index::random_access<>
  >
> person_multi;

int main()
{
```

```
person_multi persons;

persons.push_back(person("Boris", 31));
persons.push_back(person("Anton", 31));
persons.push_back(person("Caesar", 25));

const person_multi::nth_index<1>::type &ordered_index =
  persons.get<1>();
person_multi::nth_index<1>::type::iterator lower =
  ordered_index.lower_bound(30);
person_multi::nth_index<1>::type::iterator upper =
  ordered_index.upper_bound(40);
for (; lower != upper; ++lower)
  std::cout << lower->name << std::endl;

const person_multi::nth_index<2>::type &random_access_index =
  persons.get<2>();
std::cout << random_access_index[2].name << std::endl;
}
```

The interface `boost::multi_index::sequenced` allows you to treat a MultiIndex container as a list like `std::list`. The interface is fairly simply to use when defining the container: no template parameters need to be passed. The objects of type `person` are stored in the given order.

With the interface `boost::multi_index::ordered_non_unique`, objects are automatically sorted. This interface requires that you specify a sorting criterion when defining the container. Example 13.9 sorts objects of type `person` by age using the helper class `boost::multi_index::member`.

`boost::multi_index::ordered_non_unique` provides special member functions to find specific ranges within the sorted values. Using `lower_bound()` and `upper_bound()`, the program searches for people who are older than 30 and younger than 40 years. These member functions are not provided by other interfaces because they require values to be sorted.

The final interface introduced is `boost::multi_index::random_access`, which allows you to treat the MultiIndex container like a vector of type `std::vector`. The two most prominent member functions are `operator[]` and `at()`.

`boost::multi_index::random_access` includes `boost::multi_index::sequenced`. With `boost::multi_index::random_access`, all member functions of `boost::multi_index::sequenced` are available as well.

After covering the four interfaces of Boost.MultiIndex, the remainder of this section focuses on "key extractors". One of the key extractors has already been introduced: `boost::multi_index::member`, which is defined in `boost/multi_index/member.hpp`. This helper class is called a key extractor because it allows you to explicitly specify which member variable of a class should be used as the key of an interface.

Example 13.10 introduces two more key extractors.

Example 13.10

```cpp
#include <boost/multi_index_container.hpp>
#include <boost/multi_index/ordered_index.hpp>
#include <boost/multi_index/hashed_index.hpp>
#include <boost/multi_index/identity.hpp>
#include <boost/multi_index/mem_fun.hpp>
#include <iostream>
#include <string>

class person
{
public:
  person(const std::string &n, int a) : name(n), age(a) {}
  bool operator<(const person &p) const { return age < p.age; }
  std::string get_name() const { return name; }

private:
  std::string name;
  int age;
};

typedef boost::multi_index::multi_index_container<
  person,
  boost::multi_index::indexed_by<
    boost::multi_index::ordered_unique<
      boost::multi_index::identity<person>
    >,
    boost::multi_index::hashed_unique<
      boost::multi_index::const_mem_fun<
        person, std::string, &person::get_name
      >
    >
  >
> person_multi;

int main()
{
  person_multi persons;

  persons.insert(person("Boris", 31));
  persons.insert(person("Anton", 31));
  persons.insert(person("Caesar", 25));

  std::cout << persons.begin()->get_name() << std::endl;

  const person_multi::nth_index<1>::type &hashed_index = persons.get<1>();
  std::cout << hashed_index.count("Boris") << std::endl;
}
```

The key extractor boost::multi_index::identity, defined in boost/multi_index/identity.hpp, uses values stored in the container as keys. This requires the class person to be sortable because objects of type person will be used as the key for the interface boost::multi_index::ordered_unique. In Example 13.10, this is achieved through the overloaded operator<.

The header file `boost/multi_index/mem_fun.hpp` defines two key extractors, `boost::multi_index::const_mem_fun` and `boost::multi_index::mem_fun`, which use the return value of a member function as a key. In Example 13.10, the return value of `get_name()` is used that way. `boost::multi_index::const_mem_fun` is used for constant member functions, while `boost::multi_index::mem_fun` is used for non-constant member functions.

Boost.MultiIndex offers two more key extractors: `boost::multi_index::global_fun` and `boost::multi_index::composite_key`. While the former can be used for free-standing or static member functions, the latter allows you to design a key extractor made up of several other key extractors.

Boost.Bimap

The library Boost.Bimap[4] is based on Boost.MultiIndex and provides a container that can be used immediately without being defined first. The container is similar to `std::map`, but supports looking up values from either side. Consider Example 13.11.

Example 13.11

```
#include <boost/bimap.hpp>
#include <iostream>
#include <string>

int main()
{
  typedef boost::bimap<std::string, int> bimap;
  bimap persons;

  persons.insert(bimap::value_type("Boris", 31));
  persons.insert(bimap::value_type("Anton", 31));
  persons.insert(bimap::value_type("Caesar", 25));

  std::cout << persons.left.count("Boris") << std::endl;
  std::cout << persons.right.count(31) << std::endl;
}
```

`boost::bimap` is defined in `boost/bimap.hpp` and provides two member variables, **left** and **right**, which can be used to access the two containers of type `std::map` that are unified by `boost::bimap`. While **left** accesses the container using keys of type `std::string`, **right** uses keys of type `int`.

Besides supporting access to the individual records using a left or right container, `boost::bimap` allows you to view records as relations (see Example 13.12).

_____

[4] http://www.boost.org/libs/bimap/

Example 13.12

```
#include <boost/bimap.hpp>
#include <iostream>
#include <string>

int main()
{
  typedef boost::bimap<std::string, int> bimap;
  bimap persons;

  persons.insert(bimap::value_type("Boris", 31));
  persons.insert(bimap::value_type("Anton", 31));
  persons.insert(bimap::value_type("Caesar", 25));

  for (bimap::iterator it = persons.begin(); it != persons.end(); ++it)
    std::cout << it->left << " is " << it->right << " years old."
    << std::endl;
}
```

It is not necessary to access records using **left** or **right**. By iterating over records, the left and right parts of an individual record are available through the iterator as well.

While std::map is accompanied by a container called std::multimap, which can store multiple records using the same key, there is no such equivalent for boost::bimap. However, this does not mean that storing multiple records with the same key inside a container of type boost::bimap is impossible. Strictly speaking, the two required template parameters specify container types for **left** and **right**, not the data types to store. If no container type is specified, as in Example 13.12, the container type boost::bimaps::set_of is used by default which, like std::map, only accepts records with unique keys.

Example 13.12 can be rewritten as shown in Example 13.13.

Example 13.13

```
#include <boost/bimap.hpp>
#include <iostream>
#include <string>

int main()
{
  typedef boost::bimap<boost::bimaps::set_of<std::string>,
    boost::bimaps::set_of<int> > bimap;
  bimap persons;

  persons.insert(bimap::value_type("Boris", 31));
  persons.insert(bimap::value_type("Anton", 31));
  persons.insert(bimap::value_type("Caesar", 25));

  std::cout << persons.left.count("Boris") << std::endl;
  std::cout << persons.right.count(31) << std::endl;
}
```

Example 13.14

```
#include <boost/bimap.hpp>
#include <boost/bimap/multiset_of.hpp>
#include <iostream>
#include <string>

int main()
{
  typedef boost::bimap<boost::bimaps::set_of<std::string>,
    boost::bimaps::multiset_of<int> > bimap;
  bimap persons;

  persons.insert(bimap::value_type("Boris", 31));
  persons.insert(bimap::value_type("Anton", 31));
  persons.insert(bimap::value_type("Caesar", 25));

  std::cout << persons.left.count("Boris") << std::endl;
  std::cout << persons.right.count(31) << std::endl;
}
```

Besides `boost::bimaps::set_of`, other container types exist to customize `boost::bimap`. Example 13.14 uses the container type `boost::bimaps::multiset_of`, which is defined in `boost/bimap/multiset_of.hpp`. It works like `boost::bimaps::set_of`, except that keys don't need to be unique. Therefore, Example 13.14 will display 2 when searching for persons of age 31.

Because `boost::bimaps::set_of` is used for containers of type `boost::bimap` by default, the header file `boost/bimap/set_of.hpp` does not need to be included explicitly. However, when using other container types, the corresponding header files must be included.

In addition to the ones shown above, Boost.Bimap provides the following classes: `boost::bimaps::unordered_set_of`, `boost::bimaps::unordered_multiset_of`, `boost::bimaps::list_of`, `boost::bimaps::vector_of`, and `boost::bimaps::unconstrained_set_of`. Except for `boost::bimaps::unconstrained_set_of`, all other container types operate just like their counterparts from the C++ standard or from Boost.Unordered.

`boost::bimaps::unconstrained_set_of` can be used to disable one side of `boost::bimap`. In Example 13.15, `boost::bimap` behaves like `std::map`. It's impossible to access **right** to search for persons by age.

Example 13.15 also shows why it can make sense to prefer `boost::bimap` over `std::map`. Since Boost.Bimap is based on Boost.MultiIndex, member functions known from Boost.MultiIndex are available as well. Example 13.15 modifies a key using `modify_key()` - something which is not possible with `std::map`.

Example 13.15

```cpp
#include <boost/bimap.hpp>
#include <boost/bimap/unconstrained_set_of.hpp>
#include <boost/bimap/support/lambda.hpp>
#include <iostream>
#include <string>

int main()
{
  typedef boost::bimap<std::string,
    boost::bimaps::unconstrained_set_of<int> > bimap;
  bimap persons;

  persons.insert(bimap::value_type("Boris", 31));
  persons.insert(bimap::value_type("Anton", 31));
  persons.insert(bimap::value_type("Caesar", 25));

  bimap::left_map::iterator it = persons.left.find("Boris");
  persons.left.modify_key(it, boost::bimaps::_key = "Doris");

  std::cout << it->first << std::endl;
}
```

Please note how the key is modified in detail. A new value is assigned to the current key using **boost::bimaps::_key**, which is a "lambda" function that is defined in boost/bimap/support/lambda.hpp.

boost/bimap/support/lambda.hpp also defines **boost::bimaps::_data**. The member function modify_data() modifies a value in a container of type boost::bimap.

Boost.CircularBuffer

The library Boost.CircularBuffer[5] implements a circular buffer. It is a container with the following two fundamental properties:

► The capacity of the buffer is constant and is specified by the developer. The maximum size of the buffer does not change automatically. While a circular buffer is comparable to std::vector, the vector will not increase beyond this maximum size on its own.

► Like std::vector, push_back() can be called an arbitrary number of times to store data in the buffer. Because the size of the buffer does not change when push_back() is called, data will be overwritten once the maximum size is reached.

A circular buffer makes sense when the amount of available memory is limited and a container should be prevented from growing arbitrarily big. Another example is continuous data flow where old data is irrelevant as new data becomes available. The available memory is automatically reused by overwriting old data.

---

[5] http://www.boost.org/libs/circular_buffer/

To use Boost.CircularBuffer, include the header file `boost/circular_buffer.hpp`. This header file defines the class `boost::circular_buffer`.

Example 13.16

```
#include <boost/circular_buffer.hpp>
#include <iostream>

int main()
{
  typedef boost::circular_buffer<int> circular_buffer;
  circular_buffer cb(3);

  std::cout << cb.capacity() << std::endl;
  std::cout << cb.size() << std::endl;

  cb.push_back(0);
  cb.push_back(1);
  cb.push_back(2);

  std::cout << cb.size() << std::endl;

  cb.push_back(3);
  cb.push_back(4);
  cb.push_back(5);

  std::cout << cb.size() << std::endl;

  for (circular_buffer::iterator it = cb.begin(); it != cb.end(); ++it)
    std::cout << *it << std::endl;
}
```

`boost::circular_buffer` is a template and must be instantiated with a data type. For instance, the circular buffer **cb** in Example 13.16 stores numbers of type `int`.

The capacity of the circular buffer is specified when instantiating the class, not through a template parameter. The default constructor of `boost::circular_buffer` creates a buffer with a capacity of zero elements, but another constructor is available to set the capacity. In Example 13.16, the buffer **cb** has a capacity of three elements.

The capacity of a circular buffer can be queried by calling `capacity()`. In Example 13.16, `capacity()` will return 3.

The capacity is not equivalent to the number of stored elements. While the return value of `capacity()` is constant, `size()` returns the number of elements in the buffer, which may be different. Thus, the return value of `size()` will always be between 0 and the capacity of the circular buffer.

Example 13.16 returns 0 the first time `size()` is called since the buffer does not contain any data. After calling `push_back()` three times, the buffer contains three elements, and the second call to `size()` will return 3. Calling `push_back()` again does not cause the buffer to grow. The three new numbers simply overwrite the previous three. Therefore, `size()` will return 3 when called for the third time.

As a verification, the stored numbers are written to the standard output stream at the end of Example 13.16. The output contains the numbers 3, 4, and 5 since the previously stored numbers have been overwritten.

Example 13.17

```cpp
#include <boost/circular_buffer.hpp>
#include <iostream>

int main()
{
  typedef boost::circular_buffer<int> circular_buffer;
  circular_buffer cb(3);

  cb.push_back(0);
  cb.push_back(1);
  cb.push_back(2);
  cb.push_back(3);

  std::cout << cb.is_linearized() << std::endl;

  circular_buffer::array_range ar1, ar2;

  ar1 = cb.array_one();
  ar2 = cb.array_two();
  std::cout << ar1.second << ", " << ar2.second << std::endl;

  for (circular_buffer::iterator it = cb.begin(); it != cb.end(); ++it)
    std::cout << *it << std::endl;

  cb.linearize();

  ar1 = cb.array_one();
  ar2 = cb.array_two();
  std::cout << ar1.second << ", " << ar2.second << std::endl;
}
```

Example 13.17 uses the member functions is_linearized(), array_one(), array_two(), and linearize(), which do not exist in other containers. These member functions clarify the internals of the circular buffer.

As previously mentioned, the circular buffer is essentially comparable to std::vector. Because the beginning and end of a vector are well-defined, it can be treated as a conventional C array. That is, memory is contiguous and the first and the last element are always at the lowest and highest memory address. However, a circular buffer does not offer such a guarantee.

Even though it may sound strange to talk about the beginning and end of a circular buffer, they do exist. Elements can be accessed via iterators, and boost::circular_buffer provides member functions such as begin() and end(). While one doesn't need to care about the position of the beginning and end when using iterators, it becomes a bit more complicated when accessing elements using regular pointers, unless is_linearized(), array_one(), array_two(), and linearize() are used.

The member function `is_linearized()` returns `true` if the beginning of the circular buffer is at the lowest memory address. In this case, all the elements in the buffer are stored consecutively from beginning to the end at increasing memory addresses. Therefore, elements can be accessed just like in a conventional C array.

If `is_linearized()` returns `false`, the beginning of the circular buffer is not at the lowest memory address, which is the case in Example 13.17. While the first three elements 0, 1, and 2 are stored in exactly this order, calling `push_back()` for the fourth time will overwrite the number 0 with the number 4. Because 4 is the last element added by a call to `push_back()`, it is now the new end of the circular buffer. The beginning is now the element that contains the number 1, which is stored at the next higher memory address. This means elements are no longer stored consecutively at increasing memory addresses.

If the end of the circular buffer is at a lower memory address than the beginning, the elements can be accessed via two conventional C arrays. To avoid calculating the position and size of each array, `boost::circular_buffer` provides the member functions `array_one()` and `array_two()`.

Both `array_one()` and `array_two()` return a `std::pair` whose first element is a pointer to the corresponding array and second element is the size. `array_one()` accesses the array at the beginning of the circular buffer, and `array_two()` accesses the array at the end of the buffer.

If the circular buffer is linearized (`is_linearized()` returns `true`), `array_two()` can be called, too. However, since there is only one array in the buffer, the second array contains no elements.

To simplify matters and treat the circular buffer as a conventional C array, a rearrangement of the elements can be forced by calling `linearize()`. Once complete, all stored elements can be accessed using `array_one()` with no need to call `array_two()`.

Boost.CircularBuffer offers an additional class that creates a circular buffer called `boost::circular_buffer_space_optimized`. This class is also defined in `boost/circular_buffer.hpp`. Although, `boost::circular_buffer_space_optimized` is used the same way as `boost::circular_buffer`, it does not reserve any memory at instantiation. Rather, memory is allocated dynamically when elements are added until the capacity is reached. Removing elements releases memory accordingly. `boost::circular_buffer_space_optimized` manages memory efficiently and therefore can be a better choice in certain scenarios, for example, if you have a circular buffer with a large capacity that may not be needed entirely by a program.

Boost.Intrusive

Boost.Intrusive[6] is a library especially suited for high-performance applications. It provides tools to create "intrusive" containers, which can replace existing containers from the C++ standard. Intrusive containers are harder to use compared with containers like `std::list` or `std::set`. However, they do provide some advantages:

▶ Intrusive containers do not reserve dynamic memory, so calling `push_back()` does not result in dynamic allocation of memory using `new`. This is one way they can increase performance.

---

[6] http://www.boost.org/libs/intrusive/

▶ Intrusive containers use the original object, not a copy, so no memory is allocated. This provides another advantage. Because memory is not allocated, and objects are not copied, member functions like push_back() cannot throw an exception. Failed memory allocations or issues while copying objects cannot occur with intrusive containers.

The advantages are gained by more complex code, which requires preconditions to store objects of particular data types in intrusive containers. You cannot store objects of arbitrary data types in intrusive containers. For example, strings of type std::string cannot be stored in intrusive containers. To do this, one of the containers from the C++ standard must be used.

Example 13.18

```
#include <boost/intrusive/list.hpp>
#include <string>
#include <iostream>

struct person :
  public boost::intrusive::list_base_hook<>
{
  std::string name_;
  int age_;

  person(std::string name, int age) : name_(name), age_(age) {}
};

int main()
{
  person p1("Anton", 30);
  person p2("Boris", 33);
  person p3("Carl", 28);

  typedef boost::intrusive::list<person> person_list;
  person_list pl;

  pl.push_back(p1);
  pl.push_back(p2);
  pl.push_back(p3);

  p3.name_ = "David";

  for (person_list::iterator it = pl.begin(); it != pl.end(); ++it)
    std::cout << it->name_ << std::endl;
}
```

Example 13.18 prepares a class person to be stored inside an intrusive list. A list provides a mechanism to access the next element after any given element in the list. This is usually implemented with pointers. To store objects of type person in an intrusive list without allocating memory dynamically, a pointer still needs to exist to point from one element to the next.

Storing objects of type person requires the class itself to provide variables that allow the intrusive list to chain elements. This is achieved by deriving from hooks – classes provided by Boost.Intrusive – that contain the necessary variables. In order to be managed by an intrusive list, person needs to be derived from boost::intrusive::list_base_hook. This mechanism makes it possible to hide the exact requirements for an intrusive list. Nevertheless, one can assume that boost::intrusive::list_base_hook contains at least two pointers because boost::intrusive::list is a doubly-linked list. Thanks to the parent class boost::intrusive::list, these two pointers are provided by person so that objects of this type can now be chained appropriately.

boost::intrusive::list_base_hook is a template. Because it provides default values for all parameters, there is no need to pass it any parameters.

Boost.Intrusive provides the class boost::intrusive::list to create an intrusive list which can be used the same way as std::list. Values can be added with push_back() and iterated through iterators.

It is important to understand that intrusive containers store the original objects and not copies. Example 13.18 writes the names Anton, Boris, and David to the standard output stream, not the name Carl. The object **p3** itself is linked to the list causing the name change to be visible when iterating over the list.

Because intrusive containers do not store copies, objects must be explicitly removed from the container once destroyed.

Example 13.19

```cpp
#include <boost/intrusive/list.hpp>
#include <string>
#include <iostream>

struct person :
  public boost::intrusive::list_base_hook<>
{
  std::string name_;
  int age_;

  person(std::string name, int age) : name_(name), age_(age) {}
};

int main()
{
  person p1("Anton", 30);
  person p2("Boris", 33);
  person *p3 = new person("Carl", 28);

  typedef boost::intrusive::list<person> person_list;
  person_list pl;

  pl.push_back(p1);
  pl.push_back(p2);
  pl.push_back(*p3);

  for (person_list::iterator it = pl.begin(); it != pl.end(); ++it)
    std::cout << it->name_ << std::endl;

  pl.pop_back();
  delete p3;
}
```

Example 13.19 creates an object of type person with new and adds it to the list **pl**. To delete this object with delete it must be removed from the list. It is important to remove the object from the list before destroying it to keep the container from accessing invalid memory.

Because intrusive containers neither allocate nor release memory, objects managed by a container continue to exist even if the container is destroyed.

Since objects removed from an intrusive container are not automatically destroyed, additional member functions are provided. One of them is pop_back_and_dispose().

Example 13.20

```cpp
#include <boost/intrusive/list.hpp>
#include <string>
#include <iostream>

struct person :
  public boost::intrusive::list_base_hook<>
{
  std::string name_;
  int age_;

  person(std::string name, int age) : name_(name), age_(age) {}
};

void dispose(person *p)
{
  delete p;
}

int main()
{
  person p1("Anton", 30);
  person p2("Boris", 33);
  person *p3 = new person("Carl", 28);

  typedef boost::intrusive::list<person> person_list;
  person_list pl;

  pl.push_back(p1);
  pl.push_back(p2);
  pl.push_back(*p3);

  for (person_list::iterator it = pl.begin(); it != pl.end(); ++it)
    std::cout << it->name_ << std::endl;

  pl.pop_back_and_dispose(dispose);
}
```

As the name implies, pop_back_and_dispose() removes an element from the list and destroys it. Since intrusive containers do not know how to destroy a particular element, pop_back_and_dispose() expects a function or function object as a parameter. The member function calls this function or function object and passes a pointer to the object to be destroyed. Example 13.20 calls dispose(), which simply calls delete.

Only the third element in **p1** should be removed via pop_back_and_dispose(). The remaining elements in the list have not been created with new and therefore cannot be destroyed with delete.

Boost.Intrusive offers another possibility to combine the removal and destruction of elements.

Example 13.21

```cpp
#include <boost/intrusive/list.hpp>
#include <string>
#include <iostream>

typedef boost::intrusive::link_mode<boost::intrusive::auto_unlink>
  auto_unlink;

struct person :
  public boost::intrusive::list_base_hook<auto_unlink>
{
  std::string name_;
  int age_;

  person(std::string name, int age) : name_(name), age_(age) {}
};

int main()
{
  person p1("Anton", 30);
  person p2("Boris", 33);
  person *p3 = new person("Carl", 28);

  typedef boost::intrusive::constant_time_size<false> constant_time_size;
  typedef boost::intrusive::list<person, constant_time_size> person_list;
  person_list pl;

  pl.push_back(p1);
  pl.push_back(p2);
  pl.push_back(*p3);

  delete p3;

  for (person_list::iterator it = pl.begin(); it != pl.end(); ++it)
    std::cout << it->name_ << std::endl;
}
```

Hook classes can be passed a parameter to activate the "auto unlink" mode. For that purpose, the class boost::intrusive::link_mode is accessed, which is a template that expects one parameter. Passing boost::intrusive::auto_unlink causes auto unlink mode to be activated.

In auto unlink mode, elements are automatically removed from the intrusive container once they are destroyed. That's why Example 13.21 only writes the names Anton and Boris to the standard output stream.

The auto unlink mode can only be used if the member function size(), provided by all intrusive containers, does not exhibit constant complexity. By default, this member function exhibits a constant complexity, which means that no matter how many elements are stored in the container, the number of elements is always calculated in constant time. This is another option to optimize performance.

To modify the complexity of size(), you must use the class boost::intrusive::constant_time_size, which is a template that expects either true or false as a parameter. boost::intrusive::constant_time_size can be passed as the second parameter to intrusive container classes such as boost::intrusive::list to control the complexity of the member function size().

So far, two new concepts have been introduced: intrusive containers that support link modes and configuration options for the complexity of the member function size(). Even though this may indicate that Boost.Intrusive offers a lot of configuration options, there is not much more to discover. There are actually three different link modes available but only auto link mode is really worth knowing. The default mode, which is used when no link mode is specified, is a good choice in all other cases.

Intrusive containers do not offer any configuration options for other member functions. Besides boost::intrusive::constant_time_size, there are no classes worth knowing.

The last example for Boost.Intrusive (see Example 13.22) introduces another hook mechanism, and also uses boost::intrusive::set as a different intrusive container.

Example 13.22

```cpp
#include <boost/intrusive/set.hpp>
#include <string>
#include <iostream>

struct person
{
  std::string name_;
  int age_;
  boost::intrusive::set_member_hook<> set_hook_;

  person(std::string name, int age) : name_(name), age_(age) {}

  bool operator<(const person &p) const
  {
    return age_ < p.age_;
  }
};

int main()
{
  person p1("Anton", 30);
  person p2("Boris", 33);
  person p3("Carl", 28);

  typedef boost::intrusive::member_hook<person,
    boost::intrusive::set_member_hook<>, &person::set_hook_>
    person_member_hook;
  typedef boost::intrusive::set<person, person_member_hook> person_set;
  person_set ps;

  ps.insert(p1);
```

```
  ps.insert(p2);
  ps.insert(p3);

  for (person_set::iterator it = ps.begin(); it != ps.end(); ++it)
    std::cout << it->name_ << std::endl;
}
```

Strictly speaking, Boost.Intrusive offers two alternatives for supplying a class with a hook. It can derive the class from a hook class or use a hook class to define a member variable. While the previous examples derived from `boost::intrusive::list_base_hook`, Example 13.22 uses `boost::intrusive::set_member_hook` to define a member variable.

Please note that the name of the member variable does not really matter. However, for every intrusive container, a different hook class must be used. For example, the hook class to define a member variable for an intrusive list is called `boost::intrusive::list_member_hook` instead of `boost::intrusive::set_member_hook`.

The reason for the different hook classes is that each container imposes different requirements on values to be stored. It is possible to use multiple hook classes to store values in different intrusive containers at the same time. With `boost::intrusive::any_base_hook` and `boost::intrusive::any_member_hook`, classes are available that make it possible to store objects in any intrusive container without having to derive them from multiple hook classes or define multiple member variables as hooks.

By default, intrusive containers expect hooks to be defined in parent classes. If a member variable is used to define a hook, the intrusive container must be told explicitly. This is the reason for passing not only `person` as parameter to `boost::intrusive::set`, but also the type `person_member_hook`. The type is defined with the aid of `boost::intrusive::member_hook`, which is used whenever intrusive containers need to use a member variable as a hook. The class name of the value to be stored in the container, the data type of the hook, and a pointer to the corresponding member variable must be passed as parameters to `boost::intrusive::member_hook`.

Example 13.22 writes the names `Carl`, `Anton`, and `Boris` successively to the standard output stream.

Besides `boost::intrusive::list` and `boost::intrusive::set`, Boost.Intrusive provides additional, specialized, intrusive containers such as `boost::intrusive::slist` for singly-linked lists and `boost::intrusive::unordered_set` for hash containers.

Boost.MultiArray

The library Boost.MultiArray[7] simplifies managing multidimensional arrays by providing an interface similar to the containers from the C++ standard. Member functions such as `begin()` and `end()` are available to access elements via iterators, avoiding the need to use pointers, which can be confusing for arrays with multiple dimensions.

However, to introduce the basic principles of Boost.MultiArray, Example 13.23 uses a one-dimensional array first.

Example 13.23

```
#include <boost/multi_array.hpp>
#include <iostream>

int main()
{
  boost::multi_array<char, 1> a(boost::extents[6]);

  a[0] = 'H';
  a[1] = 'e';
  a[2] = 'l';
  a[3] = 'l';
  a[4] = 'o';
  a[5] = '\0';

  std::cout << a.origin() << std::endl;
}
```

To create arrays with Boost.MultiArray, use the class `boost::multi_array`, defined in `boost/multi_array.hpp`. This is the main class provided by this library.

`boost::multi_array` is a template expecting two parameters: the first parameter specifies the data type to be used by the array, and the second one specifies the number of dimensions.

The second parameter only specifies the number of dimensions, not the number of elements per dimension. Therefore, Example 13.23 declares a one-dimensional array **a**.

The number of elements per dimension is specified at run-time using the global object **boost::extents**, passed to the constructor of **a**.

In general, objects of type `boost::multi_array` can be treated like conventional C arrays that allow elements to be accessed by an index using `[]`. The one-dimensional array in the example stores six values: five characters followed by a terminating 0. The member function `origin()` returns a pointer to the first element, which can be used to print the word `Hello`.

Unlike the containers from the C++ standard, `[]` checks whether an index is valid. If the index is invalid, the program is terminated using `std::abort()`. To skip verification, the macro `BOOST_DISABLE_ASSERTS` must be defined before including `boost/multi_array.hpp`.

---

[7] http://www.boost.org/libs/multi_array/

Example 13.24

```
#include <boost/multi_array.hpp>
#include <algorithm>
#include <iostream>
#include <cstring>

int main()
{
  boost::multi_array<char, 2> a(boost::extents[2][9]);

  typedef boost::multi_array<char, 2>::array_view<1>::type array_view;
  typedef boost::multi_array_types::index_range range;
  array_view view = a[boost::indices[0][range(0, 5)]];

  std::memcpy(view.origin(), "olleH", 6);
  std::reverse(view.begin(), view.end());

  std::cout << view.origin() << std::endl;

  boost::multi_array<char, 2>::reference subarray = a[1];
  std::memcpy(subarray.origin(), ", world!", 9);

  std::cout << subarray.origin() << std::endl;
}
```

Example 13.24 creates a two-dimensional array with 2 elements in the first dimension and 9 elements in the second dimension. The array can be imagined as a table consisting of two rows and nine columns.

In order to store the word "Hello" in the first row of the table, a "view" containing exactly 5 elements of the complete array is created.

Views are based on the class boost::multi_array::array_view, a data type dependent on boost::multi_array. With a view, a particular section of an array can be accessed and treated like an independent array.

boost::multi_array::array_view is a template that expects the number of dimensions of the view as a parameter. Even though the array **a** consists of two dimensions in the example, the newly created view will ignore one dimension because 1 is passed as parameter. To store the word "Hello", a one-dimensional array is sufficient – additional dimensions would only confuse.

While the number of dimensions is specified as a template parameter, the expansion of each dimension must be specified at run-time. Rather than using **boost::extents**, boost::multi_array::array_view uses another global object called **boost::indices**.

Like **boost::extents**, **boost::indices** requires indices. Compared to **boost::extents**, which only accepts numbers, **boost::indices** also accepts ranges which are defined with boost::multi_array_types::index_range.

The first parameter passed to **boost::indices** is not a range, but the number 0. If you pass in a single number, boost::multi_array_types::index_range must not be used.

boost::indices creates a view that contains only the first element from all the elements available in the first dimension of **a** – the one with the index 0.

To specify a range for the second parameter, use boost::multi_array_types::index_range. By passing 0 and 5 to the constructor, the first five elements of the second dimension of the array **a** are accessed. The range is interpreted as starting at index 0 and ending at index 5, but index 5 does not belong to the range. The remaining four elements of the second dimension are ignored.

The view **view** represents a one-dimensional array containing the first five elements of the first row of the array **a**. However, this relation becomes irrelevant when **view** is accessed and the string is copied and reversed with std::memcpy() and std::reverse(). Once created, a view allows easy access to a section of a bigger array, acting like a regular array.

If an array of type boost::multi_array is directly accessed via [], the return value depends on the number of dimensions. Because the array in Example 13.23 was one-dimensional, individual elements of type char could be accessed directly.

However, **a** in Example 13.24 is a two-dimensional array. When accessed using the [] operator, a subarray is returned rather than elements of type char. Because Boost.MultiArray does not disclose the corresponding data type of the subarray, boost::multi_array::reference, which is not of type boost::multi_array::array_view, must be used even though a subarray essentially behaves like a view. Whereas a subarray contains all elements of each dimension and is automatically returned from a call to [], a view must be explicitly defined and can contain an arbitrary section of an array.

Example 13.25

```
#include <boost/multi_array.hpp>
#include <algorithm>
#include <iostream>
#include <cstring>

int main()
{
  char c[18] =
  {
    'o', 'l', 'l', 'e', 'H', '\0', '\0', '\0', '\0',
    ',', ' ', 'w', 'o', 'r', 'l', 'd', '!', '\0'
  };

  boost::multi_array_ref<char, 2> a(c, boost::extents[2][9]);

  typedef boost::multi_array<char, 2>::array_view<1>::type array_view;
  typedef boost::multi_array_types::index_range range;
  array_view view = a[boost::indices[0][range(0, 5)]];

  std::reverse(view.begin(), view.end());
  std::cout << view.origin() << std::endl;

  boost::multi_array<char, 2>::reference subarray = a[1];
  std::cout << subarray.origin() << std::endl;
}
```

To treat an ordinary C array as a MultiArray, Boost.MultiArray provides the class `boost::multi_array_ref`. In Example 13.25, the variable **a** provides the interface from `boost::multi_array` without reserving any memory. `boost::multi_array_ref` allows you to treat an ordinary C array, no matter how many dimensions it has, as a multi-dimensional array of type `boost::multi_array` by simply passing it as an additional parameter to the constructor.

Besides `boost::multi_array_ref`, `boost::const_multi_array_ref` can be used to treat any ordinary C array as a constant multi-dimensional one.

Exercises

1. Develop a program that associates employees with departments in a company. Store some sample records and search through them to identify the department of a particular employee, as well as the number of employees working in a particular department.

2. Extend the program by associating numbers to employees. These numbers must be unique to be sure employees with the same name are identified unambiguously. Search through the sample records to display an employee's data using a specific number.

14

Data Structures

General

There are many Boost C++ Libraries for which the definition of a container does not apply. These libraries were not presented in Chapter 13, *Containers*, and instead are introduced in this chapter.

This chapter covers the classes `boost::tuple`, `boost::any`, `boost::variant`, and `boost::dynamic_bitset`. `boost::tuple` is a generalization of `std::pair` that supports an arbitrary number of values, rather than just two. Variables of type `boost::any` behave like variables in typeless programming languages and can store any information. Variables of type `boost::variant` store information using predetermined data types and are similar to a `union`. `boost::dynamic_bitset` is similar to `std::bitset`, but supports setting the size – the number of bits – at run-time.

Boost.Tuple

The library Boost.Tuple[1] provides a class called `boost::tuple`, which is a generalized version of `std::pair`. While `std::pair` can store exactly two values, `boost::tuple` lets the user choose how many values should be stored.

To use `boost::tuple`, include the header file `boost/tuple/tuple.hpp`. To use tuples with streams, include the header file `boost/tuple/tuple_io.hpp`. Boost.Tuple doesn't provide one header file which automatically includes all others.

---

[1] http://www.boost.org/libs/tuple/

Example 14.1

```
#include <boost/tuple/tuple.hpp>
#include <boost/tuple/tuple_io.hpp>
#include <string>
#include <iostream>

int main()
{
  typedef boost::tuple<std::string, std::string> person;
  person p("Boris", "Schaeling");
  std::cout << p << std::endl;
}
```

boost::tuple is used in the same way std::pair is. As seen in Example 14.1, two values of type std::string are stored by specifying two template arguments.

While the definition of type person could have used std::pair, objects of type boost::tuple can also be written to a stream. To do this you must include the header file boost/tuple/tuple_io.hpp, which provides all the required operators. When executed, Example 14.1 displays (Boris Schaeling).

The important difference between boost::tuple and std::pair is that you can use tuples to store a virtually unlimited number of values.

Example 14.2

```
#include <boost/tuple/tuple.hpp>
#include <boost/tuple/tuple_io.hpp>
#include <string>
#include <iostream>

int main()
{
  typedef boost::tuple<std::string, std::string, int> person;
  person p("Boris", "Schaeling", 43);
  std::cout << p << std::endl;
}
```

Example 14.2 stores the shoe size of a person and his or her first and last name. All three values are placed in a tuple. When executed, this program displays (Boris Schaeling 43).

You can create a tuple using the helper function boost::make_tuple(), which works like the helper function std::make_pair() for std::pair (see Example 14.3).

Example 14.3

```
#include <boost/tuple/tuple.hpp>
#include <boost/tuple/tuple_io.hpp>
#include <iostream>

int main()
{
  std::cout << boost::make_tuple("Boris", "Schaeling", 43) << std::endl;
}
```

A tuple can also contain references, as shown in Example 14.4.

Example 14.4

```
#include <boost/tuple/tuple.hpp>
#include <boost/tuple/tuple_io.hpp>
#include <string>
#include <iostream>

int main()
{
  std::string s = "Boris";
  std::cout << boost::make_tuple(boost::ref(s), "Schaeling", 43)
    << std::endl;
}
```

"Schaeling" and 43 are passed by value and thus are stored inside the tuple directly, However, the first element is a reference to the string **s**. The function `boost::ref()` from Boost.Ref is used to create the reference. To create a constant reference, use `boost::cref()`.

Now that we have created our tuples, let's look at how to access elements. `std::pair` uses the member variables **first** and **second** to provide access. Because a tuple does not have a fixed number of elements, access must be handled differently.

Example 14.5

```
#include <boost/tuple/tuple.hpp>
#include <string>
#include <iostream>

int main()
{
  typedef boost::tuple<std::string, std::string, int> person;
  person p = boost::make_tuple("Boris", "Schaeling", 43);
  std::cout << p.get<0>() << std::endl;
  std::cout << boost::get<0>(p) << std::endl;
}
```

There are two ways to access values in a tuple. You can call the member function `get()`, or you can pass the tuple to the free-standing function `boost::get()`. In both cases, the index of the corresponding element in the tuple must be provided as a template parameter. Example 14.5 accesses the first element of the tuple **p** in both cases and thus displays `Boris` twice.

Specifying an invalid index will result in a compiler error because validity of indexes is checked at compile time.

To modify a value inside a tuple, use either the member function `get()` or the free-standing function `boost::get()`.

Example 14.6

```
#include <boost/tuple/tuple.hpp>
#include <boost/tuple/tuple_io.hpp>
#include <string>
#include <iostream>

int main()
{
  typedef boost::tuple<std::string, std::string, int> person;
  person p = boost::make_tuple("Boris", "Schaeling", 43);
  p.get<1>() = "Becker";
  std::cout << p << std::endl;
}
```

Both `boost::tuple::get()` and `boost::get()` return a reference. Example 14.6 modifies the last name and thus displays (Boris Becker 43).

Not only overloads Boost.Tuple operators to use tuples with streams, but it also defines comparison operators. To compare tuples, include the header file `boost/tuple/tuple_comparison.hpp`.

Example 14.7

```
#include <boost/tuple/tuple.hpp>
#include <boost/tuple/tuple_comparison.hpp>
#include <string>
#include <iostream>

int main()
{
  typedef boost::tuple<std::string, std::string, int> person;
  person p1 = boost::make_tuple("Boris", "Schaeling", 43);
  person p2 = boost::make_tuple("Boris", "Becker", 43);
  std::cout << (p1 != p2) << std::endl;
}
```

Example 14.7 displays 1 because the tuples **p1** and **p2** are different.

The header file `boost/tuple/tuple_comparison.hpp` also contains definitions for other comparison operators such as greater-than, which performs a lexicographical comparison.

Boost.Tuple supports a specific form of tuples called "tiers." Tiers are tuples whose elements are all reference types. They can be constructed with the function `boost::tie()`.

Example 14.8

```
#include <boost/tuple/tuple.hpp>
#include <boost/tuple/tuple_io.hpp>
#include <string>
#include <iostream>

int main()
{
  typedef boost::tuple<std::string&, std::string&, int&> person;

  std::string firstname = "Boris";
  std::string surname = "Schaeling";
  int shoesize = 43;
  person p = boost::tie(firstname, surname, shoesize);
  surname = "Becker";
  std::cout << p << std::endl;
}
```

Example 14.8 creates a tier **p**, which consists of references to the variables **firstname**, **surname**, and **shoesize**. When the variable **surname** is modified, the tier is modified at the same time.

Example 14.8 could have also been written using boost::make_tuple() and boost::ref() (see Example 14.9).

Example 14.9

```
#include <boost/tuple/tuple.hpp>
#include <boost/tuple/tuple_io.hpp>
#include <string>
#include <iostream>

int main()
{
  typedef boost::tuple<std::string&, std::string&, int&> person;

  std::string firstname = "Boris";
  std::string surname = "Schaeling";
  int shoesize = 43;
  person p = boost::make_tuple(boost::ref(firstname), boost::ref(surname),
    boost::ref(shoesize));
  surname = "Becker";
  std::cout << p << std::endl;
}
```

boost::tie() simply shortens the syntax. This function can also be used to unpack tuples. In Example 14.10, the individual values of the tuple, returned by a function, are instantly stored in variables.

Example 14.10

```
#include <boost/tuple/tuple.hpp>
#include <string>
#include <iostream>

boost::tuple<std::string, int> func()
{
  return boost::make_tuple("Error message", 2011);
}

int main()
{
  std::string errmsg;
  int errcode;

  boost::tie(errmsg, errcode) = func();
  std::cout << errmsg << ": " << errcode << std::endl;
}
```

boost::tie() stores the string "Error message" and the error code 2011, both of which are re-turned as a tuple from func(), in the variables **errmsg** and **errcode**.

Boost.Any

Strongly typed languages such as C++ require that each variable has a specific data type that defines what kind of information it can store. Other languages, like Javascript, allow developers to store any kind of information in a variable. For example, in JavaScript a variable can contain a string, then a number, and afterwards a boolean value.

The library Boost.Any[2] provides the class boost::any which, like JavaScript variables, can store arbitrary types of information.

Example 14.11

```
#include <boost/any.hpp>

int main()
{
  boost::any a = 1;
  a = 3.14;
  a = true;
}
```

To use boost::any, include the header file boost/any.hpp. Objects of type boost::any can then be created to store arbitrary information.

Please note that variables of type boost::any are not completely unlimited in what they can store; Boost.Any requires certain preconditions, albeit minimal ones. Any information stored in a variable of type boost::any must be copy-constructible. Therefore, to store a character string

---

[2] http://www.boost.org/libs/any/

in a variable of type `boost::any`, `std::string` needs to be explicitly used as shown in Example 14.12.

Example 14.12

```
#include <boost/any.hpp>
#include <string>

int main()
{
  boost::any a = 1;
  a = 3.14;
  a = true;
  a = std::string("Hello, world!");
}
```

If the application tried to assign "Hello, world!" to **a** directly, the compiler would abort with an error because character strings are arrays containing elements of type `char`, which are not copy-constructible in C++.

To access the value of variables of type `boost::any`, the cast operator `boost::any_cast` must be used (see Example 14.13).

Example 14.13

```
#include <boost/any.hpp>
#include <iostream>

int main()
{
  boost::any a = 1;
  std::cout << boost::any_cast<int>(a) << std::endl;
  a = 3.14;
  std::cout << boost::any_cast<double>(a) << std::endl;
  a = true;
  std::cout << boost::any_cast<bool>(a) << std::endl;
}
```

By passing the corresponding data type as the template parameter to `boost::any_cast`, the value of the variable is converted. If an invalid data type is specified, an exception of type `boost::bad_any_cast` will be thrown.

Example 14.14

```cpp
#include <boost/any.hpp>
#include <iostream>

int main()
{
  try
  {
    boost::any a = 1;
    std::cout << boost::any_cast<float>(a) << std::endl;
  }
  catch (boost::bad_any_cast &e)
  {
    std::cerr << e.what() << std::endl;
  }
}
```

Example 14.14 throws an exception because the template parameter of type float does not match the type int stored in **a**. The program would also throw an exception if short or long were used as the template parameter.

Because boost::bad_any_cast is derived from std::bad_cast, catch handlers can catch exceptions of this type, too.

To check whether or not a variable of type boost::any contains information, use the member function empty(). To check the data type of the stored information, use the member function type().

Example 14.15

```cpp
#include <boost/any.hpp>
#include <typeinfo>
#include <iostream>

int main()
{
  boost::any a = 1;
  if (!a.empty())
  {
    const std::type_info &ti = a.type();
    std::cout << ti.name() << std::endl;
  }
}
```

Example 14.15 uses both empty() and type(). While empty() returns a boolean value, the return value of type() is of type std::type_info, which is defined in the header file typeinfo.

Example 14.16 shows how to obtain a pointer to the value stored in a variable of type boost::any using boost::any_cast. You simply pass a pointer to a variable of type boost::any to boost::any_cast; the template parameters remain unchanged.

Example 14.16

```cpp
#include <boost/any.hpp>
#include <iostream>

int main()
{
  boost::any a = 1;
  int *i = boost::any_cast<int>(&a);
  std::cout << *i << std::endl;
}
```

Boost.Variant

The difference between Boost.Variant[3] and Boost.Any is that while Boost.Any allows you to store values of any data type, Boost.Variant lets you restrict the data types for a variable to a selected set of types. Consider Example 14.17.

Example 14.17

```cpp
#include <boost/variant.hpp>

int main()
{
  boost::variant<double, char> v;
  v = 3.14;
  v = 'A';
}
```

Boost.Variant provides a class called `boost::variant`, which is defined in `boost/variant.hpp`. Because `boost::variant` is a template, at least one parameter must be specified. One or more template parameters specify the supported data types. Example 14.17 can store values of either type `double` or type `char` in `v`. If a value of type `int` were assigned to `v`, the resulting code would not compile.

While Example 14.17 could have used a `union`, `boost::variant` allows you to store data types such as `std::string`, which is not possible with unions since unions cannot contain any class members (see Example 14.18).

Example 14.18

```cpp
#include <boost/variant.hpp>
#include <string>

int main()
{
  boost::variant<double, char, std::string> v;
  v = 3.14;
  v = 'A';
  v = "Hello, world!";
}
```

---

[3] http://www.boost.org/libs/variant/

To display the stored values of **v**, use the free-standing function `boost::get()` (see Example 14.19).

Example 14.19

```cpp
#include <boost/variant.hpp>
#include <string>
#include <iostream>

int main()
{
  boost::variant<double, char, std::string> v;
  v = 3.14;
  std::cout << boost::get<double>(v) << std::endl;
  v = 'A';
  std::cout << boost::get<char>(v) << std::endl;
  v = "Hello, world!";
  std::cout << boost::get<std::string>(v) << std::endl;
}
```

`boost::get()` expects one of the valid data types for the corresponding variable as a template parameter. Specifying an invalid type will result in a run-time error because validation of data types does not take place at compile time.

Variables of type `boost::variant` can be written to streams such as the standard output stream, bypassing the hazard of run-time errors (see Example 14.20).

Example 14.20

```cpp
#include <boost/variant.hpp>
#include <string>
#include <iostream>

int main()
{
  boost::variant<double, char, std::string> v;
  v = 3.14;
  std::cout << v << std::endl;
  v = 'A';
  std::cout << v << std::endl;
  v = "Hello, world!";
  std::cout << v << std::endl;
}
```

To process values differently, Boost.Variant provides a function called `boost::apply_visitor()` (see Example 14.21). As its first parameter, `boost::apply_visitor()` expects an object of a class derived from `boost::static_visitor`. This class must overload `operator()` for every data type used by the variable of type `boost::variant` it acts on. Consequently, the operator is overloaded three times in the example because **v** supports the data types `double`, `char`, and `std::string`.

Example 14.21

```
#include <boost/variant.hpp>
#include <boost/any.hpp>
#include <vector>
#include <string>
#include <iostream>

std::vector<boost::any> vector;

struct output :
  public boost::static_visitor<>
{
  void operator()(double &d) const
  {
    vector.push_back(d);
  }

  void operator()(char &c) const
  {
    vector.push_back(c);
  }

  void operator()(std::string &s) const
  {
    vector.push_back(s);
  }
};

int main()
{
  boost::variant<double, char, std::string> v;
  v = 3.14;
  boost::apply_visitor(output(), v);
  v = 'A';
  boost::apply_visitor(output(), v);
  v = "Hello, world!";
  boost::apply_visitor(output(), v);
}
```

Looking closely at Example 14.21, you can see that `boost::static_visitor` is a template. The type of the return value of `operator()` must be specified as a template parameter. If the operators do not have a return value, a template parameter is not required, as seen in the example.

The second parameter passed to `boost::apply_visitor()` is a variable of type `boost::variant`.

`boost::apply_visitor()` automatically calls `operator()` of the first parameter that matches the data type of the value currently stored in the second parameter. This means that the sample program uses different overloaded operators every time `boost::apply_visitor()` is invoked – first the one for `double`, followed by the one for `char`, and finally the one for `std::string`.

The advantage of `boost::apply_visitor()` is not only that the correct operator is called automatically. In addition, `boost::apply_visitor()` ensures that overloaded operators have been provided for every data type supported by variables of type boost::variant. If one of the three overloaded operators had not been defined, the code could not be compiled.

If overloaded operators are equal in functionality, the code can be simplified by using templates (see Example 14.22).

Example 14.22

```
#include <boost/variant.hpp>
#include <boost/any.hpp>
#include <vector>
#include <string>
#include <iostream>

std::vector<boost::any> vector;

struct output :
  public boost::static_visitor<>
{
  template <typename T>
  void operator()(T &t) const
  {
    vector.push_back(t);
  }
};

int main()
{
  boost::variant<double, char, std::string> v;
  v = 3.14;
  boost::apply_visitor(output(), v);
  v = 'A';
  boost::apply_visitor(output(), v);
  v = "Hello, world!";
  boost::apply_visitor(output(), v);
}
```

Because boost::apply_visitor() ensures code correctness at compile time, it should be preferred over boost::get().

Boost.DynamicBitset

The library Boost.DynamicBitset[4] provides the class boost::dynamic_bitset, which is defined in boost/dynamic_bitset.hpp. This library is used like std::bitset. The difference is that the number of bits for std::bitset must be specified at compile time, whereas the number of bits for boost::dynamic_bitset is specified at run-time.

---

[4] http://www.boost.org/libs/dynamic_bitset/

Example 14.23

```cpp
#include <boost/dynamic_bitset.hpp>
#include <iostream>

int main()
{
  boost::dynamic_bitset<> db(3, 4);

  db.push_back(true);

  std::cout << db.size() << std::endl;
  std::cout << db.count() << std::endl;
  std::cout << db.any() << std::endl;
  std::cout << db.none() << std::endl;

  std::cout << db[0].flip() << std::endl;
  std::cout << ~db[3] << std::endl;
  std::cout << db << std::endl;
}
```

boost::dynamic_bitset requires no template parameters when instantiated; default types are used in that case. More important are the parameters passed to the constructor. In Example 14.23, the constructor creates **db** with 3 bits. The second parameter initializes the bits; in this case, the number 4 initializes the most significant bit – the bit on the very left.

The number of bits inside an object of type boost::dynamic_bitset can be changed at any time. The member function push_back() adds another bit, which will become the most significant bit. Calling push_back() in Example 14.23 causes **db** to contain 4 bits, of which the two most significant bits are set. **db** therefore stores the number 12.

You can decrease the number of bits by calling the member function resize(). Depending on the parameter passed to resize(), bits will either be added or removed.

boost::dynamic_bitset provides member functions to query data and access individual bits. The member functions size() and count() return the number of bits and the number of bits currently set, respectively. Whereas any() returns true if at least one bit is set, none() returns true if no bit is set.

To access individual bits, use array syntax. A reference to an internal class is returned that represents the corresponding bit and provides member functions to manipulate it. For example, the member function flip() toggles the bit. Bitwise operators such as ~ are available as well. Ultimately, boost::dynamic_bitset offers the same bit manipulation functionality as provided by std::bitset.

Like std::bitset from the C++ standard, boost::dynamic_bitset is not a container, and therefore was not introduced in Chapter 13, *Containers* since it is missing concepts like iterators.

Exercises

1. Define a data type `configuration` that can store name/value pairs. Names are of type `std::string` while values are of type `std::string`, `int`, or `float`. Inside `main()`, store the following name/value pairs in an object of type `configuration`: path=C:\Windows, version=3 and pi=3.1415. Verify the program by writing the name/value pairs to the standard output stream.

2. Extend the program by changing the value of path to C:\Windows\System after displaying it. Verify the program by writing the name/value pairs to the standard output stream again.

15

Error Handling

General

Functions that can fail must somehow tell the caller when they fail. In C++, this is done either through a return value or by throwing an exception. A return value is usually used if the failure is not really considered exceptional in a common sense. That is, cases where the caller can check the return value and react accordingly.

Exceptions are used to indicate exceptional conditions that do not happen normally. A good example is the exception of type `std::bad_alloc`, which is thrown if dynamic memory allocation with `new` fails. Because memory can usually be allocated without any problems, it would be cumbersome to always have to check the return value.

This chapter introduces two Boost C++ Libraries that can help you manage error handling: Boost.System translates operating system-specific error codes into platform independent ones. For example, functions with a return value based on an operating system-specific type can be handled in a platform independent way. Boost.Exception makes it possible to add information to any exception so that `catch` handlers can react better to an exception.

Boost.System

Boost.System[1] is a small library that defines four classes to identify errors. `boost::system::error_code` is the most basic class and represents operating system-specific errors. Because operating systems typically enumerate errors, `boost::system::error_code` saves an error code in a variable of type `int`. Example 15.1 illustrates how to use this class.

---

[1] http://www.boost.org/libs/system/

Example 15.1

```cpp
#include <boost/system/error_code.hpp>
#include <boost/asio.hpp>
#include <iostream>
#include <string>

int main()
{
  boost::system::error_code ec;
  std::string hostname = boost::asio::ip::host_name(ec);
  std::cout << ec.value() << std::endl;
}
```

Boost.Asio provides the free-standing function `boost::asio::ip::host_name()`, which returns the name of the computer the program is executed on.

It is possible to a pass an object of type `boost::system::error_code` by reference as the sole parameter to `boost::asio::ip::host_name()`. If the underlying operating system call fails, this object contains the corresponding error code. It is also possible to call `boost::asio::ip::host_name()` without passing a parameter as you will see later in this chapter.

`boost::asio::ip::host_name()` served as a perfect example to introduce Boost.System because it was broken in Boost 1.36.0. The function returned an error code even if the underlying operating system call succeeded in fetching the computer name. The bug was fixed in Boost 1.37.0, and it is now possible to use `boost::asio::ip::host_name()` without any problems. With Boost 1.36.0 though, one could run Example 15.1 and see an error code in action.

Because an error value is nothing but a numeric value, it can be accessed using the member function `value()`. While the error value 0 means that no error occurred, the meaning of other values depends on the operating system and must be looked up in a manual.

Compiled on Windows XP with Visual C++ 2008 and Boost 1.36.0, Example 15.1 repeatedly returns error code 14 (not enough storage available to complete the operation). Even though `boost::asio::ip::host_name()` successfully determines the name of the computer, error code 14 is reported. As already mentioned this behavior is due to an error in the implementation of `boost::asio::ip::host_name()` in Boost 1.36.0.

Besides `value()`, `boost::system::error_code` provides the member function `category()`, which returns an object of the second class defined by Boost.System: `boost::system::category`.

Error codes are simply numeric values. While operating system manufacturers such as Microsoft are able to guarantee the uniqueness of system error codes, keeping error codes unique across all existing applications is virtually impossible for an application developer. It would require a central database filled with error codes from all software developers around the world to avoid reusing the same codes for different errors. Because this is impractical, error categories exist.

Error codes of type `boost::system::error_code` always belong to a category that can be retrieved with the member function `category()`. Operating system errors are represented by the system category – an object that can be fetched through the free-standing function `boost::system::system_category()`.

By calling `category()` in Example 15.2, the system category is returned. It is then possible to call, for example, `name()`, which returns `system` for the system category.

Example 15.2

```cpp
#include <boost/system/error_code.hpp>
#include <boost/asio.hpp>
#include <iostream>
#include <string>

int main()
{
  boost::system::error_code ec;
  std::string hostname = boost::asio::ip::host_name(ec);
  std::cout << ec.value() << std::endl;
  std::cout << ec.category().name() << std::endl;
}
```

Errors are uniquely identified by the error code and the error category. Because error codes are only required to be unique within a category, you should create a new category whenever you want to define error codes specific to your program. This makes it possible to use error codes that do not interfere with error codes from other developers.

Example 15.3

```cpp
#include <boost/system/error_code.hpp>
#include <iostream>
#include <string>

class application_category :
  public boost::system::error_category
{
public:
  const char *name() const { return "application"; }
  std::string message(int ev) const { return "error message"; }
};

application_category cat;

int main()
{
  boost::system::error_code ec(14, cat);
  std::cout << ec.value() << std::endl;
  std::cout << ec.category().name() << std::endl;
}
```

A new error category is defined by creating a class derived from `boost::system::error_category`. This requires you to define various member functions. At a minimum, the member functions `name()` and `message()` must be supplied because they are defined as pure virtual member functions in `boost::system::error_category`. For additional member functions, the default behavior can be overridden if required.

While `name()` returns the name of the error category, `message()` is used to retrieve the error description for a particular error code. Unlike Example 15.3, the parameter **ev** is usually evaluated to return a description based on the error code.

An object of the type of the newly created error category can be used to initialize an error code. Example 15.3 defines the error code **ec** using the new category `application_category`. Therefore, error code 14 is no longer a system error; instead, its meaning is defined by the developer of the new error category.

`boost::system::error_code` provides a member function called `default_error_condition()`, which returns an object of type `boost::system::error_condition`. The interface of `boost::system::error_condition` is almost identical to the interface of `boost::system::error_code`. The only difference is the member function `default_error_condition()`, which is only provided by `boost::system::error_code`.

Example 15.4

```cpp
#include <boost/system/error_code.hpp>
#include <boost/asio.hpp>
#include <iostream>
#include <string>

int main()
{
  boost::system::error_code ec;
  std::string hostname = boost::asio::ip::host_name(ec);
  boost::system::error_condition ecnd = ec.default_error_condition();
  std::cout << ecnd.value() << std::endl;
  std::cout << ecnd.category().name() << std::endl;
}
```

`boost::system::error_condition` is used just like `boost::system::error_code`. That's why it's also possible to call the member functions `value()` and `category()` for an object of type `boost::system::error_condition`.

The reason there are two seemingly identical classes is fairly simple: While `boost::system::error_code` is used for platform dependent error codes, `boost::system::error_condition` is used to access platform independent error codes. And by calling the member function `default_error_condition()`, a platform dependent error code is translated into a platform independent error code of type `boost::system::error_condition`.

When Example 15.4 is run, it displays the number 12 and the error category `generic`. The platform dependent error code 14 was translated into the platform independent error code 12. Thanks to `boost::system::error_condition`, the error is always represented by the same number, regardless of the underlying platform. While Windows reports the error as 14, the same error might be reported as 25 on a different operating system. If you use `boost::system::error_condition`, the error will always be reported as 12.

The fourth and last class provided by Boost.System is `boost::system::system_error`, which is derived from `std::runtime_error`. It can be used to transport an error code of type `boost::system::error_code` in an exception.

Example 15.5

```
#include <boost/asio.hpp>
#include <boost/system/system_error.hpp>
#include <iostream>

int main()
{
  try
  {
    std::cout << boost::asio::ip::host_name() << std::endl;
  }
  catch (boost::system::system_error &e)
  {
    boost::system::error_code ec = e.code();
    std::cerr << ec.value() << std::endl;
    std::cerr << ec.category().name() << std::endl;
  }
}
```

The free-standing function `boost::asio::ip::host_name()` has two versions. One version expects a parameter of type `boost::system::error_code`, and the other expects no parameters. The second version will throw an exception of type `boost::system::system_error` in case of an error. The error code of type `boost::system::error_code` which was returned through a reference parameter to the caller of `boost::asio::ip::host_name()` before is now passed in an exception to the caller.

Boost.Exception

The library Boost.Exception[2] provides a new exception type, `boost::exception`, which makes it possible to add data to an exception after it has been thrown. It is defined in `boost/exception/exception.hpp`. Because Boost.Exception spreads its classes and functions over multiple header files, the following examples access `boost/exception/all.hpp` to avoid including header files one by one.

Example 15.6

```
#include <boost/exception/all.hpp>
#include <boost/lexical_cast.hpp>
#include <boost/shared_array.hpp>
#include <exception>
#include <string>
#include <iostream>

typedef boost::error_info<struct tag_errmsg, std::string> errmsg_info;

class allocation_failed :
```

---

[2] http://www.boost.org/libs/exception/

```
  public boost::exception,
  public std::exception
{
public:
  allocation_failed(std::size_t size)
    : what_("allocation of " + boost::lexical_cast<std::string>(size) +
      " bytes failed")
  {
  }

  virtual const char *what() const throw()
  {
    return what_.c_str();
  }

private:
  std::string what_;
};

boost::shared_array<char> allocate(std::size_t size)
{
  if (size > 1000)
    throw allocation_failed(size);
  return boost::shared_array<char>(new char[size]);
}

void save_configuration_data()
{
  try
  {
    boost::shared_array<char> a = allocate(2000);
    // saving configuration data ...
  }
  catch (boost::exception &e)
  {
    e << errmsg_info("saving configuration data failed");
    throw;
  }
}

int main()
{
  try
  {
    save_configuration_data();
  }
  catch (boost::exception &e)
  {
    std::cerr << boost::diagnostic_information(e);
  }
}
```

Example 15.6 calls the function `save_configuration_data()` in `main()`, which in turn calls `allocate()`. The function `allocate()` allocates memory dynamically, but it checks whether a certain limit is exceeded. In the example, the limit is set to 1,000 bytes.

If `allocate()` is called with a value greater than 1,000, an exception is thrown, which is the case here. That's why the implementation of `save_configuration_data()` is incomplete, and the function doesn't do much. As the name of the function and a comment in the code indicate, `save_configuration_data()` is meant to save configuration data in dynamically allocated memory.

The purpose of Example 15.6 is to demonstrate Boost.Exception – that's why an exception is thrown intentionally. The exception, thrown by `allocate()`, is of type `allocation_failed`. This class is derived from both `boost::exception` and `std::exception`.

Deriving the class from `std::exception` is not necessary. `allocation_failed` could have also been derived from a class from a different class hierarchy in order to embed it in an existing framework. While Example 15.6 uses the class hierarchy defined by the C++ standard, deriving `allocation_failed` solely from `boost::exception` would have been sufficient.

If an exception of type `allocation_failed` is thrown, the requested memory size is stored inside the exception. This makes debugging easier. If more memory is requested than can be provided by `allocate()`, the root cause for the exception can be easily spotted.

If `allocate()` is called by only one function (in Example 15.6, it is called by `save_configuration_data()`), this information is sufficient to locate the issue. However, in programs that have many functions calling `allocate()`, this information is no longer sufficient to effectively debug the program. In these cases, it would help to know which function tried to allocate more memory than `allocate()` could provide. Adding more data to the exception would help the debugging process tremendously.

The challenge is that `allocate()` does not have any additional information, such as the caller name, to add to the exception.

Boost.Exception provides a solution. Data can be added to an exception at any time. You just need to define a data type based on `boost::error_info` for each bit of data you need to add.

`boost::error_info` is a template that expects two parameters. The first parameter is a tag that uniquely identifies the newly created data type. This is typically a structure with a random but unique name. The second parameter refers to the data type of the value stored inside the exception.

The sample program defined a new data type, `errmsg_info`, uniquely identifiable via the structure `tag_errmsg`, which stores a string of type `std::string`.

In the `catch` handler of `save_configuration_data()`, `errmsg_info` is used to create an object that is initialized with the string "saving configuration data failed". This object is then added to the exception of type `boost::exception` using `operator<<`. Then the exception is re-thrown.

Now, the exception carries both the size of memory that was expected to be dynamically allocated and the description of the error, which was added in the function `save_configuration_data()`. This description makes debugging even easier since it will be clear which function tried to allocate more memory than could be provided.

To retrieve all available data from an exception, the function `boost::diagnostic_informa-tion()` can be called in the `catch` handler of `main()`. For every exception passed to that function, `boost::diagnostic_information()` calls the member function `what()` and accesses all of the additional data stored inside the exception. `boost::diagnostic_information()` returns a string of type `std::string`, which for example, can be written to the standard error stream.

When compiled with Visual C++ 2010, Example 15.6 will display the following message:

```
Throw in function (unknown)
Dynamic exception type: class allocation_failed
std::exception::what: allocation of 2000 bytes failed
[struct tag_errmsg *] = saving configuration data failed
```

As can be seen, the message contains the data type of the exception, the error message retrieved from `what()`, and the description including the corresponding name of the structure.

`boost::diagnostic_information()` checks at run-time whether or not a given exception is derived from `std::exception`. `what()` will only be called if that is the case.

The name of the function that threw the exception of type `allocation_failed` is "unknown" in the message.

Boost.Exception provides a macro to throw an exception that contains not only the name of the function, but also additional data such as the file name and the line number.

Example 15.7

```cpp
#include <boost/exception/all.hpp>
#include <boost/lexical_cast.hpp>
#include <boost/shared_array.hpp>
#include <exception>
#include <string>
#include <iostream>

typedef boost::error_info<struct tag_errmsg, std::string> errmsg_info;

class allocation_failed :
  public std::exception
{
public:
  allocation_failed(std::size_t size)
    : what_("allocation of " + boost::lexical_cast<std::string>(size) +
      " bytes failed")
  {
  }

  virtual const char *what() const throw()
  {
    return what_.c_str();
  }

private:
  std::string what_;
};
```

```
boost::shared_array<char> allocate(std::size_t size)
{
  if (size > 1000)
    BOOST_THROW_EXCEPTION(allocation_failed(size));
  return boost::shared_array<char>(new char[size]);
}

void save_configuration_data()
{
  try
  {
    boost::shared_array<char> a = allocate(2000);
    // saving configuration data ...
  }
  catch (boost::exception &e)
  {
    e << errmsg_info("saving configuration data failed");
    throw;
  }
}

int main()
{
  try
  {
    save_configuration_data();
  }
  catch (boost::exception &e)
  {
    std::cerr << boost::diagnostic_information(e);
  }
}
```

By using the macro BOOST_THROW_EXCEPTION instead of throw, additional data such as function name, file name, and line number are automatically added to the exception. However, this only works if the compiler supports macros for the additional data. While macros such as __FILE__ and __LINE__ are defined by the C++ standard, there is no standardized macro that returns the name of the current function. Because many compiler manufacturers provide such a macro, BOOST_THROW_EXCEPTION tries to identify the underlying compiler and use the corresponding macro if it exists. Compiled with Visual C++ 2010, Example 15.7 displays the following message:

```
.\main.cpp(32): Throw in function class boost::shared_array<char>
  __cdecl allocate(unsigned int)
Dynamic exception type: class boost::exception_detail::clone_impl
  <struct boost::exception_detail::error_info_injector<
  class allocation_failed> >
std::exception::what: allocation of 2000 bytes failed
[struct tag_errmsg *] = saving configuration data failed
```

The code compiles without errors even though the class allocation_failed is no longer derived from boost::exception. This works because BOOST_THROW_EXCEPTION accesses a function called boost::enable_error_info(), which dynamically identifies whether or not an exception is derived from boost::exception. If not, it automatically creates a new exception type derived from the specified type and boost::exception. This is why the message shown above does not just display allocation_failed.

This section concludes with an example that selectively accesses data that has been added to an exception.

Example 15.8

```cpp
#include <boost/exception/all.hpp>
#include <boost/lexical_cast.hpp>
#include <boost/shared_array.hpp>
#include <exception>
#include <string>
#include <iostream>

typedef boost::error_info<struct tag_errmsg, std::string> errmsg_info;

class allocation_failed :
  public std::exception
{
public:
  allocation_failed(std::size_t size)
    : what_("allocation of " + boost::lexical_cast<std::string>(size) +
      " bytes failed")
  {
  }

  virtual const char *what() const throw()
  {
    return what_.c_str();
  }

private:
  std::string what_;
};

boost::shared_array<char> allocate(std::size_t size)
{
  if (size > 1000)
    BOOST_THROW_EXCEPTION(allocation_failed(size));
  return boost::shared_array<char>(new char[size]);
}

void save_configuration_data()
{
  try
  {
    boost::shared_array<char> a = allocate(2000);
    // saving configuration data ...
  }
  catch (boost::exception &e)
  {
    e << errmsg_info("saving configuration data failed");
    throw;
  }
}

int main()
{
  try
  {
```

```
    save_configuration_data();
  }
  catch (boost::exception &e)
  {
    std::cerr << *boost::get_error_info<errmsg_info>(e);
  }
}
```

Example 15.8 does not use `boost::diagnostic_information()`. Instead it uses `boost::get_error_info()` to directly access the error message of type `errmsg_info`. Because `boost::get_error_info()` returns a smart pointer of type `boost::shared_ptr`, `operator*` is used to fetch the error message. In case the parameter passed to `boost::get_error_info()` is not of type `boost::exception`, a null pointer is returned. If the macro `BOOST_THROW_EXCEPTION` is always used to throw an exception, the exception will always be derived from `boost::exception` – there is no need to check the returned smart pointer for null in that case.

16

Cast Operators

General

The C++ standard defines four cast operators: `static_cast`, `dynamic_cast`, `const_cast`, and `reinterpret_cast`. The two libraries Boost.Conversion and Boost.NumericConversion define additional cast operators specialized for certain type casts.

Boost.Conversion

The library Boost.Conversion[1] contains only two header files. The header file `boost/cast.hpp` defines the two cast operators `boost::polymorphic_cast` and `boost::polymorphic_downcast`, and `boost/lexical_cast.hpp` defines the cast operator `boost::lexical_cast`. `boost::polymorphic_cast` and `boost::polymorphic_downcast` are designed to handle type casts – usually done with `dynamic_cast` – more precisely.

Example 16.1

```
struct father
{
  virtual ~father() {};
};

struct mother
{
  virtual ~mother() {};
};

struct child :
  public father,
  public mother
{
};

void func(father *f)
```

---

[1] http://www.boost.org/libs/conversion/

```
{
  child *c = dynamic_cast<child*>(f);
}

int main()
{
  child *c = new child;
  func(c);

  father *f = new child;
  mother *m = dynamic_cast<mother*>(f);
}
```

Example 16.1 uses the cast operator `dynamic_cast` twice: In `func()`, it transforms the pointer pointing to a parent class to one pointing to a child class. In `main()`, it transforms the pointer pointing to a parent class to one pointing to a different parent class. The first transformation is called a downcast, while the second one is called a cross cast. With the cast operators from Boost.Conversion, a downcast can be distinguished from a cross cast.

Example 16.2

```
#include <boost/cast.hpp>

struct father
{
  virtual ~father() {};
};

struct mother
{
  virtual ~mother() {};
};

struct child :
  public father,
  public mother
{
};

void func(father *f)
{
  child *c = boost::polymorphic_downcast<child*>(f);
}

int main()
{
  child *c = new child;
  func(c);

  father *f = new child;
  mother *m = boost::polymorphic_cast<mother*>(f);
}
```

The cast operator `boost::polymorphic_downcast` (see Example 16.2) can only be used for downcasts. It uses `static_cast` internally to perform the cast. Because `static_cast` does not dynamically check whether the type cast is valid, `boost::polymorphic_downcast` must only be used if the type cast is safe. In debug builds, `boost::polymorphic_downcast` uses `dynamic_cast` and `assert()` to make sure that the type cast is valid. This test is only performed if the macro `NDEBUG` is not defined, which is usually the case for debug builds.

While downcasts are possible with `boost::polymorphic_downcast`, `boost::polymorphic_cast` is required for cross casts. `boost::polymorphic_cast` uses `dynamic_cast` internally because it is the only cast operator able to perform a cross cast. It still makes sense to prefer `boost::polymorphic_cast` because it throws an exception of type `std::bad_cast` in case of an error. `dynamic_cast`, on the other hand, returns 0 if the type cast fails. Instead of manually checking the return value, `boost::polymorphic_cast` does it automatically.

Use `boost::polymorphic_downcast` and `boost::polymorphic_cast` only if pointers must be converted; otherwise, you must use `dynamic_cast`. Because `boost::polymorphic_downcast` is based on `static_cast`, it cannot convert objects of a parent class to objects of a child class. Also, it does not make sense to use `boost::polymorphic_cast` to convert types other than pointers because `dynamic_cast` will throw an exception of type `std::bad_cast` if a cast fails.

While using `boost::polymorphic_downcast` and `boost::polymorphic_cast` is not really mandatory, since all type casts can also be performed with `dynamic_cast`, Boost.Conversion provides another cast operator that can be pretty useful. Consider Example 16.3.

Example 16.3

```cpp
#include <boost/lexical_cast.hpp>
#include <string>
#include <iostream>

int main()
{
  std::string s = boost::lexical_cast<std::string>(169);
  std::cout << s << std::endl;
  double d = boost::lexical_cast<double>(s);
  std::cout << d << std::endl;
}
```

The cast operator `boost::lexical_cast` can convert numbers of different types. Example 16.3 first converts the integer 169 to a string, then converts the string to a floating point number.

`boost::lexical_cast` uses streams internally to perform the conversion. Therefore, only types with overloaded `operator<<` and `operator>>` can be converted. The advantage of using `boost::lexical_cast` is that type conversions take just one line of code and do not need to use streams. This is especially important because it might not otherwise be clear in a particular case that streams were used only to convert a type. With `boost::lexical_cast` the developer's intention is clear.

`boost::lexical_cast` does not necessarily always use streams. It can be optimized for certain data types to implement a more efficient conversion.

Example 16.4

```cpp
#include <boost/lexical_cast.hpp>
#include <string>
#include <iostream>

int main()
{
  try
  {
    int i = boost::lexical_cast<int>("abc");
    std::cout << i << std::endl;
  }
  catch (boost::bad_lexical_cast &e)
  {
    std::cerr << e.what() << std::endl;
  }
}
```

If a conversion fails, an exception of type `boost::bad_lexical_cast`, which is derived from `std::bad_cast`, is thrown. Example 16.4 throws an exception because the string "abc" cannot be converted to a number of type `int`.

Boost.NumericConversion

The library Boost.NumericConversion[2] can be used to convert numbers of one type to numbers of a different type. In C++, such a conversion can also take place implicitly as shown in Example 16.5.

Example 16.5

```cpp
#include <iostream>

int main()
{
  int i = 0x10000;
  short s = i;
  std::cout << s << std::endl;
}
```

Example 16.5 can be compiled without any problem because the type conversion from `int` to `short` takes place automatically. Even though the program can be run, the result of the conversion cannot be predicted because it depends on the compiler used. The number `0x10000` in the variable `i` is too big to be stored in a variable of type `short`. According to the C++ standard, the result of this operation is implementation defined. Compiled with Visual C++ 2010, the program displays `0`. The value of `s` differs from the value in `i`.

To avoid these kind of errors when converting numbers, the cast operator `boost::numeric_cast` can be used (see Example 16.6). `boost::numeric_cast` is used exactly like the existing C++ cast operators. The correct header file must be included; in this case, the header file `boost/numeric/conversion/cast.hpp`.

---

[2] http://www.boost.org/libs/numeric/conversion/

Example 16.6

```cpp
#include <boost/numeric/conversion/cast.hpp>
#include <iostream>

int main()
{
  try
  {
    int i = 0x10000;
    short s = boost::numeric_cast<short>(i);
    std::cout << s << std::endl;
  }
  catch (boost::numeric::bad_numeric_cast &e)
  {
    std::cerr << e.what() << std::endl;
  }
}
```

boost::numeric_cast does the same conversion as C++. However, boost::numeric_cast verifies whether the conversion can take place without changing the value being converted. For Example 16.6, this means that no conversion will take place. Instead, an exception of type boost::numeric::bad_numeric_cast will be thrown because 0x10000 is too big to be placed in a variable of type short.

Strictly speaking, an exception of type boost::numeric::positive_overflow will be thrown. This type specifies an overflow – in this case for positive numbers. There is also boost::numeric::negative_overflow, which specifies an overflow for negative numbers.

Example 16.7

```cpp
#include <boost/numeric/conversion/cast.hpp>
#include <iostream>

int main()
{
  try
  {
    int i = -0x10000;
    short s = boost::numeric_cast<short>(i);
    std::cout << s << std::endl;
  }
  catch (boost::numeric::negative_overflow &e)
  {
    std::cerr << e.what() << std::endl;
  }
}
```

Boost.NumericConversion defines additional exception types, all derived from boost::numeric::bad_numeric_cast. Because boost::numeric::bad_numeric_cast is derived from std::bad_cast, a catch handler can also catch exceptions of this type.

17

Utilities

General

This chapter introduces a variety of utilities that mostly reside in the library Boost.Utility. These utilities are collected here because they do not fit in any other chapter. Not all of the utilities presented here reside in Boost.Utility. Some are maintained as stand-alone libraries. Boost.Foreach is one of them. Because this library defines only one macro, it is also presented in this chapter.

Boost.Utility

The library Boost.Utility[1] is a conglomeration of miscellaneous and useful classes and functions that are too small to justify being maintained in stand-alone libraries. While the utilities are small and can be learned quickly, they are completely unrelated. Unlike the examples in previous chapters, the code samples here are not built on each other since they are independent utilities.

While most utilities are defined in `boost/utility.hpp`, some have their own header files. The following examples include the appropriate header file for the utility being introduced.

Example 17.1 passes the function `boost::checked_delete()` as a parameter to the member function `pop_back_and_dispose()`, which is provided by the class `boost::intrusive::list` from Boost.Intrusive. While both `boost::intrusive::list` and `pop_back_and_dispose()` are introduced in Chapter 13, *Containers*, `boost::checked_delete()` is provided by Boost.Utility and is defined in `boost/checked_delete.hpp`.

---

[1] http://www.boost.org/libs/utility/

Example 17.1

```cpp
#include <boost/checked_delete.hpp>
#include <boost/intrusive/list.hpp>
#include <string>
#include <iostream>

struct person :
  public boost::intrusive::list_base_hook<>
{
  std::string name_;
  int age_;

  person(std::string name, int age) : name_(name), age_(age) {}
};

int main()
{
  person *p = new person("Anton", 30);

  typedef boost::intrusive::list<person> person_list;
  person_list pl;

  pl.push_back(*p);

  pl.pop_back_and_dispose(boost::checked_delete<person>);
  std::cout << pl.size() << std::endl;
}
```

boost::checked_delete() expects as its sole argument a pointer to the object that will be deleted by delete. Because pop_back_and_dispose() expects a function that takes a pointer to destroy the corresponding object, it makes sense to pass in boost::checked_delete() – that way, you don't need to define a similar function.

Unlike delete, boost::checked_delete() ensures that the data type of the object to be destroyed is complete. delete will accept a pointer to an object with an incomplete data type. While this concerns a detail of the C++ standard that you can usually ignore, you should note that boost::checked_delete() is not completely identical to a call to delete because it puts higher demands on its argument.

Besides boost::checked_delete(), Boost.Utility provides boost::checked_array_delete(), which can be used to destroy arrays. It calls delete[] rather than delete.

Additionally, two classes, boost::checked_deleter and boost::checked_array_deleter, are available to create function objects that behave like boost::checked_delete() and boost::checked_array_delete(), respectively.

Example 17.2

```
#include <boost/current_function.hpp>
#include <iostream>

int main()
{
  const char *funcname = BOOST_CURRENT_FUNCTION;
  std::cout << funcname << std::endl;
}
```

Example 17.2 uses a macro called BOOST_CURRENT_FUNCTION, defined in boost/current_function.hpp, which returns the name of the surrounding function as a string.

BOOST_CURRENT_FUNCTION provides a platform independent way to retrieve the name of a function. While Visual C++ and g++ support the macro __FUNCTION__ as a compiler extension, BOOST_CURRENT_FUNCTION is platform independent code.

If compiled with Visual C++ 2010, Example 17.2 displays int __cdecl main(void).

Example 17.3

```
#include <boost/next_prior.hpp>
#include <boost/array.hpp>
#include <algorithm>
#include <iostream>

int main()
{
  typedef boost::array<int, 4> array;
  array a = { { 0, 1, 2, 3 } };

  array::iterator it = std::find(a.begin(), a.end(), 2);
  array::iterator prior = boost::prior(it, 2);
  array::iterator next = boost::next(it);

  std::cout << *prior << std::endl;
  std::cout << *it << std::endl;
  std::cout << *next << std::endl;
}
```

Boost.Utility provides two functions, boost::prior() and boost::next(), that return an iterator relative to another. In Example 17.3, **it** points to the number 2 in the array, **prior** points to 0, and **next** to 3.

Unlike std::advance(), boost::prior() and boost::next() return a new iterator and do not modify the iterator that was passed in.

In addition to the iterator, both functions accept a second parameter that indicates the number of steps to move forward or backward. In Example 17.3, the iterator is moved two steps backward in the call to boost::prior() and one step forward in the call to boost::next().

Please note that the number of steps is always a positive number, even for `boost::prior()`, which of course moves backwards.

To use `boost::prior()` and `boost::next()`, include the header file `boost/next_prior.hpp`.

Example 17.4

```
#include <boost/noncopyable.hpp>
#include <string>
#include <iostream>

struct person :
  boost::noncopyable
{
  std::string name_;
  int age_;

  person(std::string name, int age) : name_(name), age_(age) {}
};

void print(person &p)
{
  std::cout << p.name_ << std::endl;
  std::cout << p.age_ << std::endl;
}

int main()
{
  person p("Boris", 33);
  print(p);
}
```

Boost.Utility provides the class `boost::noncopyable`, which is defined in `boost/noncopyable.hpp`. This class makes it impossible to copy objects.

The same effect can be achieved by defining the copy constructor and assignment operator as private member functions. However, deriving from `boost::noncopyable` explicitly states the intention that objects of a class should be non-copyable.

Example 17.4 can be compiled and executed. However, if the signature of the `print()` function is modified to take the object of type `person` by value rather than by reference, the resulting code will no longer compile.

Example 17.5

```cpp
#include <boost/utility/addressof.hpp>
#include <string>
#include <iostream>

struct person
{
  std::string name_;
  int age_;

  person(std::string name, int age) : name_(name), age_(age) {}

  int operator&() const
  {
    return age_;
  }
};

int main()
{
  person p("Boris", 33);
  std::cout << &p << std::endl;
  std::cout << boost::addressof(p) << std::endl;
}
```

To retrieve the address of a particular object, even if `operator&` has been overloaded (see Example 17.5), Boost.Utility provides the function `boost::addressof()`, which is defined in `boost/utility/addressof.hpp`.

Example 17.6

```cpp
#include <boost/utility/binary.hpp>
#include <iostream>

int main()
{
  int i = BOOST_BINARY(1001 0001);
  std::cout << i << std::endl;

  short s = BOOST_BINARY(1000 0000 0000 0000);
  std::cout << s << std::endl;
}
```

The macro `BOOST_BINARY` makes it possible to use numbers in binary form. Standard C++ only supports hexadecimal and octal forms using the prefixes `0x` and `0`.

Example 17.6 displays `145` and `-32768`. The variable **s** stores a bit sequence that represents a negative number because the 16-bit data type `short` uses the 16th bit – the most significant bit in `short` – as the sign bit.

`BOOST_BINARY` simply offers another option to write numbers. Because in C++ the data type `int` is used for numbers by default, `BOOST_BINARY` also uses `int`. To define a number of type `long`, use the macro BOOST_BINARY_L, which generates the equivalent of a number suffixed with the letter L.

Boost.Utility includes additional macros such as BOOST_BINARY_U, which initializes a variable without a sign bit. All of these macros are defined in the header file boost/utility/binary.hpp.

Additional utilities are also available, but they are beyond the scope of this book because they are mostly used by the developers of Boost libraries or for template meta programming. The documentation of Boost.Utility provides a fairly comprehensive overview of these additional utilities and can serve as a starting point if you are interested.

Boost.Swap

If you use many Boost libraries and also use std::swap() to swap data, consider using boost::swap() as an alternative. boost::swap() is provided by Boost.Swap[2] and defined in boost/swap.hpp.

Example 17.7

```
#include <boost/swap.hpp>
#include <boost/array.hpp>
#include <iostream>

int main()
{
  char c1 = 'A';
  char c2 = 'B';

  boost::swap(c1, c2);

  std::cout << c1 << ";" << c2 << std::endl;

  boost::array<int, 1> a1 = { { 1 } };
  boost::array<int, 1> a2 = { { 2 } };

  boost::swap(a1, a2);

  std::cout << a1[0] << ";" << a2[0] << std::endl;
}
```

Ultimately, boost::swap() does nothing different than std::swap(). However, because many Boost libraries offer specializations for swapping data that are defined in the namespace boost, boost::swap() can take advantage of them. In Example 17.7, boost::swap() accesses std::swap() to swap the values of the two char variables and uses the optimized function boost::swap() from Boost.Array to swap data in the arrays.

Example 17.7 writes B;A and 2;1 to the standard output stream.

---

[2] http://www.boost.org/libs/utility/swap.html

Boost.Operators

Boost.Operators[3] provides numerous classes to automatically overload operators. In Example 17.8, a greater-than operator is automatically added since it can be implemented using the already defined less-than operator.

Example 17.8

```
#include <boost/operators.hpp>
#include <iostream>

struct person :
  public boost::less_than_comparable<person>
{
  std::string name_;
  int age_;

  person(std::string name, int age) : name_(name), age_(age) {}

  bool operator<(const person &rhs) const
  {
    return age_ < rhs.age_;
  }
};

int main()
{
  person p1("Anton", 30);
  person p2("Boris", 33);

  std::cout << (p2 > p1) << std::endl;
}
```

To automatically add operators, simply derive a class from classes defined by Boost.Operators in boost/operators.hpp. If a class is derived from boost::less_than_comparable, as shown in Example 17.8, operator>, operator<=, and operator>= are automatically defined.

Because many operators can be expressed in terms of other operators, automatic overloading is possible. For example, boost::less_than_comparable implements the greater-than operator as the opposite of the less-than operator; if an object is not less than another, it must be greater.

boost::less_than_comparable assumes that two objects cannot be equal. If this isn't true for particular objects, use boost::partially_ordered as the parent class. By defining operator==, boost::partially_ordered can determine whether less-than really means greater-than or equal.

In addition to boost::less_than_comparable and boost::partially_ordered, classes are provided that allow you to overload not only comparison operators but also arithmetic and logical ones. Classes are also available to overload operators usually provided by iterators, pointers, or arrays. Because automatic overloading is only possible once other operators have been defined,

---

[3] http://www.boost.org/libs/utility/operators.htm

the particular operators that must be provided will vary depending on the situation. Consult the documentation for more information.

Boost.Foreach

Boost.Foreach[4] provides a macro called BOOST_FOREACH that works like "foreach" loops in other programming languages (see Example 17.9).

Example 17.9

```
#include <boost/foreach.hpp>
#include <boost/array.hpp>
#include <iostream>

int main()
{
  boost::array<int, 4> a = { { 0, 1, 2, 3 } };

  BOOST_FOREACH(int &i, a)
    i *= i;

  BOOST_REVERSE_FOREACH(int i, a)
  {
    std::cout << i << std::endl;
  }
}
```

BOOST_FOREACH expects two parameters. The first parameter is a variable or reference, and the second is a sequence. Of course, the data type of the first parameter needs to match the data type used by the sequence.

Anything offering iterators, for example containers from the C++ standard, classifies as a sequence. Boost.Foreach uses Boost.Range instead of directly accessing the member functions begin() and end(). However, because Boost.Range is based on iterators, anything providing iterators is compatible with BOOST_FOREACH.

Example 17.9 iterates over an array of type boost::array with BOOST_FOREACH. The first parameter passed is a reference so that you can both read and modify the elements in the array. In Example 17.9, the first loop multiplies each number by itself.

The second loop uses the macro BOOST_REVERSE_FOREACH, which works the same as BOOST_FOREACH, but iterates backwards over a sequence. The loop writes the numbers 9, 4, 1, and 0 in that order to the standard output stream.

As usual, curly brackets can be omitted if the block only consists of one statement.

Please note that you should not use operations that invalidate the iterator inside the loop. For example, elements should not be added or removed while iterating over a vector. BOOST_FOREACH and BOOST_REVERSE_FOREACH require iterators to be valid throughout the whole iteration.

---

[4] http://www.boost.org/libs/foreach/

Boost.MinMax

Boost.MinMax[5] provides an algorithm to find the minimum and the maximum of two values with only one function call, which is more efficient than calling `std::min()` and `std::max()`.

Example 17.10

```
#include <boost/algorithm/minmax.hpp>
#include <boost/tuple/tuple.hpp>
#include <iostream>

int main()
{
  int i = 6;
  int j = 5;

  boost::tuples::tuple<const int&, const int&> t = boost::minmax(i, j);

  std::cout << t.get<0>() << std::endl;
  std::cout << t.get<1>() << std::endl;
}
```

`boost::minmax()` is used if the minimum and maximum of two objects should be computed. While both `std::min()` and `std::max()` return only one value, `boost::minmax()` returns two values, causing the return type to be a tuple. The first reference in the tuple points to the minimum, and the second to the maximum. Example 17.10 writes 5 and 6 to the standard output stream.

Example 17.11

```
#include <boost/algorithm/minmax_element.hpp>
#include <boost/array.hpp>
#include <utility>
#include <iostream>

int main()
{
  typedef boost::array<int, 4> array;
  array a = { { 2, 3, 0, 1 } };

  std::pair<array::iterator, array::iterator> p =
    boost::minmax_element(a.begin(), a.end());

  std::cout << *p.first << std::endl;
  std::cout << *p.second << std::endl;
}
```

Just as the standard library offers algorithms to find the minimum and maximum value in a container, Boost.MinMax offers the same functionality with only one call to the function `boost::minmax_element()`.

---

[5] http://www.boost.org/libs/algorithm/minmax/

Please note that `boost::minmax_element()` returns a `std::pair` containing two iterators, which is different from the return value of `boost::minmax()`. Nonetheless, like `boost::minmax()`, the first iterator points to the minimum and the second points to the maximum. Therefore, Example 17.11 writes 0 and 3 to the standard output stream.

Both `boost::minmax()` and `boost::minmax_element()` can be called with a third parameter that specifies how objects should be compared. The functions can be used like the algorithms from the C++ standard.

Index

U

V

W

Y

Colophon

About the Author

Boris Schäling[6] is an active member of the Boost C++ community. He was a Boost C++ representative at the Google Summer of Code Mentor Summit 2010 and spoke at the Boost C++ conference BoostCon 2011. He leads a project to create a C++ process management library in Boost and proposes improvements and extensions to various Boost libraries from time to time.

His main interest in C++ is improving efficiency in software development projects and making C++ easier to use. He has worked as a consultant and trainer helping companies reach these goals using the Boost C++ Libraries. He has extensive international experience and is currently living in Amsterdam, the Netherlands.

About the Book

This book was authored using DocBook XML, Version 5.0. It was formatted using a customization of the standard DocBook stylesheets [http://docbook.sourceforge.net], the Saxon XSLT processor [http://saxon.sourceforge.net], and the RenderX XEP Engine [http://renderx.com].

About XML Press

XML Press[7] specializes in publications for technical communicators, their managers, marketers, and the engineers who support their work. We focus on concise, practical publications concerning social media, programming, management, XML technologies, and other topics of interest to our audience.

---

[6] mailto:boris@highscore.de
[7] http://xmlpress.net

CPSIA information can be obtained at www.ICGtesting.com
Printed in the USA
BVOW080801011211

277247BV00003B/34/P

9 780982 219195